BEYOND MEASURE

a memoir about short stature & inner growth

Ellen Frankel

PEARLSONG PRESS
NASHVILLE, TN

Pearlsong Press
P.O. Box 58095
Nashville, TN 37205
www.pearlsong.com
1–866–4-A-PEARL

ISBN-13: 978-1-59719-005-3
ISBN-10: 1-59719-005-5
Library of Congress Control Number: 2006900093

Original trade paperback

FOR BARBARA MCCOLLOUGH:

With gratitude and love,
I thank you for the wisdom you shared with me,
the compassion you showed me,
and the space you offered
that allowed me to truly grow.

AND FOR STEVE:

With love

Contents

Acknowledgements

I AM SO FORTUNATE to have
the support and encouragement of
many wonderful people in my life
who stood by me as I wrote this book. My thanks
go to my editor/publisher, Peggy Elam at Pearlsong
Press, for believing in this book, and bringing it out into the world.

Many years ago, when I first began this project, my dear friend, Ellen Reifler, offered me the time and space to formulate my ideas and willingly edited my first drafts. Her enthusiasm inspired me to continue with this work. I am forever grateful.

My gratitude goes out to Deahn Leblang, Laurie Judson, Judy Toner, Sue Fligor, Lisa Weisman, Rebecca Manley and Amy Forman for reading the manuscript, offering useful feedback, and encouraging me to keep pushing ahead with my story.

My thanks to Todd and Rosalie Miller for supporting my work and for keeping me laughing, to Beth Kaiman for her years of friendship, and to Lupe Kondo, for helping me with everything so that I had the time to work.

In the course of writing this book, an endeavor that spanned seven years, I was blessed with new friendships, which I treasure. Shelley Poulsen has an incredible spirit, and is truly an inspiration. She has enriched my life in more ways than I can express. She has read and reread this manuscript and offered invaluable feedback, and support.

Hanna Sherman has a heart of gold, and her offer to read *Beyond Measure,* at just the time I needed her input, was a wonderful gift.

Who knew that the spiritual teacher I had yearned to find, that I believed would appear to me with the shaved head of a Buddhist monk, would come to me in the form of a rabbi? He is, to me, both learned rabbi and Buddhist teacher. Rabbi Alan Ullman continues to reveal the excitement, wonder, and beauty in finding one's spiritual self, and living one's own truth. The Wednesday mornings that Shelley, Hanna,

Alan, and I spend in study sessions in Hanna's family room are sacred to me. Alan's reading of *Beyond Measure* has helped me to look more deeply into my own true nature.

I want to extend my thanks to attorneys Joe Mendelson and Andrew Kimbrell, for sharing with me their documents related to the National Institutes of Health study on the use of human grown hormone with healthy short children. My deepest gratitude, also, to those who shared with me their own stories related to short stature.

My heartfelt thanks to my high school English teacher, Joyce Grant. You inspired me to believe in myself, and I am forever grateful to have been your student.

Thanks to my parents, Lorraine and Joe Matz, for your understanding about why I needed to write my truth, and to my sister and brother, Judith and Robert Matz, for supporting me while I found my voice. I love you all.

My children, Allison and Matt, bring so much joy into my life. They have listened to me, inspired me, supported me, taught me, and gracefully tolerated me as I began my journey as a writer. Speaking my truth has included the challenging task of revealing private aspects of my life. In doing so, I hope to encourage you both to be free to live your life in an authentic way, and to reveal your truest self to the world. Follow your dreams…and go for it!

To my husband, Steve, where do I begin? You are an amazing man. I thank you for your understanding, wisdom, love, and, I must add, your much needed computer skills! I look forward to every day with you…

All living beings,
whether weak or strong,
tall, stout, average or short,
seen or unseen,
near or distant,
born or to be born,
may they all be happy.

BUDDHIST SCRIPTURES: METTA SUTRA

The urge to alter his own body is felt by man only;
animals, enjoying the advantage of healthier instincts,
do not share it.

BERNARD RUDOFSKY

You've got to do your own growing,
no matter how tall your grandfather was.

IRISH PROVERB

On Being Short

Spring 1998

I AM AT an awards ceremony
for a local arts festival. My husband
and I are sipping champagne, wandering through
the display of watercolors, hand painted furniture,
pottery and photographs. There is a good turnout
for the event, and the room is quickly filling up.

Briefly, our eyes meet. Not my husband's, but the woman standing by the harbor photograph. We stare at one another, and then quickly turn away. We busy ourselves talking with our respective partners. She glances at me once again. I do the same only seconds later. She is the first to look away. I move on to another painting, and then, ever so casually, flick my hair over my shoulder and look back at her. She is already looking my way and this time we allow ourselves a moment to acknowledge one another, to let our eyes and thoughts linger.

We share a smile. We know, we two. We've never met, yet we share a secret bond.

A few minutes later, when our paths cross again and she is focused on a vase, I let my eyes wander to her face, her back, her legs, and her shoes. Mostly her shoes. Heels? Or flats? I am comparing, of course (was taught to do it well), this woman who is within an inch of my height. Her short brown hair nicely frames her eyes. She is wearing a tailored black suit, which falls easily on her thin frame. Without those two-or-so-inch heels, I might even be half-inch taller.

She looks at me, and I look away. I know the rules. It is her turn to look.

In a crowd, I am startled by the appearance of a woman my size. We are startled by each other. When I see another my size, my body immediately adjusts; eyes focused ahead rather than upwards, shoulder and neck muscles relaxed. Equal. What must it be like to stand in such a posture all day?

Without saying a word, we both share many of the same circumstances. For instance, we know that neither of us can reach the stewed tomatoes on the shelf at the local Stop-and-Shop and that we will obsess over who will sit in front of us, blocking our view, at the theatre. We've overheard others whispering about and pointing at our short stature.

There's much more, but this is what I think about when our eyes first meet.

My husband sees me looking at this woman. He's seen this dance before, and has learned to stay out of where he doesn't belong. All 5 feet 10½ inches of him. He's the helpful person who reaches the stewed tomatoes off the grocery shelf, the one who maintains "all theatre seats have a good view." He's average, for God's sake! He can be supportive, but cannot enter this invisible club that exists in mind alone.

We know us members; we know.

Chapter One
MY SHORT PERSPECTIVE

We'll love you just the way you are if you're perfect.
"PERFECT" BY ALANIS MORRISETTE

AS A CHILD, I don't remember coming to the realization that I was short on my own. Rather, I recall snippets of conversations about my height mostly from adults who loved me. The words hung heavy in the air.

We called my step-grandmother by her first name, Julie. Upon her occasional visits, she would kiss the top of my head and say to my mother, "Look how short she is! Has she grown any this year?" Pinching my cheek, she'd declare, "You're a little doll!"

Already in a strained relationship, my mother appeared to take these comments as a personal assault, as if Julie had discovered another round of ammunition to fire at the daughter-in-law she held in disfavor. During those times my mother would look at me, her eyes rolling up and her face in a nasty grimace directed at Julie.

"She just wants to make us feel bad," my mother would tell me later.

I would wonder, alone in my room, if my growing would somehow even the score, make my parents prouder in some way. I knew that I was somehow, if not "wrong," not exactly "right," either. Too many tape measures announcing growth (or lack thereof). Too many pats on the head that made me feel foolish.

"Why, you're so tiny!" I'd hear from salesclerks in the department stores where we would buy my school clothes.

"Of course, the slacks will be too long on her," the salesclerk would confide to my mother, "but you must be used to that!" To me she might ask, "How old are you?" Whatever my answer, there was invariably a daughter, niece or neighbor who was three years younger and twice my height.

Then she'd offer, "Think of all the money you'll save when you're older! You'll be able to shop in the kids' department when you're an adult!"

The prospect of ruffled Peter Pan collars and corduroy jumpers into my later years seemed awfully unappealing.

Soon the salesclerk would go off laughing on her way to help the next (taller) customer. At least, most of them were taller. I knew because if my mother saw a short girl in the store, she would have me casually walk over to where she stood and pause for a moment. Mom would do a quick assessment and report back to me on the height differential. I hated those moments, but I loved my mother.

I never really knew what to say when comments and assessments about my height were made. I simply learned to do what girls, especially short girls, were taught to do. I'd smile. I'd stay silent and smile. And shrink a little more inside.

My mother would close the dressing room door and snicker about the salesperson. "Why does she have to say how short you are? She's just jealous. She's a large woman. I'd bet she'd love to be nice and petite like you are."

It has occurred to me as an adult that I was never asked how *I* felt about my size. I don't know if my height bothered me initially in and of itself, but I certainly hated the way it seemed to make my mother feel: defensive, inferior.

It's not that I come from a tall family who was surprised by my height. I was simply the shortest of a short family. Perhaps that is why it generated so much discussion and concern. At least, that's the way I saw it.

After all, even as an adult I have a hard time seeing, really seeing, anyone in my family as particularly short. When I talk to them, I still look up; it's all relative, literally and figuratively. Being the shortest of a short family renders everyone else if not actually tall, not all that short, either.

I learned to be concerned about my weight in a similar way to learning discomfort around my height: through conversations and concerns between family members about my body and in my presence. These notions were reinforced in peer groups and in the culture at large.

I WAS STANDING in our kitchen with the red brick tile, sucking on a watermelon candy. I loved those candies. The little dimple in the hard, oval shaped center was the perfect place to let my tongue wash back and forth over the sugary smoothness. I would turn the candy over in my mouth and listen for the hard "click" against my molars. I tried to suck it until it disappeared, but more often than not bit it towards the end, where the thinness rendered it almost transparent.

I was examining a shelf of miniature animals playing musical instruments, which my mother had been collecting. Pewter mice with flutes, ducks with violins, little porcelain bears playing drums. I was counting how many string instruments there were as I reached into the glass jar on the counter for another watermelon candy.

Judy, my older sister, rolled her eyes at me as I took another piece. I ignored her as I unwrapped the candy and popped it into my mouth, savoring the sticky sweetness.

"Look at Ellen," she said to my mother, "she's getting fat."

My tongue left the groove in the dimple and I froze. My mother looked alarmed.

"Really?" she asked my sister. "Do you think she's gaining too much weight?"

"Yes," Judy declared. "Look at her stomach!"

My mother eyed me up and down. Judy glanced at the jarful of candies and then back at me.

"It's a little candy!" I said defensively. "How can that be fattening?"

Judy assured me that one piece of candy was packed with calories and I'd already had two. "I'm sure you've had other snacks besides the candy, too!"

My mother continued to look worried.

Kids learn to be preoccupied with dieting early. I was ten and my sister was thirteen. I spit the candy out.

Later that afternoon my mother took Judy and me shopping at

the clothing store Best & Co. I remember that afternoon with surprising clarity.

Standing alone in the dressing room, a stack of slacks and sweaters waiting to be tried on, my mother and sister still sifting through the racks. I looked at myself in the full-length mirror. I was wearing pinkish mauve corduroy jeans. The brand name was called "Pretty Please;" it said so on the silver snap. (As if one were making a wish: to be pretty, please.) The matching shirt was a short-sleeved clingy sweater in horizontal mauve, pink and white stripes. That was before I learned about the dangers, the taboo, of horizontal stripes.

I hadn't seen it before, or consciously felt it before, but now I did. I took the white flesh on my stomach in my hands and rolled and squeezed it as hard as I could. I remember wishing I could take a knife and slice it off, making my belly flat and acceptable.

I took my nails and dug them into my skin until they left tiny white scratches. I saw my legs as stubby, my thighs as fat, my breasts too big, and puberty in too much of a hurry, beyond the understanding of a mere fifth-grader. I felt tears burn my eyes and the panic set in.

That day, in the little dressing room at Best & Co., I began to truly hate my body size. I now considered myself officially "too short" and "too fat."

Twenty-five years later

I TOOK MY CHILDREN to the town pool yesterday. It was hot, and they were happy splashing in the cool, unheated water. I felt free because Allison, my eight year old, and Matt, my six year old, only needed my watchful eye as they swam, as opposed to my body being used as their flotation device.

I hadn't even worn a bathing suit. In my adult years, I have discovered that unheated pools are too darn cold for anyone over the age of eighteen (unless it is a paid babysitter) and have come to know that "hazy, hot and humid" is not actually a good thing, despite what my kids and their friends might believe.

On this day I ran into Kathy, a woman I knew because our children had once attended the same pre-school. A professor of psychology at a local college, we "re-met" each other professionally when I gave a lecture on eating disorders during grand rounds at a local hospital a few years ago. As the topic was covered in her coursework, she had asked me various questions after my presentation, and from time to time, upon bumping into each other at the local Stop-and-Shop or T.J. Maxx, we would often continue our discussion.

Yesterday was no different, and as we discussed various aspects of eating issues she mentioned that she no longer could find my name in the Massachusetts Eating Disorder Directory. I informed her that I had left my job last May.

"But you love that field!" she exclaimed. "Why'd you leave?"

I told her I had wanted to take some time off to write, and was working on a book about heightism.

"What?" she asked. "I missed that."

"Heightism."

Kathy looked at me doubtfully. "Heigh wha?" she asked again.

"Heightism; the discrimination against people of short stature."

Kathy stared at me blankly and then laughed. "Heightism." She said this hesitantly, as if lacing her foot in an unheated pool, unsure if she really wanted to test these waters. Then she offered some advice.

"Menopause. Menopause is really big right now; you should write about menopause."

I thanked her for the suggestion, but reiterated that I was writing about heightism.

"But why would you leave the eating disorder field to write about that?" she asked incredulously.

I threw up my hands around my body, indicating my presence, my short stature.

"Yeah, but you're not zaftig and short. You're thin and petite. You're cute! If you were fat, then I could imagine that you would be unhappy about your size."

"Don't you think that assumption has a lot to do with the power issues in our culture?" I asked. "Think about all of the girls and women who develop eating disorders in an attempt to gain power. It's such a contradiction. The person suffering with anorexia nervosa only begins to feel powerful when her body becomes smaller, weaker, and when she takes up less space."

"That's true," Kathy agreed. "And fat women are teased."

"Right. The space they take up is seen in a negative way. Almost like an imposition."

I explained to Kathy why I disliked the way in which being short is equated with being "cute." This societal view is consistent with our culture's comfort with small women. In a culture dominated by men, where women occupy a subordinate status, my physical size is nonthreatening to the status quo. The adjectives that go along with being "petite" (e.g., silly, sweet, acquiescing) are not about to threaten the powers that be.

Then I shared with Kathy a conversation I recently had with Jody Abrams, the activism director of the local National Association for the Advancement of Fat Acceptance (NAAFA) chapter. Ms. Abrams explained that in our culture, women fear being fat, and men fear being short. A tall man, even if he is fat, is more desirable than a short man without a "weight issue." For women, being short is less an issue, but being fat is deplorable.

In other words males, consistent with their status in our society, are expected to take up space and to dominate. Females, on the other hand, occupy a second-class citizenship in this culture, and are expected to take up less space, and less room. As a result, women and men will experience different pressures and challenges in dealing with their particular body type and the demands and expectations of our culture.

Kathy thought about this for a moment. "You know," she began, "I'm very sensitive to the issues of short people. I'm not that tall myself. I'm 5 feet 6 inches and I wish I were taller, but I come from a really short family; a family of Weebles."

I had to hold my tongue.

"Yeah," Kathy continued, "my family is just a bunch of Weebles. My mother is probably taller than you—around 5 feet—but ooh," she gestured girth with her hands around her middle, "she is round. And she hated being short her whole life. My father is about 5 feet 7 inches, and my older brother was furious that we were the same height. People would ask if we were twins and that made him crazy. After all, he was older and a guy! In college I remember making this rule for myself that I would only date men 6 feet or taller."

I was thinking that this woman better not have tenure.

"How tall is your husband?" Kathy asked.

"5 feet 10½ inches," I answered. She nodded in approval, relief written across her face. "So at least your kids may inherit some of his height. You really left the eating disorder field?"

"Well, yes and no. I see this as one large issue of the politics of body size. Of how height and weight are perceived in our culture, and the consequences of those perceptions. You know, some cultures favor fat women as the cultural ideal. Others favor short stature and show a bias against tallness." As Kathy and I continued our conversation, I told her that I was hoping to speak with Robert Reich, and that he is currently teaching at Brandeis University.

"Oh!" she said, tapping her head as if to encourage her memory, "I know who you mean!" She was gesturing with her hand near her hip, palm down, to indicate his stature. "That little guy, that little Secretary of Labor guy. God, he's really short, but I understand he is brilliant."

"Help!" I wanted to shout to the lifeguard.

FOR YEARS I SPECIALIZED in the treatment of eating disorders. Working predominately with girls and women of varying ages, we looked at the underlying reasons for starving themselves, for bingeing and purging and for eating compulsively. We examined the symptoms and discussed the emotional and physical toll they exacted. Together we wrestled with the contributing factors, including the psychological, familial, cultural, and political components of these disorders. I was also active in prevention, and often spoke to schools and universities about eating disorders.

Often, I would use personal examples of my own history, which involved, at various times, restrictive eating, use of diuretics and diet pills, and compulsive eating. There was always an interesting catch for me, however. Most of the other therapists I worked with in the field of eating disorders had been in treatment for, and had recovered from, a full-blown eating disorder. They were survivors both internally and externally; they knew they had a serious problem, and the people in their lives validated that experience by seeking professional help. I didn't feel entitled to be part of that group.

For starters, though I had engaged in disordered eating behaviors, they failed to meet the criteria for an eating disorder in the *Diagnostic and Statistical Manual of Mental Disorders*. (In other words, my chances for insurance coverage would have been bleak indeed). Secondly, I had never received treatment for my eating problems and obsession with food, dieting, and weight loss. In fact, I had been behaving in ways that to some extent are expected from teenage girls.

The development of an eating disorder has a lot to do with the striving for power and control, and an exaggerated response in seeking the cultural ideal. When I look back now, I can see that the disordered eating and poor body image I experienced spoke to other aspects of my size than simply body weight.

I often spoke with students about these issues. For example, I would explain that whenever I thought about losing weight, or attempted to lose weight, I would imagine myself shedding pounds and getting thinner. But—and this is crucial—I imagined myself tall and thin.

The image I had of myself losing weight was of a tall, leggy, thin woman walking along the seashore, my long blonde hair swaying gently in the breeze, my blue eyes as crystal clear as the turquoise sea. I would be, in essence, Sea Time Barbie. Never mind that I am 4 feet 8 ½ inches tall with red hair and brown eyes. These were mere details.

As it turns out, I was not alone. According to Joni E. Johnston, author of *Appearance Obsession*, " . . . 90% of all American girls ages 3–11 have a Barbie doll, an early role model with a figure not attainable in real life . . . A significant number of teenagers describe their 'ideal girl' as being 5'7" tall, weighing 110 pounds and having blue eyes and long blonde hair. Many of them also describe her in terms of her resemblance to Barbie."[1]

I tell the students that much of my eating and body concerns stemmed from issues related to my height, and that my preoccupation with changing my body had taken the socially sanctioned route of dieting. Just as dieting fails to address the underlying issues with which a person with an eating disorder must contend, so too did dieting fail to alter my feelings of inadequacy and poor body image, both of which had much to do with being short in a culture that reveres tallness.

It was, in hindsight, much easier to wrestle with the question of where on a continuum my "disordered eating" fell and whether I was "entitled" to belong to the group of professionals who had recovered from an eating disorder, than to easily and readily discuss another aspect of size: stature. It is my height that makes me a member of a short stature "club," my height that is often ridiculed. My weight falls easily on the scale, but my height falls below the lowest percentile of the bell-shaped curve.

THE BELL-SHAPED CURVE. It's a funny thing. The essence of this curve is its normal distribution. Take height. The bulk of the population will be in the middle of the curve, fewer will fall away from the center, and still fewer will fill in the tail ends. Our culture likes the middle. We seem to have trouble with those who fit elsewhere, especially when they take a seat on the tail ends.

Now, the bell-shaped curve is something I need to talk about. I harbor no ill will toward its refusal to accommodate my height. Okay, sometimes I do look at its distribution longingly. Maybe if I occupied just a smidgeon of a spot. Maybe just on weekends, or vacations. But the "No Vacancy" sign flashes before me.

This is the way the curve works. Let's say you fall into the fifth percentile for height. This means that of one hundred people the same age, ninety-five of them will be taller than you. This tail end (five percent) is a necessary part of the bell-shaped curve. Six million Americans fall into the fifth percentile or below for height. Males in the fifth percentile are 5 feet four inches tall and females in the fifth percentile are just about five feet.

Each year, ninety thousand children are born into the third percentile or below. These people, short in stature, have increasingly been referred to in the medical community as the "abnormally short" even in the absence of any medical problem contributing to their shortness. Many are short because genetically, they were programmed to be short.

So basically, from a medical perspective, occupying a necessary tail end of a "normal distribution" renders you "abnormally" short. But at least you have lots of company.

The pharmaceutical companies have jumped on this social bias, and are currently targeting very short children for medical intervention in an attempt to make healthy short children taller. They calculated that they have a built-in population to treat that could make them rich.

There will *always* be a bottom fifth percentile, third percentile, or first percentile; that's the nature of the curve. Even if people were taller on the average, some would still fall into the lowest percentiles. The "abnormally short" percentiles.

Now, THE SHORT PERSON in this culture will rarely look upon his or her height as a positive. After all, there is status in stature.

Studies have revealed a bias favoring tallness in politics. For example, from 1904–1984 the taller candidate won the U.S. presidential elections 80 percent of the time, and only two presidents in the entire history of the United States have been shorter than the nation's average height at the time of their presidencies.

During the 2000 Presidential election with Vice President Al Gore and Gov. George Bush battling it out in one of the closest races since WWII, each candidate looked for any possible edge they might find. Height was no exception. During the debates, "There was extensive pre-debate about what kind of chairs to use for the discussion; stationary, or ones that swivel. Andrew Card, the Massachusetts native and debate chief for the Bush campaign, said there was also talk about whether the seats should be adjustable. Card said the Gore team wanted fixed-height chairs, apparently to accentuate the vice president's slight height advantage over Bush."[2]

The business world also favors tallness. One study found a positive relationship between newly hired MBAs' height and starting salaries. Specifically, tall men (6 feet 2 inches and above) received a starting salary 12.4 percent higher than graduates of the same school who were less than 6 feet. The researcher noted that favoring the taller individual and paying him a larger salary occurred even when the shorter applicant was a man of higher intelligence."[3]

David Kurtz, an Eastern Michigan University marketing professor, asked 140 recruits to make a hypothetical hiring choice between two equally qualified applicants, one 6 feet 1 inch tall, and the other 5 feet 5 inches tall, for a sales job. Seventy-two percent "hired" the tall one, twenty-seven percent expressed no preference, and one percent chose the short one.[4]

In his book *The Height of Your Life*, Ralph Keyes quotes the successful John Kenneth Galbraith (6 feet 8 inches) as saying that "the bias towards tallness and against shortness is one of society's most blatant and forgivable prejudices."[5]

ANOTHER AREA WHERE height prejudice exists is in dating. When one hundred women were asked to evaluate photographs of men whom they believed to be tall, average, or short, all of them found the tall and medium men significantly more attractive.[6]

I remember watching an episode of *20/20* that aired in 1996. It was about dating and short men.

An experiment was set up to test the theory that short men are less desirable to women than tall men. *20/20* recruited tall and short men and lined them up behind a two-way mirror. Groups of women were then asked to look at the lineup to choose a date. Despite being told positive attributes about the short men—that they had interesting careers, elite educational backgrounds, were very rich—the women always chose the tall men.

To see what it would take for the women to pick Rob, with a height of 5 feet 3 inches, the experimenters told the women that he was a doctor, a bestselling author, and a champion skier who had just built his own ski house. All of the women insisted he was too short to date. Then the experimenters gave Rob a promotion and made him chief of staff at a prestigious hospital. One woman said she would date him at that point.

The next challenge was exploring what it would take to get Stu, with a height of 5 feet, a date. The researchers told the women that he was a venture capitalist who had made millions by the age of twenty-five, but the women still insisted he was too short to consider as a date. When the women were asked if there was anything they could be told about Stu to make him irresistible, one woman said that perhaps if the other candidates for a date were murderers or child molesters, she might go out with Stu. The other women, laughing, agreed with her sentiments.

AND THEN THERE is the world of sports. Of American sports, noted English sportswriter Paul Gardner said, "Americans have made it very clear they find big men much more entertaining than small men.

There is a long-standing American idea that bigger means better…one of the reasons why football is cherished is because it is one of the few areas of life where the idea actually works."[7]

It's worth noting that the American obsession with emphasizing size in sports hurts the smaller athlete as well as the bigger one. The pressure is great for athletes to conform to the cartoon image of The Incredible Hulk. The result is the widespread abuse of steroids at all levels of athletic activity. For example, estimates of steroid abuse among professional football players, particularly linebackers and linemen, run as high as fifty percent.[8]

So THE PERSON in the lower percentiles (five percent or below) for height often wishes he/she were taller and at a higher percentile because of a cultural bias against short people. Compare this with weight. Those who fall into the bottom five percent (meaning that of one hundred people in that age group, the individual will be thinner than ninety-five of them) are held up as cultural ideals, at least for women.

With height, you have five percent of the population labeled "abnormal" and being the victims of social prejudice, with medical technology supporting that prejudice, while with weight, you have ninety-five percent of the (female) population trying to squeeze into the lowest percentiles, where ultra thinness is held up as perfection. The pharmaceutical companies have drugs (i.e., diet pills) to support this bias as well.

This equation is most unwelcome news, especially for women, for whom the cultural ideal is quite rigid. Unfortunately, the pressure to conform to an unrealistic ideal is being increasingly felt by men as well. Still, males have historically been given greater leeway in appearance acceptability. For instance, men who are rounder in size are often said to be "cute and cuddly like a teddy bear." Have you ever heard a round woman described in such a way?

The female societal ideal is very tall (top five percent) of height and very thin (bottom five percent) of weight, but only five percent of the population would naturally look like this. It's like we're all trying to sit in the Chinese splits, reaching for both extremes at the same time.

FOR THE MAJORITY of the population, despite diet after diet, and medical interventions, it is impossible for their bodies to accommodate the current ideal body image. And it *is* current. By today's standards, Marilyn Monroe would be considered fat.

Researchers have tracked the height and weight of Miss America winners and found that many had a Body Mass Index (BMI—a measure of weight relative to height in which "normal" is considered 18.5–24.9) that would qualify them as being undernourished by World Health Organizations standards. The authors found that height increased two percent while BMI decreased by twelve percent. In 1941, Miss America had the highest BMI (among the winners studied) of 22.4. By 1986, Miss America had a BMI of only 16.9.[9]

The average fashion model is 5 feet 11 inches tall and weighs 117 pounds, while the average American woman is 5 feet 4 inches tall and weighs 140 pounds.[10]

THE THING IS, we are comparing our body size to an ideal that is elusive, subjectively based, and subject to change. Our bodies are smart. They don't take readily to changes that go against their nature. The fact that ninety-five to ninety-eight percent of dieters who lose weight will regain that weight within one to five years attests to that.

The highly sought after seats on the height and weight bell-shaped curves are a result of cultural biases that basically say, "Most of you flying coach (in the middle) are safe. Our first class members (tall and thin) will be catered to, premier. But those of you who fill in the tails of the short and fat ends, perhaps you'd best fly stand-by. You, we're not so comfortable with."

WE ARE A SOCIETY obsessed with outer appearance, and the belief that a tall, thin body will bring success, happiness, and respect. A $50 billion diet industry is happy to pedal this myth, along with the belief that permanently occupying a different space on the bell-shaped curve is possible with enough willpower and, of course, their newest product. It's what keeps them growing, and booming.

Isn't it amazing that an industry that sells a product (dieting) that fails at least ninety-five percent of the time is so successful? To tell you the truth, I don't know many other businesses that could thrive with such a dismal failure rate.

Could you imagine buying a vacuum cleaner that never picked up dirt? What if, after you complained to the manufacturer on and off for twenty years, he/she was still able to assure you that the vacuum cleaner was just fine? What if the owner of the shop told you to simply go back home, plug in the vacuum and just keep moving it back and forth over that living room carpet with more determination and willpower? But dust and dirt still litter the rug, and you blame yourself instead of the product. Meanwhile, the only one who is "cleaning up" is the owner of the vacuum store.

That's the bottom line with the diet industry, which is bad enough. But now a new industry has emerged. I call it a "growth industry." Literally.

As a culture, we glorify tallness the way we glorify thinness, and we stigmatize shortness the way we stigmatize fatness. Because physical appearance is emphasized so greatly in our culture, the medical industry has increasingly stepped into this arena for a piece of the action. Cosmetic surgery is at an all-time high. New diet drugs frequently step in to replace outgoing prescriptions that have proved dangerous.

It takes a lot of alterations and money to try to move to a different percentile on the bell-shaped curve. There is also a boundary that is crossed as we move into the world of bioengineering. Especially when our children are the subjects. Especially when the children are healthy children who happen to be short.

There is a name for using medical technology in an attempt to physically alter traits deemed socially less desirable: eugenics.

In our culture, shortness is viewed as a liability. Just ask kids on the school playground. Or the short businessman who is paid less than his taller colleague, or our politicians.

Former Secretary of Labor Robert Reich writes, "With rare exceptions, senators are always tall and big-shouldered. Heightism is rampant in American politics. I'm tempted to stand on my chair, but that would be uncabinetlike. I have to remain content to hear the oath and watch the backs of senatorial necks."[11]

Even our language reveals a bias against shortness. We "belittle" someone, or we "cut him down to size." Compare this with our adoration for tallness: When we admire someone we "look up to him." If someone is successful, we say he is "riding high in the saddle."

A determined tall person is often admired. A determined short person is often said to have a "Napoleon Complex."

Because social prejudice against short people is so ingrained in our culture, it is often invisible. Heightism is the last acceptable area of prejudice in our society. Few people are willing to look at the seriousness of height prejudice and the consequences of this discrimination.

The medical industry understands this. Frighteningly enough, many in the medical and pharmaceutical communities believe that because of the social prejudice against short stature, medically attempting to make healthy short kids taller through repeated human growth hormone injections is an appropriate pursuit.

As a matter of fact, our tax dollars have already helped pay for a government-funded study to determine the safety and efficacy of that practice. Short, healthy kids were the guinea pigs. Most people never knew the study was happening.

Andrew Kimbrell, author of *The Human Body Shop,* writes that the solution to prejudice is education for those who are its purveyors, not the genetic engineering of their victims.[12] But the government doesn't see it that way. Despite repeated injunctions attempting to stop a National Institutes of Health study in which healthy short children were injected with growth hormone to see if that would make them taller, the study continued to its conclusion in 2001.

As a short kid, I grew up during the emerging practice of trying to "grow" kids for their own good. I remember, back in the sixth grade, talking with my mother and pediatrician during my annual physical. My mother was concerned about the co-ed parties that were the rage of middle school that year. I watched them commiserate about the upcoming teen years they were both witnessing in their kids.

The comment I remember as though it was yesterday was when the conversation shifted to my size. Laughingly, Dr. Silverman spoke to my mother while looking at me, "Just be sure that when Ellen is ready to date, she falls in love with someone tall. Then when she gets married she won't have to worry about her kids being too short."

My parents relied on the expertise of doctors. I grew up thinking they were godlike. They healed. They helped my younger brother's asthma, they prescribed medication, they reassured. They even made house calls. How could I, back then, have known that doctors have prejudices of their own?

As part of our culture, physicians practice medicine based on certain cultural assumptions. I did not know that then.

I left the doctor's office that day wondering if Howie, my sixth grade love, was tall enough to make up for my obvious deficiencies.

Chapter Two
A PINCH TO GROW AN INCH
& OTHER TALL TALES
(OR WHAT I DID ON MY SAN FRANCISCO VACATION)

IN 1971 I WAS in the fifth grade at Highcrest Elementary School in Wilmette, Illinois. I already wore a training bra, had just gotten my period, and was short. I remember boys like David Gold and Scott Birch who used to pull the bra straps of the few girls wearing them and snap them against our skin. Oh, how I wished that I were one of the girls still wearing the safety of a cotton undershirt.

There was some sex education that year. The girls and boys were separated during class to learn about their respective puberties. At one point in this curriculum, the boys and fathers had a special night of in-depth discussion. The next day, I remember hearing how my name had come up often during their talk. Apparently the lecturer told the young boys, teetering on the verge of complete hormonal meltdown, that some girls mature more quickly than others. "They develop breasts and . . ." one kid yelled out, "Like Ellen Matz!" I then became an unwilling example, star of the evening.

Even then, when friends told me of it, I felt embarrassed and violated. From their accounts, it appeared that the boys were allowed to continue discussing my puberty with the implicit consent of adults present. The last comment stuck with me. "I mean c'mon," one boy said," "you are the shortest girl with the biggest boobs!" He roared with laughter.

The middle school years were hard. On the outside, I seemed happy enough. I had friends, I was a cheerleader, and I did well in school. But inside, I felt desperate. I believed I wasn't "good enough;"

not tall enough, thin enough, pretty enough. I would stand in front of the mirror for hours at a time in our small, blue-tiled bathroom, the night hours ticking away. I experimented with different ways of wearing my hair, pink eye shadow, lip gloss. I held my stomach in and looked at my side reflection.

There was always a voice inside of me that compared me to others. I always lost.

What made these years extra confusing for me was that I had a passion for spiritual matters, but lacked a place for that passion to be nurtured. As a kid, I would check out books at the public library on comparative religion. I would ride my bicycle to different churches (I was raised Jewish) and try to listen to the services.

The only Bahai Temple on this continent happened to be in my hometown. One of my favorite ways to spend an afternoon was to ride my bike to the Bahai Temple and walk around in the beautiful gardens for which they are known. In the springtime, red and yellow tulips would explode in clusters while manicured trees and bushes created a refuge. I would go inside the temple, where nine pillars of white-lace concrete formed the ceiling, and sit and think. Oftentimes I would bring a notebook and pen and would hike on out of the Temple across the street to a forested area with a stream. There I would sit and write poetry.

My family and relatives encouraged none of this behavior. It didn't help matters when I bought a copy of the *New Testament* (I can hear my ancestors: "What 'New?' The 'Old' one was fine") with my allowance, and then proceeded to read it cover to cover.

Later that year, I figured out a way to leave Sunday school during third period. Our synagogue was in Chicago, about a forty-minute drive from our house. Sunday school consisted of three one-hour periods. One semester I dropped my third period elective class and was supposed to see the secretary in the school office to choose another class. I never went.

Instead, I would leave the building after second period, stop at the corner deli for a soft plain bagel and a salami stick, and then walk a few blocks this way or that way to an interesting-looking church. There I would find a vacant seat in the back row and listen to the service. I would return back to the hallways of my Sunday school just as the end of school bell rang. Until the synagogue and my parents caught on, it was great. Technically, for a few months during third period, *I* didn't exist, which had a nice Buddhist ring to it.

I was supposed to be a nice Jewish girl, interested in nice girl-type things. I drove my parents crazy those years when I insisted on wearing a gold necklace with an Egyptian ankh charm on the chain. The little loop making the life sign was quite small, and my parents worried it would be mistaken for a cross. Of course, the teachers at my Temple didn't like my necklace either.

Once in Sunday school I mentioned a parable from the Gospel According to Matthew. The teacher asked me where I had learned that information. I proudly answered that I had read the *New Testament*.

She didn't share my enthusiasm. The next week she had the Rabbi visit our class. He told me that Christians believe Jesus was the Son of God, and that Jews don't believe this is true.

"What do you believe?" he asked. "Do you believe that Jesus is the Son of God?"

"Aren't we all the children of God?" I replied.

The Rabbi did not look impressed.

THE PROBLEM FOR ME was that I had an inner life that yearned for spiritual awakening, but that very yearning was discouraged. The outer life and the outer me faced an equally difficult challenge.

The focus of many adults, including my parents, was on my physical appearance, particularly my height. They worried that I would be at a disadvantage in life because I was short. I learned to feel badly about my height. About being small.

But internally I felt almost—dare I say?—too big! I wanted to be like the Buddha, to sit and meditate. I wanted to follow the words of Jesus. To me, Jesus and Buddha were the same. They were awake, aware. They didn't talk about the importance of appearance. In fact, outer appearances, they taught, were often deceiving. Instead their focus was inside, in the heart.

I wanted to be devoted to the task of unlocking the inner realm. After reading *Siddhartha* by Herman Hesse, I had fantasies of living in the wilderness, by a stream or river. In fact when I was a kid and we would take a driving trip, I always kept my eyes open for options on where this magical spot might exist.

When I was in junior high school, we took a family vacation to upstate New York. One of the shops we visited had a small, ivory meditating Buddha on a black piece of wood. I had never seen a statue of a Buddha before. When I first laid eyes on it, my heart skipped a beat. I remember that it cost ten dollars. I wanted it so badly. Seeing it felt like seeing a long lost friend.

My parents at first said, "No." I didn't put it down the whole time we were in the store. At some point, my parents asked me to give it to them. I handed it to my mother, who then handed it to my father.

"Joe," she said. "Why don't we buy this for her?"

It meant so much to me. To this day, the statue sits on my dresser. It was a moment in which I felt held and validated.

Perhaps they didn't understand my longing anymore than I did at the time, but that was beside the point. Their purchase will always be, for me, a symbolic gesture of accepting my needs and me without interference. It served as a reminder that my heart often understood things, yearnings and stirrings, much quicker than my mind. It reminded me to trust that "gut" feeling you sometimes get. Like that old phrase, "Lose your mind and come to your senses." I am grateful for that moment.

BUT FOR MOST of my childhood, the problem was really twofold: a spiritual body that felt large and expansive that my parents, Rabbi, and other adults in my life often tried to shrink or reduce, and a physical body that my parents, relatives, and doctors worried was too small (i.e., short) and wanted to make bigger.

Of course, at that age, I didn't understand the conflict as clearly as I do now. What I experienced instead was that something was wrong with me both inside and outside.

I figured this because my restless yearning seemed to upset a lot of people, and I had no friends who shared my interest in religion and/or spiritual matters. I began, on some level, to doubt the integrity of this spiritual quest, and part of me bought into the notions others expressed regarding this behavior: that I was only looking for attention, trying to rebel, or was simply listening to the albums *Jesus Christ Superstar* and *Godspell* too much.

I am grateful that deep, deep down, my yearning remained.

WHILE AN INNER LIFE was not encouraged, my outer life was. Appearances counted.

Though my parents wanted me taller, feeling it would make me happier; they emphasized my "cuteness." When you are "petite," people sort of expect you to act silly. Cheerleading fit this.

Of course, the pressure for boys is to act big and powerful, so they often find it helpful to hang out with girls like me, small, silly, and acquiescing. On the outside, that's where the rewards were.

I would "go steady" with a boy and fall not so much "in love" but "in obsession." It was like finding a place to store my passion, yearning, and devotion, which sought expression somewhere.

I didn't have the resources to find a spiritual haven for those stirrings that uplifted me, confused me, all the while angering the adults in my life. I found instead a place to put this part of me in the more socially acceptable place for teenage girls: with teenage boys. While my parents and their friends would laugh and call me "boy crazy," I feared I was simply "crazy."

Sometimes, at night, I would cry so much it hurt. I would take the plastic off the dry-cleaning with its warning to avoid putting the bag over the head for fear of suffocation. I would sit down on my closet floor with the closet door closed, and I would put the plastic over my head.

I didn't want to die. I just needed a very concrete way of telling myself that despite what everyone seemed to think, I was not happy. That something inside of me felt like it was dying.

I GREW UP in a comfortable suburb on the north shore of Chicago. We are a short family as a whole. My father is 5 feet 6 inches, my mother stands at 5 feet 1 inch, my older sister is 4 feet 11 inches, my younger brother has a height of 5 feet 3 inches, and I stand at 4 feet 8½ inches.

I remember once my sister coming home from the endocrinologist with my mother. She was about 13 or 14 years old at the time. I was playing in her room when they returned. As my sister placed her new clogs with the four-inch heels in the closet, my mother said that the doctor had confirmed that Judy was through growing. That was fine, mother had insisted, and as they were near the mall, they had stopped at the shoe store on the way home from the doctor's office.

The lesson was not lost on me. I surmised that they had stopped at the shoe store to buy the inches my sister's bones were unwilling to give.

Later that day, my mother told me she had made an appointment for me with the same endocrinologist. The doctor had asked my mother if she had other younger children at home. Perhaps he felt badly because he couldn't help my sister grow taller. When my mother mentioned my age, he seemed encouraged. "When a child has not completed puberty," he had explained to my mom, "there are sometimes things we can do to increase growth."

Though I have little memory of it, I did meet with this endocrinologist. I had some tests done, and upon receiving the results, he informed my mother that nothing could be done to increase my height. That genetically, I was simply programmed to be short.

Recently, I talked with my mother about this doctor. My mother remembers him fondly. She told me that this doctor was "only 5 feet 2 inches or so" and hated being short. That's why, the doctor had explained to her, he chose to specialize in endocrinology. He wanted to do what he could to help short people.

I thought perhaps he would have found therapy useful. Maybe deep down he had dreams of becoming a painter, but instead kept replaying his unresolved height issues for his whole career.

When I shared my musings, my mother remained loyal to the doctor and to her convictions. "Well, I think it's wonderful. He really cared."

A FEW MONTHS after meeting with the first doctor, my mother heard of another endocrinologist in Chicago of whom people were raving. He was gaining a good reputation for adding inches to short kids' height.

Parents were flocking to his practice, trying to help their children gain an extra edge (or inch) in life. Parents were doing this out of love and concern for their children's' well-being. But good intentions are not always enough.

In my case, I would rather have had my parents talk with me about how I felt about my height, and focus at least as much about my growth on the inside. Instead I, like many other short people I know, came to view my height negatively as a result of so much attention and intervention regarding stature. For many of us, the result was a sinking sense of self-esteem, and a pressure to try to compensate for a lack of inches.

The second endocrinologist that I had an appointment with was also the doctor of my second cousin Donna, the granddaughter of my infamous step-grandmother Julie. Donna was said to be "growing like a weed." I'm sure my mother must have felt some pressure from that development.

I met with this endocrinologist for close to a year. He put me on his special "treatment," a treatment he used frequently with short, healthy children. Because I, and others like me, am short due to genetic makeup rather than any underlying medical problem, his solution was to put us on a high protein diet.

Each morning, my mother was told to prepare me a breakfast of eggs, meat (ham, bacon, or sausage), toast, milk and juice. Each morning. Every morning.

Now, taking a pre-teen who was developing early, who was already concerned about her weight and was carrying around a poor body image, and then making her eat an extra thousand calories at breakfast was perhaps unwise. I wasn't hungry for it and I didn't want it.

Every morning, faced with the task of eating "The Lumberjack Special," I felt unacceptable. It was like taking medicine for a sickness. I started the day with the belief that my height, my body, "*me*" was in some way wrong. There were days when I longed for a bowl of Raisin Bran, some Frosted Flakes.

One week, during the summer, my parents went on vacation and I stayed with family friends. I remember "Aunt" Phyllis being informed of my "special" breakfast, and each morning she dutifully cooked that meal. She introduced me to corned beef hash, and assured me that it counted as breakfast meat.

I felt like a burden. I felt embarrassed by the amount of food I had to eat in an attempt to gain inches. I feared instead that I was simply gaining weight.

Each month, my mother and I would drive into Chicago for the endocrinologist's appointment. He would measure me. When I hadn't grown, his face would show disappointment. He would encourage my mother to continue the breakfasts.

JUST LAST YEAR I met a woman who has a short son. This is thirty years later, different doctor, and different city.

The endocrinologist recommended her son eat a high protein breakfast. Her family is kosher. She wondered if feeding her son the bacon should take precedence over a religious observance.

I told her that there was no evidence that a high protein diet resulted in added inches.

I WANTED TO PLEASE the doctor. I wanted to please my mother. I kept eating the breakfasts, and I kept on not growing.

In between the monthly check-ins, my mother would measure me. "Ellen," she'd call. "Why don't you stand against the garage door? Let's see if you grew."

I would walk on over to the oak door between the kitchen and the family room that led to the garage. My mother would arrange me to make sure my heels were against the dark wood of the door, my head was straight, and I was still. She would then take a wooden ruler and place it horizontally on my head and against the door. I could feel the imprint on my scalp, and on my soul.

"Stand up straight!" she would encourage. Holding a pencil in her other hand, she would mark my height, moving the pencil back and forth, and have me step away.

"Look, Ellen! I think it's a little bit higher!"

"It looks the same," I'd say.

"Well, I think it might be a little higher."

Over the months, and eventually over the years, the pencil mark grew darker with repeated measuring.

A few years ago, my parents sold that house. I had returned home from Boston to help them pack. During a quiet moment when no one was home, I walked over to that garage door.

I stood against the hard wood, stood straight with my heels backed against the door. Closing my eyes, I could almost feel the ruler pressing on my head. I could feel the hope and dread rising inside me, just like when I was young.

I turned to look at the door. The pencil marking was still there.

Later that day, when my parents returned, I thought about showing them the pencil marking on the door. I didn't.

I know, as parents, they were simply doing what they thought was best for me. Out of love and out of concern. They had the blessings and support of our pediatrician, various endocrinologists, friends, and the culture as a whole, which encouraged parents to thin out their rounder offspring and grow their shorter children. Give them that extra "edge" that everyone is looking for.

Pointing out the marking would have put my parents on the defensive. And I don't think they could understand how something they did out of love caused me so much pain.

I carried that damn garage door mark within me for years. A black spot that I associated with failure despite my successes.

MY COUSIN DONNA continued to eat her high protein breakfasts, and over time reached a final adult height of 5 feet 1 inch. When my step-grandmother Julie and Donna's mother would tell my mother about Donna's "progress," they would wonder out loud why I had failed to grow.

My mother would answer with the logical conclusion, "Donna was probably going to grow anyway, with or without the breakfasts."

It made sense; Donna's parents were both taller than my parents. Still, this sound reasoning fell by the wayside when it came to my height. My mother continued scrambling the eggs and frying the bacon. While I didn't grow in inches, I did add some pounds to my short stature that succeeded in making me increasingly obsessed with my weight.

During this period, another significant event took place.

HAVING A GOOD MEMORY, it surprises me that I am unable to recall the specifics, even the season in which it happened. In hindsight, it is almost as if this event were timeless, suspended in my personal history without context.

Perhaps, at the age of eleven, full of pubescent insecurities and self-doubt, this part of the story so affected me that I was unable to find a place to file it away. I had no heading in my personal reference upon which to place it, and so, even as an adult, it continues to elude me. The memory is clear, but detached, lacking understanding and comprehension, the way it must have felt to me at the time.

One day, my mother told me we were taking a trip, just the two of us.

"Where?" I had asked excitedly, imagining places like Disneyland.

"San Francisco," she had answered.

"San Francisco," I had replied, "what are we going to do there?" Already Mickey Mouse and the Dumbo ride had faded from view. "How come no one else is going?"

"I talked with the endocrinologist and he told me that there is a special doctor in San Francisco who will be able to determine if you are done growing. If you're not, they may be able to give you shots that will make you taller. It's called growth hormone therapy."

I don't remember ever talking with my mother about it again until we were on the plane. I have no recollection of ever discussing the impending trip with my father, sister, or brother, nor do I remember how much time passed between learning of the trip and actually going. It may have been a day, a week, six months; I do not know.

What I can recall is getting off the plane and waiting at baggage. This was the first time I had ever been to California, and I had my eyes set for the one thing that did matter to me: teen-age idol Bobby Sherman.

"Do you see him?" I kept asking my mother. "I should have a paper and a pen just in case. For his autograph. That looks like him, don't you think?" I'd ask as each 5 foot 9 inch brown-haired, blue-eyed male that walked by held the possibility of uniting me with my true love.

To an eleven year old, it was simple. I knew everything there was to know about Bobby Sherman. I'd even been to two of his concerts (I wondered if he would recognize me) and had written several (as yet unanswered) letters. I was a proud card-carrying member of his fan club. He lives in California. I'm flying to California. Chances are, I figured, that we would meet. (Interestingly, his #1 hit song was called "Little Woman.")

The next memory I have of this trip takes place in the taxi from our hotel to San Francisco's Children's Hospital. I remember that the cab driver was nice. He kept looking back at me, smiling. He had asked where we were from, and my mother had told him Chicago.

When we arrived at the hospital and mom was paying the fare, I remember how he kept wishing us good luck. His big, hairy hand had grabbed my small one as I exited the cab, and squeezing it, he whispered to me, "God bless."

In the big lobby of the hospital waiting room, I had been impressed. The chairs and carpet looked shiny and clean, and that was something that I had always liked: organization and cleanliness. As I was surveying my surroundings, my mother motioned for me to come over.

"That was so embarrassing," she whispered conspiratorially.

"What?" I asked. I was looking out the spotless window to get a view of the city. Bobby Sherman could be anywhere, I had realized. California was one big state.

"That taxi driver," my mother said. "He must have thought that something was really wrong with you. He kept telling me how he hoped everything would all work out and that he would pray for you."

She continued this monologue while I just sat there. I felt as inanimate as the connecting chairs in the waiting area.

"Well, of course," she figured out loud, "he must have thought something was terribly wrong with you. After all, Chicago is a big city with plenty of doctors, yet we flew across the country to get to this hospital. Isn't that crazy? He'd never imagine that you're fine…"

I think I felt comforted by that image of the taxi driver. I was just as bewildered by my predicament. If I really was fine, then why was I at a hospital? And why was I at a hospital so far from home?

My next memory, more like a frozen snapshot, really, is of meeting with a doctor or nurse who asked me the age at which I first detected pubic hair. I froze. It was like a pop quiz. I wasn't sure what pubic hair was! Did it mean under my arms, or "down there?"

I remember what felt like a sea of faces waiting for me to answer. I guessed. My heart pounded as I waited to see if I had passed.

Someone nodded and made a note on the chart. Relief! I have no idea what I answered.

There were some X-rays, and a blood test. By noon, I remember the doctor telling my mother that it appeared I would not be a candidate for growth hormone therapy because my bones were just about done growing.

The doctor told my mother she could stop the high protein breakfasts; they would not help me to grow taller. He told me I was "adorable" and that "good things come in small packages."

We left the hospital, passing other patients waiting to be seen. Many of them were dwarfs. My mother told me how lucky I was, and how beautiful. I felt confused.

I'VE TALKED A LOT about my mother in association with my height. I think this is a function of the role mothers play in their children's lives.

As a culture, we tend to blame mothers for a myriad of childhood hurts. But this is like blaming the victim herself. How many mothers take on the emotional challenges of child rearing practically by themselves because the father is focused on concerns outside the home?

Because so much of the father's role is tied up in this culture with being financially successful and "taking care of the family," the father often misses out on really being a part of the family. My dad was preoccupied with his own work and life, so that day in and day out, it was my mother who cared for our physical and emotional needs. She worked full-time and also took care of my grandmother.

She looked at the unforgiving culture we live in and thought she was doing the right thing for me in trying to make me taller. When I didn't grow taller, she listened to the culture and told me how lucky I was to be petite.

She focused on how much harder it was going to be for my brother. Society tells us that. Short girls can always try for cute; short boys can simply try to survive.

While the focus in our family was on increasing height, we didn't really talk about our own feelings, perceptions and experiences about being short. Mixed messages about stature were all over my family, like shadows you couldn't catch.

But those shadows have impact, and the thread that weaves itself through each generation will affect family members in different ways. It's not blame, it's life. In my family, we measured our shortness, inch by inch, and then denied its importance.

I NEVER DID MEET Bobby Sherman. Years later, I learned how fortunate I was not to have received growth hormone treatment.

During that time, human growth hormone was harvested from the pituitary glands of human cadavers, some of which were infected with a rare brain virus called Creutzfeldt-Jakob Disease. Once infected, the virus lays dormant in the brain tissue for years.

Kids who were infected with the virus at ten years of age may not have any symptoms until they are in their thirties. Once activated, the virus causes a rapid degeneration of brain cells, resulting in severe neurological damage and death. In 1985, several fatalities were traced to human growth hormone derived from infected cadavers.

Fortuitously, the synthetic genetically engineered hormone had just become available, providing an unlimited supply of this once scarce commodity. This abundant supply has implications for the way in which the "healthy short population" was targeted as a new market for pharmaceutical companies looking to increase profits.

Human Growth Hormone (hGH)

HUMAN GROWTH HORMONE (hGH) occurs naturally in the body and plays a key role in the growth of human tissue. Beginning at birth, hGH is produced in the body, and various levels of the hormone are secreted until death. Along with other chemical processes, hGH promotes the building of muscle and bone as well as the growth of cells that enable organs and tissues to grow and repair themselves.

A protein hormone, hGH is responsible for two major functions. First, it promotes skeletal and tissue growth—primarily in the arms and legs—and soft tissue growth. During childhood, puberty, and adolescence, hGH promotes development of the bones, muscles, liver and kidneys as well as the immune system. hGH also allows for the shrinking of fatty tissue. Growth hormone enables the muscles and bones to use amino acids, the core building blocks of protein, for growth. Without growth hormone, or with a deficient supply, children are unable to reach their full potential and body type.

Second, hGH plays an important role in metabolism, or the way in which the body uses energy. It stimulates the release of fat from body tissue and then signals heart and muscle tissue to use fat for energy instead of blood sugar.

It's INTERESTING TO ME that for the most part, up until 1985, doctors pretty much accepted the fact that many healthy kids who were short as a result of genetics would grow up to be healthy short adults.

In 1958, human growth hormone began to be used to treat the medical disease of hypopituitary dwarfism. Hypopituitary dwarfism is an actual medical disease. Children who suffer from it are unable to produce sufficient growth hormone in their bodies, and one consequence of this deficiency is the inability to reach their full height potential. Because their bodies fail to produce enough growth hormone naturally, a different source of hormone was needed to make-up for the inadequate production. This medical disease is in contrast to constitutional or familial short stature, which refers to those who inherit their shortness from short parents, the same way red hair or hazel eyes are inherited.

Sometimes the child who is deficient in growth hormone and the child who produces adequate amounts of growth hormone will be the same height. Medically treating the growth hormone deficient child with growth hormone treatment is a medical response to an underlying condition that poses various health concerns. Medically treating the non-deficient short child with growth hormone treatment is an example of using a medical treatment to support and reinforce a social prejudice—in this case, short stature.

To TREAT A GROWTH HORMONE DEFICIENT CHILD prior to 1985, one would need fifty to one hundred cadavers per year to provide enough hGH to treat a single child. The National Pituitary Agency was in charge of collecting cadaver glands from pathologists and distributing them to physicians. The supply was so scarce that only the neediest children had access, and were then involved in research studies.

In October 1985 Genentech, Inc. of San Francisco created the first recombinant human growth hormone to receive approval from the

Food and Drug Administration (FDA). Genentech named its product Protropin.

Genentech had an "orphan drug" permit for human growth hormone. Orphan drug permits are issued to pharmaceutical companies to encourage research for drugs to deal with diseases suffered by relatively few people. By ensuring the company has a grace period without market competition, the company enjoys a financial incentive for an otherwise unprofitable endeavor.

Genentech's orphan drug permit expired in 1992. Today, Eli Lilly and other biotechnology companies in the United States and abroad are also manufacturing human growth hormone. For the small population of children with classical growth hormone deficiency, for whom hGH treatment was developed, the results have proven beneficial.

In 1993, the FDA had approved only two childhood conditions for treatment with human growth hormone, classical growth hormone deficiency and chronic renal insufficiency. Despite this, only four out of ten children receiving growth hormone treatment at that time fit these categories.

What is crucial to explore are the many other recipients of human growth hormone treatment whose parents are, according to Barry B. Bercu of All Children's Hospital in St. Petersburg, Florida, "driven by a cultural heightism that permeates American society."[13] The theory is that if human growth hormone can help add inches to children deficient in its production, why not give short children who *do* make enough growth hormone on their own extra doses of growth hormone in an attempt to add inches to their height?

Increasingly, with the encouragement of leading pharmaceutical companies, pediatric endocrinologists are prescribing hGH for healthy short kids in an attempt to make them taller. And their profits bigger.

Growth hormone treatment costs approximately $20,000 per year and lasts an average of five years. To treat the fourteen- to twenty-thousand children in the U.S. who suffer with classic growth hormone deficiency (the FDA approved treatment), the cost would be approximately $182 million annually. If non-growth-hormone-deficient children below the third percentile are deemed eligible for growth hormone treatment, the number of treatment candidates jumps to 1.7 million children at an annual cost of $22 billion.

To pharmaceutical companies, healthy short children have become a huge target market. There will always be, say, a bottom third percentile of a growth chart. These children will provide a built-in population for treatment. The potential for profit is enormous.

So is the potential of exacerbating a social bias against short stature. Will parents of short children now feel added cultural pressure to "do something," like a child's crooked teeth needing braces?

THE SAFETY AND EFFICACY of this treatment for healthy, nondeficient children of short stature remains uncertain, and serious health risks do exist. The treatment itself consists of the parents administering an injection to their child six days per week over an average of five to ten years. Even in those studies that show a small percentage of children obtaining a taller final height than without treatment, the effects are so small as to question whether the risk of treatment is prudent.

For example, a study reported in *The Lancet* noted that the treatment-associated increase in final height was about one inch, and failed to justify the widespread use of human growth hormone treatment for normal, short children.[14] Still, the widespread use has continued.

Chapter Three

A Case in Point:
The Personal is Political
& The Political is Personal

From 1988 to 2001 a study
was run at the National Institutes
of Health with your tax dollars, and with mine.
When I tell people what I have learned about it,
they are shocked.

It is my intention to tell you the truth about a prejudice against short people that includes researchers and doctors attempting to physically manipulate healthy short children's height because of the assumption that taller is inherently better and will lead to a happier, more successful life.

Even if you have not sought or received treatment as a short person in an attempt to "grow you," the fact that such practices are going on has an impact on people everywhere. When a social bias is treated with a medical solution, we as a nation are entering frightening territory.

Imagine if you read the following:

Associated Wire—Dark skin may be correlated with poor psychosocial adjustment and contribute to problems in living, experts have suggested, but a medical technological breakthrough called Human Color Hormone (Hch) may provide a solution to the problems of African-Americans.

A new report revealed today that manifestations of racism continue to seep across our nation. Statistics reveal that discrimination in the workplace and in housing is increasingly evident.

African-Americans are underrepresented in politics and corporate America, and over-represented in prisons.

Research shows that whites enjoy a lower infant mortality rate and a higher chance of graduating from high school. New evidence also suggests that African-Americans may suffer from a low sense of self-esteem and demonstrate poor psychosocial adjustment when compared with whites of similar age.

As researchers have concluded that it is hard to be black in white America, Human Color Hormone (Hch) is being offered as an exciting new solution. Costing approximately $20,000 per year, the treatment would entail an individual being administered an injection six days per week intramuscularly for an average of five years.

In clinical trials it appears that for some subjects, some of the time, skin color does change a shade lighter, though of course it is still obviously black. But researchers claim that while African-Americans as a whole are discriminated against, those with "lighter black" skin appear to fare better, at least in some areas, and that lighter pigmented skin should increase self-esteem.

While the long-term side effects of the treatment are largely unknown and may include quite serious health risks, researchers are excited about this treatment as a method of dealing with the problem of racism.

At least two major pharmaceutical companies will manufacture the new drug, and Wall Street is predicting great success for early investors.

The National Institutes of Health is currently looking for medically healthy African-American children as subjects for a study assessing the safety and efficacy of Hch.

The scary part of this fictitious report is that medically treating the victim of a social prejudice is already happening.

For more than fifteen years, endocrinologists have treated healthy short kids with hGH in an off-label fashion. "Off-label" refers to the practice of allowing physicians to use an FDA approved drug for a condition other than which it was originally intended.

It was emotionally difficult for me just being considered for human growth hormone treatment. I can only imagine what it must be like for a child to receive a shot six days a week because our culture doesn't look favorably upon short people.

THE NATIONAL INSTITUTES OF HEALTH has reclassified short stature as a disease in need of treatment. In 1988 the NIH began looking for eighty healthy short children for an experiment to see if hGH treatment for this group of children was effective (i.e., increased their height) and safe.

Here is a real letter from the U.S. Department of Health & Human Services:

> Clinical Center Study of Short Stature
>
> Dear Colleague:
>
> The Developmental Endocrinology Branch of the National Institutes of Child Health and Human Development (NICHD), one of the National Institutes of Health in Bethesda, Maryland is continuing to recruit children with non-growth-hormone-deficient short stature for a placebo controlled trial of the effect of growth hormone treatment on final adult height.
>
> The NICHD seeks children 9 to 14 years of age who are prepubertal or just starting puberty. Each child's initial height must be less than the median height of children 2 ½ years younger (2.5 SD [standard deviations] below the mean height for age). Health should be normal. Children with prior growth hormone or androgen treatment, or current Ritalin or steroid treatment, are not eligible to take part. Children will be evaluated to determine that their growth hormone secretion is normal.[15]

Another letter reads:

> The National Institutes of Health in Bethesda, Maryland is conducting a study to determine whether growth hormone is an effective treatment for children who are extremely short but are not growth-hormone-deficient.
>
> Our study involves children (boys age 10–16 years, girls age 9–15 years) who are below the first percentile for height. They must be otherwise healthy and cannot have received any previous treatment for their short stature.[16]

The NIH, in conjunction with Eli Lilly, a pharmaceutical company manufacturing human growth hormone under the name Humatrope, funded and carried out an experiment entitled "A Randomized Double-blind, Placebo-controlled Trial of the Effect of Growth Hormone Therapy on the Adult Height of Non-Growth-Hormone Deficient Children with Short Stature."

According to the consent form for participation in this study, "At this time, it is not known whether Humatrope treatment in such children will increase adult height or whether these children will simply grow faster and reach the same adult height sooner. Thus, the purpose of this study is to learn whether short children who receive Humatrope will be taller as adults than short children who will not receive this hormone. This study will also help show if Humatrope is *safe* [my italics] for this use."[17]

In order to scientifically validate the results, a randomized, placebo-controlled, double-blind study design was used. The term "randomized" ensures that each child has an equal chance of being in the treatment group or in the control group. That means that of the eighty subjects in the experiment, forty would be in the treatment group and would receive Humatrope. The remaining half would comprise the control group and would receive a placebo, a similarly appearing medication from which the hormone had been omitted. In this way, the experiment would be "placebo-controlled." By comparing the final heights of the children in these two groups, it should be possible to assess whether long-term growth hormone therapy would increase the adult height of short children.

This study was also "double-blind," meaning neither the subjects nor the doctors would know which children were receiving Humatrope or a placebo. Only Eli Lilly and the NIH pharmacy would have that information. The purpose of a double-blind research design is to avoid unconscious bias on the part of investigators.

In the consent form, the investigators explained the procedures of the study prior to entry, and upon entering the experiment:

Prior to entry of this study, your child will be admitted to the Clinical Center at The National Institutes of Health.

Depending on the test results that are available from previous evaluations of your child, we may recommend certain tests that physicians use to understand why children are not growing well. These may include tests to measure stimulated growth hormone responses such as arginine, insulin or L-Dopa tests. As part of these tests, we may ask your child to take a hormone pill (estradiol) each day for 3 days or a single injection of testosterone 5–14 days just before the growth hormone tests. These hormones improve the growth response to tests in some children who might otherwise have to return to the hospital to have tests repeated. Your child will also receive the following procedures related to this study. The procedures will take three days:

1. Medical history and physical examination.

2. Standard blood tests to evaluate blood cell count, liver, kidney and thyroid function.

3. Standard urine tests.

4. Tests of growth and bone maturity.

A. Ten measurements of standing and sitting height of your child and of each parent.

B. Measurements of head circumference and arm span.

C. A left wrist X-ray and left knee X-ray to measure bone age, an index of bone maturity.

D. A Study of cartilage thickness in the left knee. This is called imaging by magnetic resonance (MRI).

E. Photographs with clothes off. These photographs will be kept in a medical file and used only to provide a record of growth and development in children so that small changes can be detected later by comparing photographs. The child's eyes will be covered in the picture.

5. Measurement of blood hormone levels. One-fourth teaspoon to one teaspoon of blood will be obtained every 20 minutes for twenty-four hours.

6. A thyropin releasing hormone (TRH) test will be performed. This will include blood samples every 15 minutes for three hours.

7. Behavioral questionnaire—you will be asked to fill out a 30-minute questionnaire known as "The Child Behavior Checklist" about your child's behavior. Your child will be asked to fill out a self-perception questionnaire and

may participate in psychological testing.

8. Evaluation for other causes of short stature will include a 72-hour stool collection, a xylose absorption test, a dietary history and a social service evaluation."[18]

I CLOSE MY EYES and I am back at San Francisco's Children's Hospital, where the endocrinologist is determining whether human growth hormone might help me grow taller. I want my mother to release me from the massive concrete building itself, and from the pressure to grow into something I'm not. I imagine what it would be like to spend three days in the hospital being considered as a possible subject for the NIH experiment.

Three days of being prodded and probed and measured. I picture myself scared, standing naked in front of strangers as they click away with their cameras, taking pictures of me as if I were a hostage or the victim of child pornography.

The humiliation of having my body, bursting with the rush of puberty, exposed; the budding breasts, the small triangle of pubic hair, the coldness of the bare floor and the starkness of fluorescent lighting. I can see the intravenous tubes threaded in my blue veins, collecting my crimson blood repeatedly throughout the day and night, the nurses collecting my stool samples.

All because I am a perfectly healthy child with a genetic makeup that included red hair, brown eyes, and short stature.

AFTER THESE STUDIES were completed, the child was sent home. Whether or not the child would be accepted into the study depended on the results of the initial evaluations. The consent form states, "If these results suggest a significant cause of poor growth requiring treatment outside this study, you will be appropriately referred. If no *abnormalities* (my italics) are found, your child will be scheduled to enter the treatment phase of the study."[19]

Upon entering the study, the child would be followed for a six-month baseline period. After this time, the child would receive injections of either Humatrope or placebo. The parents would learn to give the injections using the same type of syringe and needle that are used to give insulin to diabetic children. The treatment would be continued until final adult height had been attained.

Children usually complete their growth between fifteen and eighteen years of age. Therefore, the child would participate in the study for four to seven years.

The middle school years are a time of rapid change. Puberty, with its physical and emotional upheavals, is typically a trying time for youngsters. Body image concerns, insecurities, and self-esteem are in the forefront during this period. Under the best of circumstances, this is a challenging period.

Being placed in the role described above must certainly have exacerbated the normal struggles of this developmental stage. The child would have already experienced peer teasing around his/her height. Nicknames like "shrimp" and "peewee" are common. How, then, must the child have felt when he/she read the NIH consent form explaining why he/she was being considered for the experiment? "Your parents have brought you to the National Institutes of Health because you are shorter than most children your age."[20]

The comparisons and value judgments are hard enough on the school playground. Now the child hears those same sentiments from the doctors and researchers to whom his/her parents have turned for help.

MANY DOCTORS across the country voiced grave concerns about the NIH experiment. Psychiatrists supporting the Physicians Committee for Responsible Medicine's position against the use of human growth hormone with healthy short children pointed out that the entire experiment could be a potential source of lifelong problems for participating children.

The child could conclude that part of his parents' acceptance of him has to do with his height, and that's why they were subjecting him to painful, frightening procedures. Psychiatrists have pointed out the potential difference in a child's perception of procedures inflicted upon him when he is healthy and procedures implemented in the case of an illness or deficiency of a hormone. In the latter case, it can be explained to the child that the purpose of treatment is to make him healthy and well.

On top of this, psychiatrists have wondered, what does the child conclude if the injections do not bring about increased height—that he is forever unacceptable?

PEDIATRICIANS SUPPORTING the Physicians Committee for Responsible Medicine have explained that the NIH experiment was a counterproductive approach for both the subjects in the study and as a means of dealing with the problems stemming from short stature more generally. The study was based on the premise that the problem was the child's height and that by adding inches, the problem would be solved. It ignored the bias against short stature itself, these physicians claimed, which was at the root of problems associated with short stature. The study thus shifted the focus from a social problem into a medical problem.

Pediatricians concerned about the NIH study focused on the discomfort of daily injections, and the way the treatment reinforced the notion that short stature is a serious medical problem. Because many children receive no short-term, let alone long-term, growth effect from hGH treatment, the child's disappointment might worsen a negative self-image. Doctors also pointed out that there are potentially serious risks—such as cancer—involved in human growth hormone treatment.

WHILE THE EFFICACY OF hGH for classic growth hormone deficiency has been well documented, its ability to increase the height of non-deficient, healthy short children is far less certain.

Think of it like an antibiotic. If you are suffering from a strep throat, antibiotics are clearly indicated. When taken properly they will successfully cure the infection. But if you didn't have a strep throat or any type of bacterial infection and you took the medicine anyway, what would be the effect? Would it be in any way helpful? Harmful? Neutral?

If somebody has a vitamin deficiency, supplementing the body with additional doses of the vitamin is beneficial; you are providing the body with a replacement for what it was lacking. But taking extra doses of a particular vitamin that is not lacking in the body is not necessarily good. More doesn't necessarily mean better, and, in fact, too much of a particular vitamin may be downright harmful.

There is no quick assessment available for the efficacy of hGH treatment in those already producing adequate amounts of growth hormone. Growth is a painstakingly slow process, and it is difficult to attribute growth to the treatment per se.

JOHN, A FRIEND OF MINE, was a slow grower as a child. Despite having parents of average height, he consistently fell around the fifteenth percentile for height throughout his childhood and teen years.

His pediatrician suggested that the parents meet with an endocrinologist to discuss the possible use of growth hormone (which, was, at that time, pituitary derived and scarce). After considerable discussion, it was decided that they would not treat John medically, and would let nature take her course.

John experienced a growth spurt during his late teens and into his early college years. His final adult height is 5 feet 11 inches.

Had he been given the growth hormone treatment, would his eventual growth spurt have been attributed to the drug? Chances are, many would believe his increasing stature was the result of hGH, thereby offering anecdotal "proof" of the effectiveness of hGH in non-deficient children.

EVEN IN EXPERIMENTAL DESIGNS with control groups, determining that increased growth is attributable to hGH is tricky business. One's predicted adult height and actual attained height may vary by as much as three inches in either direction.

Research has found the response of healthy short children to hGH therapy has been best during the first year of treatment, with efficacy falling off during subsequent years of treatment. What many observe is that an increase in growth velocity seems to occur, but that does not necessarily result in a change of final adult height.

In other words, healthy short children treated with hGH may simply reach their final adult height quicker, but not taller. It reminds me of the saying, "Wherever you go, there you are."

To date, it appears that hGH administered to healthy children may add one or two inches to final height in some children, but whether the increased inch or so is attributable to the hGH therapy itself is unclear. You also have to figure that those who claim the extra inch is a result of treatment have spent approximately $100,000 for that inch. The ways in which the child may have suffered are less easily calculated.

Will an extra inch make any real difference? The person is still short, but now the child has had the extra physical, emotional, and financial burden of treatment, as well.

THE NIH OFFERED two major reasons for conducting the more-than-a-decade-long study, which cost up to $40,000 per year just for the drug for some patients. One justification the NIH offered was that around the country, doctors were already giving the growth hormone to healthy short children. While the FDA had not approved hGH for use with the population of healthy short children at the time the study was conducted, it was (and still is) legally permissible to prescribe any FDA approved drug in an off-label fashion for other uses.

Dr. John Lantos, a biomedical ethicist, estimates that if the ninety thousand healthy children falling below the third percentile in height in the U.S. each year were to receive growth hormone for five years, it would cost approximately $8-10 billion a year, adding a financial dilemma to an already complicated ethical issue.

Supporters of the NIH study maintained that it was necessary to prove whether the drug was safe and effective for the healthy children already being given the treatment off-label. Dr. Neil Barnard, President of the Physician's Committee for Responsible Medicine, called that reasoning silly and irresponsible. Barnard noted that many high school kids take anabolic steroids and bulimics abuse diet drugs, but we don't then force normal, healthy children to take these drugs to find out their effects. Barnard has discussed the social prejudice against short stature, emphasizing that it is a social issue that should be dealt with socially.

Giving short children injections to "cure" their shortness is itself a stigma, because you are telling these kids there is something wrong with them.

I SPOKE WITH Ellen Leschek, a pediatric endocrinologist involved with the NIH study. She too, offered the rationalization that the research was necessary, as many doctors around the country were prescribing the treatment for healthy short children.

When she asked me my height and I replied 4 feet 8½ inches, she told me that as a child, I would have been eligible for the study. When she asked my children's height, I told her that they fell into the fifth percentile. (My height, on the other hand, fell below the bottom of the curve). She told me that they still had space for subjects, and explained that my children's shortness qualified them as potential participants.

I choose, rather, to think of it this way:

Their shortness qualifies them for full participation in life, the joys and the sorrows, the excitement and the tedium. The pictures I take of them will celebrate who they are, not a naked subject being evaluated for an experiment. I won't collect their blood for study, but I will wash and bandage a skinned knee, will celebrate my daughter's menarche.

I will offer them my thoughts on growing up short, and will ask them to share with me their own thoughts and experiences. We will celebrate our bodies and our strength and the diversity of people.

And, in our lives, we will practice not evaluating others and ourselves concretely, through inches, but through the ongoing growth of being open, curious, and caring human beings.

I didn't tell Dr. Leschek this.

I did decline her offer.

ARTHUR CAPLAN, director of the Center for Biomedical Ethics at the University of Minnesota, has stated, "The right response to the random prescription of growth hormone for children is to stop it, not to study it."[21]

In an interview with the *Los Angeles Times*, Jeremy Rifkin, president of the Foundation on Economic Trends, a biotech watchdog, said, "It is the first time the NIH has exposed healthy children to risk in order to make a scientific point. I have no objection to medical uses of growth hormone, but they have reclassified a social issue as a medical problem. The NIH has no mandate to experiment on children simply because they are the victims of discrimination."[22]

THE SECOND REASON that the NIH offered in support of this study was that extremely short people "may be harmed by deeply ingrained prejudices resulting in stigmatization and impaired self-esteem."[23] Micheala Richardson, media representative of the NIH, was quoted in the *Wall Street Journal* defending the study, stating, "These kids are not normal. They are short in a society that looks at that unfavorably."[24]

The study itself replicated the cultural bias against short stature. Because there is no medical issue for healthy short children, those in favor of using hGH for this population must rely on non-medical rationalizations and justifications for treatment.

According to Arthur Levine, scientific director of the National Institute of Child Health and Human Development, "I don't think this is the same as having freckles or blond hair; short stature can cause considerable anxiety to a disabling degree in children."[25] Levine has had personal experience in this matter, as he stands 5 feet 4 inches tall. He continues, "It has to do with psychology of body image. Although it is not a disease per se, it still is something that can compromise health."[26]

How about the many ways the "psychology of body image" and the "considerable anxiety to a disabling degree" are exacerbated by the decision to consider hGH and the treatment itself?

WHILE MUCH RESEARCH has been done investigating the psychosocial issues related to short stature, the research results must be read with care. It is critical to distinguish between any inherent problems associated with shortness itself, and the difficulties that arise from the acts of prejudice and discriminatory behaviors to which the short person is subjected.

Justification of hGH therapy with this segment of the short population has often rested upon the supposed psychiatric sequelae of being vertically challenged. The theory is that human growth hormone treatment would address the psychosocial problems of short children by an increase in psychosocial functioning and self-esteem. Given the rigors of the NIH study, this seems, to me, absurd.

Many studies have found no correlation between short stature and psychosocial functioning. In studies that do find an association, difficulty is often attributed to a cultural bias against short stature, rather than anything inherent in being short itself.

For example, adults tend to baby and overprotect short children, resulting in a process called "juvenilization." In other words, short kids are presumed to be younger than their chronological age as a result of their physical appearance.[27] In a self-fulfilling prophecy, treated younger, these kids may act younger, feel less is expected from them, and respond accordingly.

If a teacher expects less of a shorter child, difficulties may occur in academic performance. The child may act younger, avoid challenges and responsibilities, and learn that behaviors related to height-age perceptions offer attention. Thus, academic and behavioral issues may, in fact, be based on developmental expectations of the child rather than something intrinsic in his height.

In a 1995 study led by Gregory Zimet of the Indiana University School of Medicine, the researchers investigated the psychological adjustment of non-growth-hormone-deficient short children. They found no evidence of significant dysfunction in clinically referred children with short stature, and thus saw no justification for the use of growth hormone in the healthy short population. What the kids in the study did reveal, however, was that short stature was a stressor in these children's lives because of the heightism in our culture and the continued sanctioning of discrimination against short people.

For example, they were often teased and ridiculed by others about their size.[28] In a study five years later, researchers found that short adolescents were at greater risk for being teased and bullied as compared to their taller counterparts.[29]

THE ADULT RESPONSE to a short child's height may be incomprehensibly strong and immediate. One mother I know told me of a discussion she had with the principal of a private school to which her pre-teen had just applied. While his strong intellectual and social abilities were apparent, the principal asked the mother with alarm, "Do you think he will grow? He's so short!"

With such an inappropriate initial outburst, one can only wonder how the principal will react in the future, and what messages she will send to her staff and students.

Even our wonderful pediatrician has made such remarks, despite his disapproval of using hGH with healthy short kids. When my daughter had an annual physical a few years ago, he measured her height. While doing so, he asked Allison if she was the shortest in her class.

"No," she had answered. "Jackie is shorter."

"Oh good!" our doctor had replied. "As long as you're not the shortest. You don't want to be the shortest."

THE DECISION FOR hGH treatment has much to do with doctors' and parents' belief of the need for treatment. As treatment must begin before puberty, the recipients of treatment are, by definition, minors.

One study explored the way in which physicians' beliefs impacted upon their decision to prescribe human growth hormone to healthy children. Those who believed that the emotional well-being of the child would be affected by their short stature, and who believed that growth hormone would have a positive effect on emotional well-being, "even if it doesn't have a major effect on adult height," were more likely to use growth hormone treatment.[30]

The theory is that hGH therapy can help these youngsters feel more "normal" if their height is increased, or even if simply the rate of growth is increased despite final adult height remaining unchanged. Some experts in the field recommend that the therapeutic goal itself be defined in terms of how short-term acceleration of growth would benefit the patient socially and psychologically.

One study investigated whether parents and children held different feelings about being short. As the well-being of children is often assessed by talking with parents and/or teachers, it is important to explore whether their responses are consistent with the child's own perceptions. The researchers found that children mostly rated themselves as having a "rather positive perception of their well-being, although their parents rated their children's well-being as lower."[31] The authors note that this discrepancy may be due to parents' increased sensitivity to potential stresses the child may face, or a symptom of their worry about future problems.

In justifying the NIH study, Micheala Richardson stated, "These kids were referred to the study by parents who are concerned about the height of their children."[32]

Especially noteworthy is the research finding that children have high and unrealistic expectations of the effect of growth hormone treatment.[33] Now the child must face two added burdens: the first being defined as a patient, and second, the fantasy that the drug will actually make him or her tall.

The decision to use growth hormone therapy is often an agonizing one for parents. Social bias, cultural pressure, and their own personal history influence parents in the decision making process. Perhaps they feel that an extra inch or two would have made a difference in their own lives.

Parents are trying to do right by their children and provide them with every advantage, while at the same time weighing the risks against the benefits. Often unrealistic expectations are born from the myth of a "quick fix," influencing their decision to spend $20,000 per year in an attempt to make their short kids taller.

Despite parents' best intentions, the child's self-esteem is bound to suffer with so much intervention around his or her stature: the extensive medical tests compounded with years of injections. The child may experience the lack of hoped for inches as an added "failure" to his/her already "unacceptable" height, and his/her feelings of not "measuring up."

MEANWHILE, LITTLE ATTENTION is directed toward alleviating the bias against short people.

Making fun of short people is rarely, if ever, taken seriously. The costs on people's lives are huge, and our children, used as guinea pigs in experiments to make them taller, represent the extreme of that prejudice.

Many researchers themselves demonstrate a tendency to look at short stature as a disease, which influences the conclusions they draw. For example, Deborah Young-Hymen reviewed studies offering positive and adaptive characteristics displayed by short children. Yet in her final analysis she concludes, "Though at first glance short stature is not life-threatening or physically a prohibitive *illness,* by definition 3% of our pediatric population fall below the growth chart percentiles and are therefore considered to be short stature. A *diagnostic entity* of this magnitude deserves continued research and medical exploration to further our understanding of this *condition* and to help these youngsters achieve more adequate and developmentally appropriate psychosocial adjustment and competence."[34] (My italics.)

Of particular concern in the NIH study was that final adult height was being used as the criterion to determine efficacy. Although the researchers of the study echo Young-Hymen's goal of improved psychosocial functioning as a stated objective, the study lacked any plan to actually measure that variable.

After the extensive medical intervention the child must have undergone in the NIH research protocol simply because of a social bias, it is not unreasonable to wonder if psychosocial adjustment would be *poorer* after the study!

To BE HONEST, I find more trouble in the concept of the growth curve itself.

I fall three standard deviations below the mean of American heights, and am not included in the "normal" curve. However, in Japan, Vietnam, and the Phillipines, my height would be closer to the average.

Many of the "problems" short children exhibit stem from the prejudice and discrimination directed toward them by others. Placing blame on the victim of societal prejudice and directing efforts at changing his/her height ignores the cultural bias against short stature and its various manifestations.

In defending the NIH study, Marsha Love, deputy branch chief at the Office of Research, demonstrates the willingness to use medical technology to support and reinforce social prejudice. Instead of examining the prejudice directed at short people, she supports trying to change the unpopular characteristics of children.

Love states, "Short stature is perceived as a major developmental abnormality. It can cause a whole myriad of problems when you're different—from having hair that's too curly or straight to wearing glasses at a very young age. Those can be changed over time, but short stature is there."[35]

The medical lengths she supports the government taking in trying to change the "unchangeable" point toward the extreme bias against short stature that pervades our country.

IN HIS ARTICLE *Small is Beautiful,* Thomas Samaras, a longevity researcher and author of the book *The Truth About Your Height,* states,

Society's adulation of height has caused millions of children and adults incredible pain and suffering. It will continue to produce pain in parents and short children of future generations. Therefore, a change in attitude toward shorter stature will produce a much healthier society. If we do nothing else, let's change our attitudes so that personal worth becomes entirely independent of height. This in turn will stifle any future height competition among young people.[36]

Yet in that same article he writes, "Short children do endure harm, stigmatization and impaired self-esteem due to deeply ingrained prejudices. For *very short children,* a safe, effective growth hormone can minimize much suffering."[37] [My italics].

I spoke with Mr. Samaras via telephone about this contradiction, and he understood my frustration. I felt he negated much of his argument by the statement supporting growth hormone treatment for "very short" children.

He offered that many people had edited the article. I suppose he meant that since many editors went over his work and the statement was left in, it was justified to reside on page 29.

I think Samaras's statement proves the point that a cultural bias is so ingrained in our psyche that even in writing about the detrimental effects of heightism, such bias seeps through.

Does "very short" mean those in the fifth percentile? The third percentile? The first percentile? Or those off the chart, as in my own case? Isn't he once again arbitrarily defining what constitutes "too short" and turning healthy children into sick patients?

Contradictions are evident again in Melvin Crumbach's statements. A pediatrician and growth disorder specialist at the University of California at San Francisco, Crumbach maintains "…in most cases the hormone does not make a huge difference. If it costs a couple of hundred thousand dollars to put 5 centimeters—about 2 inches—on a child, is that the best way we can spend our health care dollars?"[38]

But at another point he states that, "Shortness is not a disease… But children who are so short that they fall at the extreme bottom of the *normal statistical curve* [my italics] really are abnormal and an extra bit of height can be a big help to them."[39]

IN THE NIH EXPERIMENT, the height requirements for admission into the study were actually quite arbitrary. Carol Tauer, professor of philosophy at Minnesota's College of St. Catherine, explains:

The protocol's criterion for 'short stature' has changed several times. When the study was first proposed in 1984, growth hormone was scarce, so the children admitted as subjects were to be extremely short, with current or predicted adult height at least 3.00 standard deviations below the mean. In 1987, with biosynthetic growth hormone available, the inclusion criteria was changed to 2.5 standard deviations below the mean, and later amended to 2.25 standard deviations. These variations cover a range of approximately two inches with respect to adult height. And interestingly, though the protocol simply speaks of "the mean" and "adult height," it is assumed that the male and female means will be treated separately. For North American males, an adult height of 2.5 standard deviations below the mean is 5'3," and for females it is 4'10 ½." So the standards for adult "short stature" vary by about two inches across the three proposed criteria, and all three differ by 4.5" for males vs. females.[40]

The changes in height criteria for inclusion in the study covered about two inches. At this point, the most "optimistic" studies of hGH with non-deficient children offer one or two inches in growth. What kind of difference will one or two inches make?

THE DEFINITION OF "short stature" is culturally determined and variable. It is influenced by the availability of pharmaceuticals and the profit motive.

Keep in mind that targeting a bottom percentile as "too short" and deeming that population as eligible for growth hormone therapy ensures an endless supply of "patients" in need of treatment. No matter what ranges of heights a distribution covers, there will always be some people at the bottom of the curve.

The inherent sexism in the politics of body size is also evident. According to the NIH panel there is substantial evidence that extreme short stature carries distinct disadvantages, including functional impairment. The NIH maintains that children and adults with extreme short stature may experience difficulty with physical aspects of the culture generally designed for individuals taller than themselves, such as driving a car or other daily tasks.

But males and females do not drive different cars, reach different shelves, or turn on and off different light switches based on their gender. Therefore, to rationalize the NIH experiment and its gender differences in height criteria for "abnormal stature" on the grounds of physical impairment is quite literally a stretch. Even if physical impairment were a serious problem, it would be far less costly financially, physically, and emotionally to alter the physical objects rather than the human body.

As Carol Tauer notes, seventy-five percent of healthy short children receiving hGH are wealthy white boys. There is status in stature. We live in a culture dominated by tall, wealthy white men. Gender and race issues are mingled into the height prejudice in many ways. The costly genetic "enhancement" of white boys further widens the gap between rich and poor, white and non-white, male and female.

Questions of justice come into play. If hGH is considered effective and safe for use in healthy short children, who will have access to this costly therapy? How much greater will the prejudice against short people become? Will it now be assumed that short people should "do something about it?" Will those parents who are unable to pay for hGH feel guilty and experience the double pain of "not measuring up?" Citing equal access, will insurance companies carry part of the burden?

Is this how we want to spend our limited health care dollars?

FINALLY, THE PRACTICE of counteracting height prejudice by turning the victim into a patient in need of medical treatment is itself startling. Again, I am reminded of Andrew Kimbrell's assertion, "The solution to prejudice is education for those who are its purveyors, not the genetic engineering of their victims."[41]

The question I am asking is this: Is modern medicine being used to promote social norms rather than health?

According to Jeremy Rifkin's Foundation on Economic Trends, and the Physicians Committee for Responsible Medicine, the answer is "yes." Together, these organizations filed a series of formal legal petitions with the National Institutes of Health in the early 1990s, demanding that experiments involving children and human growth hormone be stopped.

The petitions charged the NIH with widespread abuse of children in the human growth hormone experiments, and with violating federal regulations on the treatment of children in research. Petitioners charged that the NIH's experiments using hGH were a gross violation of federal regulations protecting children, and violated all traditional ethical norms controlling the use of children in research.

NIH regulations require that experiments using minors as subjects must meet certain standards to avoid causing harm and medical exploitation of children. For example, no experiments are permissible with children unless they are conducted to cure a serious disease and pose only minimal risk to children.

The NIH hGH experiments, however, put children at great physical and psychological risk for a purely social, rather than medical, issue. The sole purpose of the NIH research with healthy short children was to test whether the drug increases height, and does so safely.

The NIH hGH studies were funded in part by Eli Lilly, one of the leading manufacturers of human growth hormone. Eli Lilly and Genentech together sell over $250 million of hGH annually.

The companies were looking to expand the use of hGH, and were hopeful that the research on hGH for healthy short children would provide the basis for gaining FDA approval for treatment with this large population. Not only is the population large, it is unlimited as well, since it is built into a bell-shaped curve.

Jeremy Rifkin has stated, "It is shocking that the NIH is using children as guinea pigs in order to expand the market for genetically engineered hGH. We are calling on Director Bernadine Healy and others at the NIH to obey their own regulations, and to comply with common laws of decency, by stopping this exploitative and abusive research program."[42]

In that same document Neal Barnard, director of the Physicians Committee for Responsible Medicine, stated, "This is a grossly irresponsible use of federal funds. The NIH is supposed to conduct research to increase the health of Americans, not to abuse children in the name of private profit for a couple of companies."[43]

As a result of the joint petitions filed by Rifkin and Barnard on behalf of their organizations, the NIH convened an external advisory panel, the Human Growth Hormone Protocol Review Committee. They concluded that the protocol addressed an important health issue and was not in violation of any of the applicable Department of Health and Human Services regulations cited in the petition to halt the study.

The committee recommended that an independent Data Safety and Monitoring Board (DSMB) be convened to conduct an independent review of the study on a regular basis. This board would be composed of pediatric endocrinologists, ethicists, an attorney, biostatisticians, and a physician with extensive clinical trial experience.

The Human Growth Hormone Protocol Review Committee was given the initial mandate of reviewing a series of questions and reporting to the director of the NIH within a month. By May 1993 the NIH was given the green light to resume recruiting short children for its hGH study, along with the panels' recommendation that the research continue with some modifications.

Bernadine Healy, outgoing director of the NIH, granted permission for the studies to resume. Form letters were sent to pediatricians and pediatric endocrinologists letting them know that the NIH was continuing to recruit children for these experiments.

The DSMB offered several justifications for the continuation of the hGH experiment with non-deficient short children. For starters, they noted that healthy short children were already being prescribed hGH in an off-label fashion, despite questions of safety and efficacy of the treatment with this population. It is estimated that up to half of the approximately fifteen- to twenty-thousand children currently being treated with hGH in the United States are children who do not have classical growth hormone deficiency. The committee hypothesized that this number would likely increase in the future, especially as Eli Lilly lost the last "orphan drug" permit in 1994.

Once other pharmaceutical companies produced hGH, the hefty $20,000 annual price tag was expected to drop significantly. According to the NIH, the greater availability and lower competitive cost would likely result in increased hGH prescriptions for healthy short children regardless of whether hGH received FDA approval for this usage.

Because parents would be able to find a doctor willing to prescribe hGH, the theory was that the study was needed to decide once and for all if hGH is safe and effective in the healthy short population. Here, I am reminded again of Arthur Caplan's statement, "The right response to the random prescription of growth hormone for children is to stop it, not to study it."[44]

The board also supported the research based on a justice and equality argument. Since these healthy short children may be the same height as a child with a growth hormone deficiency, they suffer the same "functional impairment and psychosocial stigmatization" as growth hormone deficient children. They stated, "It could be considered unjust to deny them access to treatment simply on the basis of an imprecise definition of deficiency."[45]

The issue then is whether the non-deficient-growth-hormone children could expect the same benefits from treatment with hGH that the children with growth hormone deficiency receive, which is the question this research is designed to answer. However, these children differ in important ways.

The growth hormone deficient kids suffer from an underlying medical problem that affects the body's health in different ways. The non-growth-hormone-deficient kids have no underlying medical problem. They simply present as a variation on the norm with regard to height.

The decision to medically intervene on the healthy child's stature is socially based due to height discrimination and prejudice.

IN DETERMINING whether the NIH study could continue, the review board focused on questions of whether the short stature protocol complied with the federal regulations on research involving children. Under the Department of Health and Human Services (DHHS), specific conditions must be met to satisfy the requirements to conduct or fund research involving children.

The first section (46.404) of the federal regulations specifies that DHHS may conduct or fund research with children provided that the risk to the subjects is no greater than minimal risk. For example, "The probability and magnitude of harm or discomfort anticipated are not greater…than those ordinarily encountered in daily life or during routine physical or psychological examination or tests."[46]

All members of the review board agreed that the risk to subjects in the short stature experiment went beyond minimal risk. Since the study could not be justified under that section, the review committee examined section 46.406. This section allows DHHS to conduct or fund research with children that involves greater than minimal risk as long as the intervention offers the subjects a chance of direct benefit. As Carol Tauer explains, certain provisions must be satisfied:

> The risks are only a minor increase over minimal risk.

> [The research interventions are] "reasonably commensurate with those inherent in the subject's actual or expected medical, dental, psychological, social or emotional situations.

> The expected knowledge is of vital importance for the understanding or amelioration of the subject's disorder or condition.

> The parent and child both consent to participation in the study.[47]

It was under these provisions that the review committee approved the continuation of the study.

It is mind boggling that the review committee agreed that the risks were "only a minor increase over minimal risk." The members theorized that any serious problem would be detected and dealt with quickly so that the child would be safe. But since the synthetic version of hGH had only been introduced in 1985, there hadn't been sufficient time to assess the "long-term" effects of treatment that lasts an average of five to ten years.

And, as Carol Tauer reports, the dosages being administered in the study were higher than those used when hGH was scarce. Higher doses were now being used to increase growth in those already producing adequate amounts of growth hormone in an attempt to create and sustain growth.

Indeed, Levine, NIH director of Child Health and Human Development, *defended* the importance of the study by stating, "No one knows what the long-term side effects in a large population might be . . . our intention is only to serve the nation's best interest. It could be that growth hormone doesn't work…and could be dangerous. We don't know."[48]

BUT HERE IS WHAT we do know. The *Journal of the American Medical Association* reports of the following known potential adverse effects of hGH therapy: allergy, impaired glucose tolerance, pseudo-tumor cerebri (a condition of the brain simulating the presence of an intracranial tumor, probably due either to vascular congestion or to a swelling of the brain), hyperlipidemia, slipped capital femoral epiphysis, transient peripheral edema, severe kidney damage, exaggeration of scoliosis and leukemia.[49]

In a letter to *The Lancet,* it was reported, "Although there is experimental evidence for a cause-and-effect relationship between growth hormone and acute leukemia, the incidence of leukemia among patients treated with growth hormone is not known."[50]

Jeremy Rifkin refers to conclusions drawn by the Lawson Wilkins Pediatric Endocrine Society, an American society of pediatric specialists, that growth hormone could double the risk of leukemia in children. He states, "The FDA and NIH have known about the possible causal link between hGH treatment and the increased risk of contracting leukemia, but have neither suspended the commercial sale or experimental use. The FDA has not even taken the minimum precaution of informing doctors of the possible increase of risk to their patients. . .I'm sure parents would want to know if their children were twice as likely to contract leukemia as a result of hGH treatments."[51]

Rifkin further declares, "The risk of leukemia to those being treated with hGH can no longer be ignored. It is grossly irresponsible for corporations and researchers to test humans with the drug while its link with a variety of cancers is still being explored. We are calling on all those who are subjecting children or the elderly to hGH treatment to stop until the evidence of the drug's health impacts are better understood."[52] The fact that healthy short children are receiving the drug for a social rather than a medical issue heightens this concern.

Other potential side effects of hGH treatment include hypertension, headaches, fevers, spontaneous bone fractures, flu, vomiting and stomach problems. A small percentage of patients can be expected to form antibodies against growth hormone that can *interfere* with growth. Short-term acceleration of growth from hGH therapy may hasten puberty and bone aging so that final adult height may actually be *less* than it would have been without intervention. Similarly, stopping treatment before adult height is reached may render the child shorter than he/she would have been without treatment.

Growth hormone causes the liver to manufacture chemicals that have effects on various parts of the body. One of the chemicals, insulin-like growth factor (IGF-1) is thought to play a role in breast cell growth, and many doctors are concerned about a possible connection with the development of breast cancer. IGF-1 acts to stimulate cell division, especially in the breast and colon. If any cancer cells are stimulated by IGF-1, its presence may help the cancer to grow and spread. IGF-1 may also play another role in cancer by preventing cells from self-destructing as they normally do, a process called apoptosis. This often leads to pre-cancerous conditions.

Serious risks involve hGH's effect on blood sugar. The body typically uses glucose (circulating blood sugar derived from recently digested carbohydrates) as energy. Human growth hormone releases fat into the bloodstream and then triggers cells to use fat rather than glucose. Over time this action may result in abnormally high blood sugar levels (hyperglycemia). Eventually diabetes may result, in which the body no longer metabolizes glucose properly. Growth hormone increases the metabolism, or the rate at which the cells of the body burn food as fuel. Some children may become unusually lean, losing body fat and becoming inappropriately muscular.

THE BODY IS extremely complex, and the interaction of hormones on various functions is not fully understood. I've talked to parents using hGH with their children and have discovered some disturbing evidence that at least in these cases, the doctors prescribing the treatment focused little attention on potential side effects.

In one case, the mother was told that there had been some concern of an association with leukemia, but the possibility was discounted as "enormously remote." The doctor made no mention of other potentially harmful consequences from hGH treatment.

Another parent was never told of the possibility that the hormone could stunt growth all together. She was unaware that her son could end up shorter than would have been the case without any treatment at all. This woman was also surprised to hear about the possibility of impaired glucose tolerance and hypertension, both of which already ran in her family.

Another mother wondered if the testosterone the endocrinologist suggested for her then eight-year-old son in order to "jump start" a growth spurt may have decreased his final adult height after all, which her son's physician now suspects. After a few years of hGH therapy and the earlier treatment with testosterone, she wonders how much damage was done to her son's growth process, not to mention his self-esteem, altogether.

Still another parent I spoke with told me that her twelve-year-old son developed a worsening of his scoliosis during the first year of hGH treatment. Neither her pediatrician nor pediatric endocrinologist told her of the possible risk of exaggeration of scoliosis as a possible side effect of the treatment. Despite the diagnosis in his chart and the deterioration of his condition, doctors allowed her concern as to what was causing this worsening to remain a mystery. It wasn't until a year later, upon doing some of her own research on the growth hormone, that she learned of the connection.

Instead of focusing on these issues and risks, the DSMB directed their risk concerns on the pain, discomfort, and inconvenience of the large number of shots (six- to eleven-hundred) given to each child. Special concern was focused upon the control group subjects, who lacked the potential benefits of the injections. The committee, in its infinite wisdom, decided that they were, however, imposing an adult perspective, and lacked data to suggest that children receiving the injections experienced them as unduly burdensome.

I don't know about you, but my children begin obsessing about their yearly physical and any accompanying shots by the time their birthday invitations are dropped in the mail. A review of the literature suggests that children in fact find the shots painful, may resist them, and may develop angry feelings at their parents for giving them the injections. The unrealistic fantasy that these shots will actually make them tall also brings distress, since little if any change in height is gained.

THE CONSENT FORM regarding the placebo group appeared purposefully misleading in guiding the children's understanding about the injections. It was not clear that for years they might be getting shots of saline solution rather than a drug that might add inches to their height.

For example, the consent form told the child, "Half of the children in this study will receive shots that contain placebo. Placebo does not contain Humatrope or any other medicine. We need to use placebo with some children in order to be sure that our study works correctly. Some children will grow taller and faster just by coming to the hospital and being checked by a doctor."[53]

In reviewing section 46.406b of the federal regulations governing research on children, the board determined that the child's experience in the NIH hGH study was commensurate with undergoing hGH treatment in a practice setting. However, for the children entering the NIH study, it was mandatory that the child had not received any prior treatment with hGH.

Tauer raises an important argument on this point. She explains that a serious problem in satisfying the criteria of 46.406b "is the question of whether growth hormone treatment, or any other drug therapy ought to be the actual or expected response to short stature. To conclude that provision (b) is satisfied by the NIH protocol, the review panel had to make the assumption that a burdensome and costly drug therapy is an appropriate and, in fact, expected clinical recommendation for treating the condition of short stature."[54]

This value-laden assumption lurks behind the board's interpretation of 46.406b. The original authors of 46.406 were referring to children with a particular disease for which treatment is part of their lives. But children who are discriminated against because they are short in a height-obsessed culture do not fall into that category.

Lynette Lamb, managing editor of the magazine *Utne Reader,* states, "Is there no end, then, to what we'll subject ourselves and our children to fit society's increasingly stringent physical requirements? We say it is for their own good, but what are we teaching our offspring about tolerance for human diversity when we go to such extremes to fit them into that 40 long?"[55]

Concerning section 46.406c of the federal regulations governing research on children, the board agreed that the NIH study did promise to yield knowledge "vital to understanding or ameliorating the disorder or condition under study."

If we are willing to refer to healthy short children as suffering from a disorder or condition simply because of a cultural bias against short stature, what will be next?

The committee made the point that very short stature is a statistical rather than a medical abnormality. Can a child undergoing extensive medical intervention because of a cultural bias make this distinction? Can you? Can anyone help but internalize feeling "abnormal" under these conditions?

APPROVING THE NIH STUDY under these provisions sets a dangerous precedent. Medicalizing a variation of the norm and using medical technology to support and reinforce a social prejudice scares me.

Rifkin poses the following questions: "What about fat people? What about different skin pigmentation? What about young girls whose breasts won't grow to the size society desires? This experiment moves us onto a very dangerous journey that starts with "enhancement" and ends up with eugenics."[56]

Rifkin voiced these concerns back in 1992. He was right on target. Just as short people have been reclassified as sick and in need of treatment, so too have fat people been increasingly viewed as disease-ridden and in need of medical care.

Fat people have been ridiculed and blamed for having a body type that differs from the cultural ideal. As treatment for this "disease" they have been encouraged to take diet pills. In 1997, six million people were taking the prescription diet drugs fen/phen and Redux when the FDA pulled the drugs off the market due to safety concerns. Serious complications, including death, were attributed to the diet drugs.

Gastric bypass surgery is another "treatment" offered to those whose body type is deemed unacceptable. There has been a growing demand for the surgery. In 1992, 16,200 people in the United States underwent the surgery. By 1997 that number had increased to 23,100 and in the year 2000 the figure was up to 63,100.[57] Gastric bypass surgery is gaining acceptance for treating fat children, some as young as thirteen years of age.

The death rate from gastric bypass surgery is reported to be one in a hundred to one in two hundred, although recent studies have indicated an even higher mortality rate. From 1997–2000, Medicare collected data on 16,155 patients undergoing the procedure. Analysis of the data revealed that two percent of gastric bypass surgery patients died in the first month after surgery, almost three percent died within the first three months, and nearly five percent died within the first year.[58]

The obsession with altering the body to fit a societal image of perfection has crossed a boundary that is scary. Our culture has come to celebrate going under the knife in an attempt to manipulate the body in a subjectively more favorable light.

Evening television features programs on "extreme makeovers" in which contestants engage in a "before" and "after" series of surgeries in their quest for beauty. The American public is following suit. In 2003, nearly 8.3 million surgical and non-surgical cosmetic procedures were performed in the U.S., representing a twenty percent increase from 2002. Since 1997 there has been a 293 percent increase in the total number of cosmetic procedures. The top five surgical cosmetic procedures in 2003 were liposuction, breast augmentation, eyelid surgery, rhinoplasty, and breast reduction.[59]

What is the legacy of this age of "extreme makeovers?" What messages are we sending to our children about what is important in life?

ON JUNE 10, 2003, Eli Lilly asked the FDA to approve hGH for healthy short children. Lilly based its request on the two studies it sponsored: the NIH experiment, and a randomized open-label European trial involving 239 children.

In the NIH study, which ended in 2001, researchers found that kids who received three hGH injections a week for four years grew an average of one and a half inches more than children receiving placebo injections. Six shots a week at higher doses in the European study produced gains of two to four inches.

But these numbers must be read with care. While the NIH study began with seventy-one subjects, by the conclusion of the study there were only thirty-three subjects included in the data results: nineteen getting hGH (Humatrope) and twenty getting a placebo. The large dropout rate, along with the fact that adult height is predicted within a plus or minus three-inch range, brings into question the meager reported height gain.

The larger doses given in the European study raise further concerns about safety levels and long-term risks in a drug that has only been available for a relatively short period. Neal Barnard summed it up when he stated, "Hormones are like spider webs. You pull one strand and it affects everything else."[60]

The fact is, each inch costs thousands of dollars, and a short child who gains an additional inch is still a short child. Is there a qualitative difference in being in the world at 4 feet 10 inches instead of 4 feet 9 inches?

ON JULY 25, 2003, the FDA gave final approval to the use of human growth hormone in the treatment of healthy short children at the low end of the normal curve. The new approval allows treatment for healthy short children with an expected adult height of less than 5 feet 3 inches for men and 4 feet 11 inches for women.

Social prejudice against short stature is real. The NIH study is an example of the extreme of this discrimination. Our government funded this experiment and then approved the use of a drug because our culture has a bias against short people.

I have a problem with this.

On Being Seen

Chapter Four

Body Talk

God, grant me the serenity to accept the things I cannot change,
The courage to change the things I can change,
And the wisdom to know the difference.
Reinhold Niebuhr

March 2, 1997

I am sitting on a balcony overlooking the beauty of Provi-denciales, a small island of Turks and Caicos. The palm trees sing gently in the breeze and the waves caress the sand and the blueness surrounds.

The view is breathtaking in the golden morning sun, and I laugh silently to myself that, arriving late last night, I complained to my husband, Steve, that we didn't get a water view after all.

"It's dark, Ellen. I'm telling you that's the ocean." He's pointing to a darkened direction and straining to look off the deck.

I doubt him. I know he's tired and trying to appease me. He's sure I'll insist we return to the long line winding around the hotel lobby with weary travelers wanting to register and begin their vacations.

"I promise tomorrow you'll wake up and see a beautiful water view," he assures me before falling asleep. After all, it's very late and we had a long travel day. Before falling asleep, I strain to hear a wave or a splash that will confirm my husband's promise. This morning, I wake up early like a child on Christmas. Did Santa come? Will I really wake up looking at the turquoise sea?

Ah, he was right. I smile and drift off happily to sleep once again, no longer straining to hear the waves.

On the flight last night, I met a lovely woman who was traveling alone to a Club Med down the beach from where we are staying. She was excited, having just celebrated her 29th birthday and deciding that the future was hers to take. With Stephanie on the aisle and Steve at the window, I sat in the middle talking to my new airplane buddy and watching my husband pretend he wasn't listening, a book opened in his lap.

Women bond quickly. Before long I knew about her childhood, past traumatic relationships, and form of birth control. She and Steve were both in the investment business, so they exchanged a few comments and stories. But mostly, Steve read James Patterson's *Silent Witness* while Stephanie and I chatted. She had decided she deserved a vacation on the islands whether she was involved with someone or not, and I applauded her. She decided that adventures don't always come knocking at your front door; sometimes you had to seek your own, and I commended her.

She asked what type of work I was in, and I briefly told her of my work with women suffering with eating disorders, and my interest in heightism. We talked about women and their bodies, about a culture that dictates tall and thin as the true measure of beauty. We were in agreement about the tremendous pressure women experience in this society.

She offered that in her field, being a woman is hard enough, for so long males have dominated the industry. She was grateful that she is 5 feet 6½ inches tall because "being short and a woman in this field would be an uphill battle."

Her mother is less than five feet tall, she told me, and she is at least five inches taller than her sister. She understood how hard life could be when so much prejudice exists against short people, but the prejudice itself is mostly ignored.

I told her that the big conference rooms with the lovely executive tables and chairs were meant for tall people. That short men and women have to let their feet dangle from the chair, above the ground, suspended. That such "inconveniences" over and over, in various situations, can knock away at you, whether consciously or unconsciously. Sometimes those "inconveniences" are even manufactured by people whose prejudice against shortness is startling, especially in the way that the prejudice is simply ignored.

I told Stephanie about a recent story I read about the control tower at Washington D.C.'s National Airport (now called Ronald Reagan Washington National Airport). A $25 million state-of-the-art control tower had one really big "shortcoming:" the tower was built so that controllers under 5 feet 5 inches tall couldn't see over some of the countertops onto the runways below. Ten percent of the sixty controllers fell into that category. Apparently while designing this $25 million state-of-the-art control tower, the designers overlooked these employees.

The initial recommendation in dealing with this problem, I told Stephanie, didn't have the state-of-the-art feel that surely went into the original costly plan for the control tower. The administration officials discussed having controllers who measured below 5 feet 5 inches tall stand on specially constructed boxes, or even plastic soda crates. That way, they would be able to see planes on the field and ascertain whether the runways were clear for takeoffs and landings. The Controllers Union rejected that solution because they worried controllers might fall off the boxes, and wondered why, with a $25 million tower, workers needed to be standing on Coke crates in the first place!

The average height for American women is 5 feet 4 inches tall, so many future female employees would have the same problem in that job as would short men.

What was really amazing to me was that the counters contained electronic equipment. Federal guidelines require that tower personnel clearing aircrafts for arrivals and departures have clear views of the runways below them. There are more than eight hundred takeoffs or landings at National each day. If the counters require a minimum height above 5 feet 5 inches, this is no small consideration. It goes beyond the discomfort of dangling feet off conference chairs and shelves that require an upper body workout to reach.

Many people jokingly call short folks the "vertically challenged." In this case, workers became "vertically challenged" by the arbitrary decisions of those involved in designing the tower, who simply ignored their biases against short stature (and not even a bias solely against the short, as the average woman would fall below the height requirement).

"So what happened?" Stephanie asked.

"Oh, eventually the Federal Aviation Administration acknowledged that the countertops were built too high and had to pay $10,000 in repairs. The new tower's opening was delayed for about a month."

"Unbelievable," Stephanie murmured, shaking her head, her layered brown hair caught in static on the back of her seat.

We moved on to other subjects. Thai food, snorkeling, Oprah Winfrey. Later, Stephanie told me how much she would like to be in a committed relationship and eventually marry.

"I mean, I don't have that many absolutes, I'm not overly picky about requirements," she said, and then continued. "I mean, of course, he has to be taller than I am—I wouldn't want to date a guy who is shorter than I am. But that's pretty easy because I'm not that tall; I'm only a little over 5 feet 6 inches tall."

I wanted to SCREAM! But I didn't.

It always surprises me, but it shouldn't. After all the things Stephanie said during our long conversation, I thought we were on the same page. I wasn't angry, just weary. Heightism is pervasive, but it is also invisible. There has been so little talk about its existence that people have continued in their prejudices and biases without exploring these feelings and their effects on others.

I hope Stephanie had a wonderful week at Club Med. I know she would have loved to meet someone there and fall in love. I just hope she didn't walk past Mr. Right because he's short.

My friend Scott, who is 5 feet 4 inches tall, has met many a Stephanie. He once told me, "As far as the women, and hanging out at the beach are concerned, nobody wants the short guy. Everyone wants the big, tall one. No one's looking at the small guy."

March 5, 1997

I'M BACK on the deck. The view is still breathtaking, but my heart is not in it.

It is 1:00 P.M. I am sitting in the farthest corner of the balcony, where there is shade. Sitting cross-legged in the chair, a cool white terrycloth towel is draped over my legs, and I am dressed in shorts and a T-shirt. My hair is pulled back in a ponytail and my head is covered with a denim baseball cap. I wear sunglasses. I have put on suntan lotion with an SPF of fifty, just in case the shade is deceiving.

Yesterday I was in a slinky bikini. Careful to use sunscreen and wear sunglasses, I luxuriated on the beach, the breeze keeping the air deceptively cool. I read, dipped into the inviting sea, sipped a Sprite, and took a stroll. I was vacationing, island style. Three days had passed, and I was happy.

Around 3:00 P.M. yesterday my right eyelid started hurting. I put some extra lotion on, and then applied some to my left eyelid as well. Another chapter went by, a refreshing beer. A trip to the bathroom. My eyelids were red now. The sunscreen had worked, but I was developing a heat rash on my arms and thighs, along with sore, swollen eyes. I asked Steve if he wanted to go up early from the beach; I had had enough sun. We decided to shower and then do some shopping for souvenirs for our children.

My eyes continued burning and swelling. I was glad I'd come up early from the sun. I had learned my lessons well from past experiences. I have fair skin, prone to heat rashes and burns, so I apply sunscreen early and often to avert a crisis.

We played slot machines at a casino in the early evening, and then went to dinner at a lovely outdoor restaurant overlooking the sea. We enjoyed a bottle of Pouissey Fusse, letting the cool, dry liquid tingle down our throats and render the evening mood hot. Then a beautiful woman walked in with a group of four men.

The woman was very tall, about 5 feet 10 inches, and very thin. She wore a stunning black pantsuit and strappy black sandals. The top was a silky, long-sleeved blazer that had only one button down a V-neck at her cleavage. Then the jacket just fell away, separating on either side in a flowing, tailored sort of way, revealing a flat, muscular stomach. She had long, silky blonde hair and sparkling green eyes. Her skin was flawless and very tanned. Every inch of her looked sun-kissed. Her makeup was perfectly finished, with silver spun rose lips and pearly white teeth. All eyes in the restaurant moved toward her, men and women alike.

"She must be someone famous," Steve remarked. It was too difficult to look at this woman and think otherwise. "She's very composed," he added.

"She looks familiar; maybe she's a model," I offered. We went back to eating, to the wine, but we, like others in the restaurant, kept sneaking peeks at her. Never had I seen someone so stunning, so otherworldly.

Why am I telling you this? Because in the middle of the night I could feel my eyes swelling from the sun the previous day. When I woke at 6:30 A.M. and went into the bathroom, I saw a horrible reflection. My forehead was swollen, my right eye practically swollen shut, the eyeball sucked into my face. The left eye was bad, but not quite as bad as its companion. All resulted from the combination of wind, heat, sun and fair skin.

I lay in bed with ice wrapped in towels over my forehead and eyes. I turned on the television and imagined the pictures that went with the sound. I showered and dressed and we ate breakfast at the indoor restaurant rather than on the terrace.

Steve felt badly, but I told him to go on down to the beach. That I would be fine. And then, I regressed. I said it wasn't fair that my skin was so sensitive and that there was nothing to do on this stupid island at this stupid hotel, and that on our next vacation I'm picking Alaska.

Steve hugged me and offered some suggestions on how I might spend the day, but nothing would suffice. I didn't want to hear how he thought I should spend the next day or two; he, with a deep tan, had no right to try to help. The problem was Steve was acting rational while I wanted to hear nothing of the sort.

Then, during my tantrum, I let all my feelings out. That woman at the restaurant last night could sit in the sun all day if she wanted. She could use baby oil for her tan without even getting a hint of a burn. I want to be her on vacation! I want to be tall and thin in a white French bikini with a golden tan. Like the ad for the hotel where we're staying. Like the *Sports Illustrated* swimsuit edition. Like the television commercials that promise it's better in the Bahamas!

I wanted the package deal, the package promise: an all-inclusive vacation where, besides your water sports and meals, you get to look like the ideal woman, society's model of perfection! Sure, I knew intellectually this was an unrealistic cultural invention featuring capitalism at its best, mother of the eating disorder epidemic, but I'll be damned at just how hard it is to refuse to let it get to you.

Steve knows me. He let me go on until I ran out of steam.

"Maybe that's the package you feel like you want, Ellen," he said. "But I signed up for a different all-inclusive deal. Water sports, meals, sure. But my package included a 4 foot 8½ inch woman with sensitive skin, one who, after having a day or two in the shade, will come snorkeling with me on the beach."

As I SAT in the corner of the deck looking pretty much like an advertisement put out by dermatologists warning about the risks of skin cancer, I realized how much a part of me still wanted to sign up for that other package. Despite what I know about eating and body issues and the fallacy of thinking that a certain number on the scale or tape measure is the promise to happiness, the culture and its biases affect us all in different ways and from time to time.

I don't want to be tall and thin because being tall and thin are intrinsically better characteristics, but because we live in a culture that offers rewards for those meeting this subjective criteria, and punishments for those who differ.

Sometimes I let my desire for a quick fix get the better of me. Sometimes when I see a very tall woman, I will find myself bargaining silently, like I am at an auction or flea market. "She must be 5 feet 10," I reason. "If only I could have a mere three inches or so, she would still get to be tall, and I would be a little less short!"

I imagine the clothes that would fit off the rack, and the leggy look I would exude as I stroll down the beach. I think about how nice it would be to not have people pointing at me and laughing at my shortness. I fantasize that if I were tall I would be more successful, sexier, and happier.

And then I stop and realize that I am again playing the "change your shape, change your life game." A game that has no end and no winner because who you are goes way beyond how you look, and how you look is impermanent.

AT TIMES WHEN my children are walking with their classmates, I find myself doing an automatic scan of the height differential and where my children fall in the grouping. And then I stop myself, and instead listen to the harmony of laughter.

I know I'm not the only parent who has struggled with issues related to height. My friend Audrey often brings her five-year-old, Craig, to our house. One day she was telling me about his latest checkup at the pediatrician's. She said everything was fine except her son was still "S-H-O-R-T." She spelled the word out in a whisper.

"Why are you spelling the word 'short?'" I asked her.

She nudged her head in the direction of her son. "I don't want him to hear. I don't want him to know he is short. I don't want to give him a complex."

It is true that as much as height and weight shouldn't matter, they often do. Our feelings are greatly influenced by the societal ideal.

Despite struggling to defend ourselves against an enormous diet, pharmaceutical, and fashion industry, we still feel its force. These messages are everywhere, on billboards, television, magazines, and buses. A short, fat man might promote Dunkin Donuts, but it is the tall, thin, and sleek male and female models that entice us to buy luxury cars and sophisticated colognes.

It's hard to escape from the cultural forces that tell us one body type is the ideal. That tall is better than short, and thin is better than rounder. Those forces creep up on you without you realizing, and all of a sudden you're in the grips of those biases.

Last week, Steve and I took our children and our teen-age nephew, Dan, to lunch. Dan is 6 foot 1 inch tall and still growing. He was discussing his feelings about being taller than his parents and many of his teachers. He then asked Allison and Matt if they thought they were going to be short or tall when they grew up.

Matt was busy eating his French fries and didn't say too much. Allison said she thought she would be on the short side, "but probably taller than mom."

I offered that it's hard to predict just how tall someone will grow, but at this point, they both appeared to have inherited my shorter height as opposed to their father's taller height. My husband looked at the kids and said, "Sorry, guys."

My mouth fell open even before he struggled to take his foot out of his own mouth.

"I can't believe I just said that," he offered.

Later I told him that despite his insistences that I am perfect as I am, that my shortness is a non-issue, I think that heightism and weightism pervade our culture and influence us all at different times and in different ways. The worst thing we could do, I suggested, is to ignore the impact it plays. When you do that, you end up feeling that something is wrong with you, rather than that something is wrong with a culture that rewards some body types at the expense of others.

I think as a culture, we have been brainwashed to view tall, short, fat, and thin people as being totally different from each other. As competition, instead of as a garden full of different types of blooming flowers. What binds us all together is our humanity and the way in which cultural stereotypes regarding bodies have influenced us in one way or another.

FOR MANY YEARS I ran therapy groups for women suffering with eating disorders. Those with anorexia nervosa and/or bulimia worked together in one group, and those dealing with compulsive eating comprised the other. As it happened, on one weeknight I ran two groups back to back. From 6:00–7:30 P.M. I saw those struggling with anorexia and bulimia, and from 7:30–9:00 P.M. I saw those struggling with compulsive eating.

Outside of the group room was a small reception area. One door served as exit and entrance. During the initial meetings, a curious tension filled the office. Those women leaving the 6:00 group, most of whom, despite their protests to the contrary, were extremely thin, would pass through the reception area where the women of the 7:30 group were waiting. These women were all women of size.

I would observe the silent rules and behaviors the women in these two groups created. Hurried glances at each other, followed by quickly averted eyes. The sudden urge by those who were seated to search their pocketbooks for something that never materialized. Shifts in the chair. The pulling of a jacket more fully over the body.

The women exiting the 6:00 group seemed to huddle together, their bodies somehow more substantial when walking in pairs of two or three. It was hard for the seated women not to notice the bony limbs and thready veins that throbbed from the arms of the women exiting the group room. The women with anorexia nervosa and bulimia would glance at the women filling every inch of the chairs in the waiting room and then walk more swiftly to the door, a mixture of fear and apology in their pale faces.

During the first week, the women in the compulsive eating group looked uncomfortable. There were six members and myself. After they had seated themselves, I closed the door and sat in my chair. A few women got up and moved to different chairs, or tried sitting on various sections of the couch. One woman groaned as the love seat sank a few inches when she lowered herself into the cushion. Getting situated with girth was hard. I understood. My feet didn't reach the ground on my chair. Did they notice?

A few eyes challenged me. A glare, almost. A silent protest that said, "How the hell are you going to help us?" In their minds I was part of the "other" group, the 6:00 group. The thin group. Someone who didn't have a "weight problem." Someone who couldn't possibly understand what it was like to be fat. Someone who wasn't teased, or laughed at, or assigned attributes strictly based on stereotypes of body size. Someone who wasn't told to try to "do something" about her size to look more "acceptable."

I had met each group member individually during an assessment interview. Each member understood that the goal of this group was not weight loss. All group members had been in numerous diet programs and had lost and regained weight many times. This group was a non-diet approach to food, founded upon the research showing that diets don't work. That deprivation itself leads to a cycle of bingeing, self-loathing, and weight gain.

The group was about understanding the reasons that led to compulsive eating. It was about learning what they were truly hungry for: Love? Companionship? Meaningful work? Power? The group was about understanding what the deprivations were about, and where the guilt was coming from and why. It was about distractions. How did a focus on weight, food, and diet allow them to ignore more pressing issues? It was about exploring the way in which an eating disorder kept them in a box by living a constricted life. It was about challenging the cultural ideal of perfection, the stereotypes about being female, and the politics of body size. It was about acceptance.

I think a combination of these issues brought each woman to the group. But I think that after watching the thin women from the 6:00 group depart, and looking at me alone in the room with them, they would have been happy at that moment to leave.

After introductions, I asked them each to write down on a small piece of paper one thing they hoped to get out of the group, and one thing they feared in joining the group. I asked them not to put their names on the paper. Each member folded the paper and put it in a small basket I had placed in the center of the room. I then asked each person to pick a piece of paper and open it, making sure it was not her own.

Next, I asked each woman to read what the other person had written, one at a time, out loud. The common hopes and fears instantly helped the group feel more united and less alone. One theme that emerged as a group concern dealt with me as the group therapist. As the similarities of their own hopes and fears helped create a bond between the women, it also enabled them to work together in expressing their discomfort with my size.

"How can you understand what it's like to be our size?" one wondered.

Another group member offered, "You probably weigh now what I weighed when I was ten years old."

Still another chimed in with, "I think I was born weighing more than you!"

I remember leaning back in my chair, my feet striving to anchor at least the toes of my shoes on the floor, and saying, "Tell me. Tell me what it's like to be you, day in and day out. Tell me what it's like to be fat."

Week after week they spoke of a low self-esteem. They spoke of feeling like they were not good enough, worthy enough, or loveable enough. They didn't fit in. The women talked about the painful, hurtful comments people made about their size. About the assumptions people make if you are fat.

They talked about being passed over for promotions and the difficulty of living fat in a society that fears fat to the same intense degree it loves thin. They talked about their longing to be able to go to the beach in the summer and swim in the ocean, but how they would never dare because even just the thought of a bathing suit was enough to put them over the edge.

They talked about how no matter what you look like, we live in a society that insists that with enough time and money spent, you could look "better."

And over time, an interesting thing happened. When the 6:00 group passed the 7:30 group in the reception area, no longer were the women such opposites. Rather, they were the extremes of the same coin. Through the group process, and the many discussions that took place in each group on the political, cultural, relational, and personal experience of body size, they realized that while the outward symptoms and physical appearances were different, the internal struggles and issues were the same.

Both feared being visible and invisible, in control and out of control. Both feared not measuring up or being "good enough." Both resented the cultural pressures to fit an unrealistic goal of perfection, and in their own way, each rebelled against this pressure.

Now they acknowledged each other with nods and smiles as they passed. Jaws were no longer as clenched and eyes no longer cast downward. My height was seen in the same light. Together, as well as separately in our own unique way, we shared a history (HERstory) of differing from a subjective, cultural view of "right."

This was a great insight. One to hold onto, because people will try to tear it down one comment at a time.

I REMEMBER picking up at the airport a well-known therapist who specialized in compulsive eating. She was to be the keynote speaker at an eating disorders conference hosted by the agency for which I worked. She had written two books and staked her career on body acceptance. She also knew my sister professionally, though we had never met.

As I walked up to greet her at the gate and introduce myself, she stopped and exclaimed, laughing, "Oh, my gosh, look at you! You're even shorter than your sister!"

I didn't say anything, just sort of smiled and laughed, but I was pissed. I had footnoted her on many a term paper. Had admired her convictions about challenging the rigid cultural ideal. Her ease in commenting about my shortness before even saying hello baffled me, but attested to the continued sanctioning of height prejudice.

Would she make such comments about weight? She has based her reputation on size acceptance. She would never think of saying to someone "you're even fatter (or thinner) than your sister."

That's the invisible built-in bias of height prejudice. It's painful. And it's real.

My decision to treat eating disorders was itself a way of dealing further with the conflicts I experienced around my own body size. On the one hand, my shortness elicited the concern of my parents and different doctors. On the other hand, when the experts reported that nothing could be done to change my height, the doctors and my parents emphasized how much easier it would be for me as a short female.

My mother worried about my brother's height. "Make sure to keep an eye on your brother at school," my mother would say to me. "Those girls, they call him little Bobby. Maybe they just like him, but I don't want them to pick on him. Look after him and take care of him."

I am ten years old and my brother is seven. I see the girls at school. "Little Bobby!" They call out. I don't remember his reaction. I can only see myself wanting to protect him, and not knowing how.

It seemed that the adults in my life wanted to change my height, but at the same time told me that I was just fine. The messages were confusing.

I felt that my brother's height elicited concern about how he could make it in a world that ridiculed short men, and that I was supposed to be somehow grateful I was female and could get by on being " little and sweet." Still, I was reminded that something was "wrong" by the comments and continued measuring by both my parents and doctors, as well as by the teasing from peers and strangers regarding my height.

It wasn't just the hurtful teasing from strangers and students that was hard, but the constant comments from friends that were painful reminders that I was somehow seen as "less-than." Adding to this situation were the numerous expectations that I act in a certain way because of my shortness: as silly, childlike, compliant. Like the hurtful comments didn't matter. Like I was just supposed to laugh it off with a silly grin. Like I couldn't call these acts what they were, acts of prejudice, and have them taken seriously.

My interest in treating eating disorders had a definite connection to my predicament. Despite the seriousness of anorexia nervosa and bulimia, the fact that they have the highest fatality rate of any psychiatric illness, many people continue to make light of these conditions. Some look at anorexia nervosa as girls who simply take dieting too far.

People joke about anorexia and bulimia. They make fun of people who are fat. I've often heard friends complain about their weight and jokingly say "I wish I could be anorexic for a week."

I chose to specialize in a field in which the severity of the disorder/ problem is overwhelmingly clear and potentially deadly, but is often ridiculed, or not taken seriously. I chose to work in an area in which the body concretely plays out the refusal to abide by the dictates of a culture obsessed with one perfect, unattainable ideal body, yet at the same time yearns for the rewards promised to those who are viewed as "acceptable."

It is no wonder my passion lay with these disorders and these dilemmas. In a culture that reveals its biases by the tendency to round up one's height, (5 feet 1½ inches becomes 5 feet 2 inches) and round down one's weight (123 pounds becomes 120 pounds), so many of us become caught in a cycle of confusion. Of wanting to conform, and wanting to hold our own ground. Of wanting to be seen, of wanting to be taken seriously.

Of wanting to simply be.

By MIDDLE SCHOOL, I was eager to lose weight. After my year of thousand-calorie breakfasts came to an end, my dieting began in earnest. I figured that if I couldn't make my height more acceptable, at least I could have control over my weight. I wanted to be thin.

A neighbor across the street, Mrs. Mulkin, was 4 feet 10 inches and forever on a diet. She used to tell me that being short was hard, but being short and fat was horrible.

Mrs. Mulkin told me that as I grew older, I had better be diligent about counting calories. "When you are short," she would teach, "every pound gained shows."

I was a quick learner. My mind was equally preoccupied between counting calories and fantasizing about how the "new me" would change my life.

I persisted in my quest for a body that fit more closely with the models that decorated the glossy covers of my *Teen* and *Seventeen* magazines. I didn't know that those perfect and carefree looking models that stared seductively out of the magazine pages had been airbrushed. I didn't know that airbrushing could offer a bigger bust line, a smaller waist or longer legs.

Even if I did know of these things, I don't know if it would have mattered. Most of my friends were dieting, too. We bought into the fantasy that the perfect body would bring us the perfect life. Suppressing the initial panic we experienced at the realization that we were "too fat," we willingly spent hours poring over articles suggesting methods for losing unwanted pounds. We thought we were acting grown-up.

Our diet obsession was a rite of passage. It was what we saw our role models do: big sisters, mothers, college-aged cousins, and favorite aunts all did it. We were coming of age by coming apart. Separating our wholeness into disconnected limbs and body parts that were too wide, or big, or, well, just not "right." We were simultaneously "too much" and "not enough."

We accepted these contradictions and negative appraisals without question or fight. The energy for the fight was harnessed for our individual battles with our bodies, not against the culture that orchestrated the war and allowed the industries (diet, fashion, and eventually medical and pharmaceutical) to profit enormously from the emotional and physical carnage left in its wake.

From the images in our magazines, the stars on our favorite programs, and the commercials squeezed in between, we learned that being thin and tall held the promise of "having it all." We learned that once a woman, or girl, attained a certain figure, she would be glamorous and successful in both her career and her relationships. Wine glasses would toast her, mouths (by both males and admiring females) would proclaim "oohs and ahhs," strangers would buy and present her with flowers, doors would open for her, colleagues would listen to (and applaud) her ideas, beach parties would await her along with moonlit nights, and she would stay forever youthful, beautiful, and sensual.

Of course, because every diet has an equal and opposite binge, my friends and I spent a fair number of days breaking our diets with piping hot pizza oozing with cheese, cream-filled donuts, slice-and-bake cookies (always sliced, perhaps not always baked) and any other temptation we had defined as off limits during our period of diet and deprivation.

We were dutiful consumers who followed the extremes of deprivation and indulgence marketed to us, keeping the economy healthy and blaming our supposed lack of willpower for our despair.

DURING HIGH SCHOOL I became more involved in dance. With the tall, thin ballerina as my role model, the dissatisfaction with my body grew in proportion to the long legs and lithe bodies of my various dance instructors and peers.

The world of dance is an exaggeration of the cultural ideal, very tall and very thin. The norm wasn't simply the everyday diets and binges I had come to view as a fact of life. It grew to an obsession in the world of dance, theatre, and performance.

Dressed in leotards, with mirrors reflecting not only my image but also that of all the other dancers around me, I'd compare. And fret. Cindy's arms are so graceful, Carol's legs so long, Shari's stomach so tight. And Cindy, Carol, and Shari are all on diets. They are unhappy with their bodies.

"God," I think. "If these girls believe they need to lose weight, what must they think about me?" The thought that Jan or Nancy might be admiring an aspect of my body, or my abilities, escaped me. The fact that we were all unhealthily obsessed with our bodies escaped all of us.

My high school dance teacher was constantly dieting and wishing she were taller than her 5 feet 4 inches. Once, when I told her that I coveted a smaller chest, she pulled me aside and ushered me into the bathroom. From her dance bag she pulled out a beige cotton Ace bandage.

Ms. Nash told me to pull down my leotard, and then she took the bandage and wound it around and around and around, over my chest, and around my back. Over my chest and around my back. Over my chest and around my back, until my breasts were fully bound.

After fastening the bandage closed, she had me pull up my leotard and return to class. She smiled at her handiwork, and I smiled at my newly flattened bust, the image of a more "perfect" dancer's body.

As I danced, I tried to smile through the shallow, difficult breaths I struggled to take, feeling as if a dead weight were suffocating my chest. I saw my flat self reflected in the mirror. "Now," I thought to myself, "how can I make my legs look longer and my stomach seem flatter?"

Recently I came across an article in a magazine selling a more expensive version of my high school binding experience:

> Karl Lagerfeld's words are sure to make any red-blooded woman catch her breath. "It's smaller! Narrower! Skinnier! Tighter!" he announced triumphantly, referring to the latest silhouette he sent down the runway at his recent Chanel Couture Collection.

> Naturally, Karl offers some sartorial aid to achieve this somewhat unnatural form. He has designed a body-shaping slip made with a corset-like construction, promising it would skim two dress sizes from a woman's body. It's intended to be worn under his narrow, square shouldered silhouettes, what the designer calls elongated elegante. "It's not a corset," Lagerfeld notes, "It's a caress."[61]

Oh yeah, right. This designer may be selling a more chic version of the binding used by my dance teacher, but they are both delivering the same message: The female form is unacceptable and must be shrunk, skimmed off, or diminished in some fashion.

TODAY, PEOPLE CONTINUE to seek a thinner body through increasingly drastic means. Women are willingly going under the surgeon's knife for liposuction as a weight loss method.

Since its introduction in the U.S. in 1982, liposuction has been one of the most popular cosmetic procedures. Some plastic surgeons have reported that models represent a significant portion of their practice, generally coming with complaints about their lower abdomen or thighs. Photographers who claim they cannot get a good angle in their swimsuit shoot often recommend the procedure. This is to whom we are comparing ourselves.

As a culture, we attempt to diminish the severity of this relentless pursuit of unrealistic thinness and the extreme measures to which we turn. We give it a cute name, like "a tummy tuck." As if slicing off part of our flesh was merely an alteration, like taking up the hem of a dress. As if it were the most natural thing in the world to cut up our bodies to fit the latest ideal body image.

EVEN HEIGHT, a characteristic believed to be virtually unchangeable, is being subjected to treatment methods for purely cosmetic reasons. Growth hormone treatment is not the only method being used to try to "grow" people.

Xia Hetao, a doctor in China, lengthens legs. Dr. Hetao explains that he has received many letters from people saying that life has been hard for them because they were born short, and are looking for a way to grow taller and alleviate their suffering.

He offers a procedure that entails slicing a thighbone in half and inserting a steel rod supported by a metal frame on the outside of the bone. The patient then cranks the mechanism wider every day, forcing the leg to grow longer as it attempts to heal the gap with new bone.

The pain is excruciating, and most people can't stand it for long. But Hetao notes that one young man gained 6½ inches. This procedure has also been used in the United States.

EACH CULTURE HOLDS a particular image or role model of perfection, and its members compete within that environment to reach ever closer to that elusive body in ever more drastic ways. Now, competition appears to exist even between cultures themselves.

Only recently the Chinese learned that on average, the Japanese have become taller than they. For centuries, the Chinese have referred to the Japanese as "dwarfs." One of China's solutions, issued from Beijing, is to make it compulsory that every child, from nursery school on up, must drink a quarter-pint of milk daily in an effort to promote growth. The children (most of whom are lactose-intolerant) are not keen about this requirement. Yet the Chinese have accepted it as a necessary evil if the Chinese are to become a taller nation. Chinese magazines featuring tall, lanky models and basketball stars reinforce the increasingly strong pressure for its citizens to achieve a taller height.

AS TEENS, WE ALL TRIED, in one way or another, to will our bodies to conform. We were encouraged in these endeavors. Another dance teacher suggested diet pills to curb our appetites. Still another swore by her one-day-a-week fast.

I tried most suggestions. My friends and I would pop diet pills the way others popped breath mints. I would visit the drug store, looking up and down the "diet aid" section. The promises were appealing. I was a willing consumer. I bought Dexatrim and Prolamine, sometimes Promathene for variety.

At first, I took the recommended dosage. But soon I heard of dance friends who would double the dose. I had a close friend, Mandy. She told me that for a few days she had even tripled the dosage and wasn't hungry at all. In fact, she claimed, she had increased energy without eating!

Both of us had fifth period free. We met in the girl's bathroom and downed the pills. Then we drove down to the coffee shop a few blocks from school. Mandy and I ordered coffee with Sweet'n Low.

Between the diet pills (which are mostly caffeine) and the coffee, my hands shook through American History and Algebra. I took that as a good sign. A "losing weight" sign. A "feeling sort-of-sick and suffering, so good! I'll get thinner" sign.

Months of diet pills led into a fasting trial. For four days I ate nothing, drinking only water, diet coke, and coffee with my trusty Sweet'n Low. My friends thought I was on a diet where I ate breakfast and dinner, but no lunch. I told my parents I was on a diet where I ate breakfast and lunch, but no dinner.

At 3:00 A.M. going into the fifth day of fasting, I woke up in utter terror. My heart was pounding, I could barely breathe, and I was freezing.

It took me fifteen minutes to crawl to my parent's bedroom next door. I woke up my mother. She made me tomato soup in the middle of the night.

IT BEGAN TO SET IN that diets would render me thinner, but never taller. I could be short and thin, that was the most I could hope for.

I would never be "right" enough. I seemed to gravitate towards those who reinforced this belief by comparing me to others where I would inevitably "fall short."

At that time, I was unable to question such comparisons and assumptions. Already my parents and numerous doctors had been involved in the minutiae of my height and body size. I had been measured repeatedly and subjected to endless comments about my stature. I took it as a given: I didn't "measure up."

Despite my academic successes, my hobbies and interests, despite having friends, deep down I felt something was terribly wrong with me. I simply wasn't good enough.

My boyfriend at the time, a very tall dancer whom I thought I loved, in hindsight proved to be my enlisted persecutor. He too embarked on endless diets, which inevitably led to binges. In fact, Jeff liked to smoke pot because he would get the "munchies" and binge. His uninhibited state made room for the physical sensations demanding attention. Simply put, the drug gave Jeff permission to eat in the foodless world he had created.

When he wasn't high, the binges that inevitably occurred as a result of deprivation were dealt with through vomiting. Jeff told me that because I was short, I had to watch every ounce. Jeff told me that I should try sticking my finger down my throat, too.

Other girls had boyfriends who encouraged them to take up skiing, who bought them flowers, told them they loved them, took them to the prom. I figured that was for other girls. I was wrapped up in the drama of trying to "measure up." This, I reasoned unconsciously then, was best served by falling for a guy with whom you had to prove your worthiness. Again and again.

What was the use in falling for someone who already thought I was great? Certainly no challenge in that. And what's wrong with him, I would reason, if he thinks I'm so terrific? I was too short, not skinny enough. So I made sure I "fell in love" with a boy who willingly reminded me of my "shortcomings" and pointed out to me the girls at school who he believed were beautiful.

Comparisons. I was used to that.

I aimed to please. I tried to vomit with Jeff. I'd stick my fingers down my throat and gag and gag, but nothing came up. I remember once trying to throw up at his house one afternoon before varsity cheerleading practice. I gave up quickly, as all that happened was that my eyes became red and teary.

Jeff told me my mascara was running. "Make sure you buy the

waterproof kind," he advised. Jeff suggested I wear a different style of shorts for practice, "a little looser in the stomach and shorter in the leg. It will give you the illusion of looking taller and thinner than you are."

Oh.

I was forever on the scale. On, off, on, off. There was always a place on the tiled bathroom floor that would increase weight, another that would decrease the number. I would move the scale; adjust. Step on. Step off. Move. Pee. Try again. I'd take the best three out of five results. I'd go out for a run and weigh myself upon my return, before grabbing a glass of water to rehydrate myself, and possibly move the scale accordingly.

I wanted control. If I couldn't change my height, at least I could be thin, a little more acceptable, a little more okay.

Someone once told me that diuretics (water pills) work great for losing a quick few pounds. My father had a bottle of Diuril, a prescription diuretic, to treat his high blood pressure. For years, I would steal a pill when I felt "too bloated."

I spent a summer in Israel when I was sixteen years old starving myself in order to look what I thought would be more acceptable. If Jeff thought I was thin (i.e., good enough), then I would have succeeded.

I was so used to looking at other people's reactions to my size as a gauge to how "okay" I was, I became hyper-attuned to others. How often I would walk down the street and hear people laugh as they whispered, "she's so short!"

THROUGHOUT THE YEARS, I have been stopped on the street and have heard the following remarks (this is merely a sample of a quite extensive list):

"How's the weather down there?"

"You must have drunk a lot of coffee and smoked a lot of cigarettes as a kid to stunt your growth like that!"

"Hey! It's a munchkin."

"A little Smurf!" "No," his friend says, "it's a Smurfette!"

"Just how tall are you?" (To which I would usually reply, "not very.")

"Hey, they said you can stand up now!"

"Are you still sitting down?" (When he passes you on the next street corner.)

"SHRIMP!"

"She looks like a midget!"

"Did you see her? (Giggle, giggle) She's so short!" And they keep turning around to stare.

From contemporaries I have heard:

"Gosh, Ellen (chuckle, chuckle), my daughter Cindy is only in the fifth grade and she is already taller than you are!" (Chuckle, chuckle.)

And, "Ellen, I love standing next to you because you make me feel so tall." (From Lisa, who is about 5 feet 1 inch tall.)

From another contemporary:

"I thought *I* was short. I want to hang out with you!" She rests her arm on my head and says, "Finally, I can use somebody as my arm rest! I hate being short and having people make comments about my height to me, don't you? That's why it's so nice to be with you; I get to be the tall one for a change!" (She is 5 feet).

SOMETIMES PEOPLE ASK MY HEIGHT, and when I reply 4 feet 8½ inches, they say, "I didn't know you were that short!" Which is like saying, "Gosh, I didn't' know you were that fat!"

Recently I was at a friend's fortieth birthday celebration at a lavish hotel in Boston. I went to use the restroom while the band took a break. Apparently a lot of women had the same idea, because when I walked out of the stall, there was a long line for the two bathrooms.

Before I even made it over to the sink to wash my hands, my friend's mother-in-law said to the women standing near her, "That's Ellen! Didn't I tell you she was so short! Just look!"

Suddenly all eyes were upon me as this woman demanded, "How tall are you?"

Stunned, I answered. I turned to leave and the eyes followed me. I heard whispers and giggles.

This woman was large. I'd never say to her, "There she is! Look at how fat she is. How much do you weigh?"

Why do people think it is okay to confront me and laugh at my height? Even worse, why am I supposed to smile at their comments because after the teasing, I am declared to be "little and cute?"

As A CHILD, a teen, and into my early adult years, I often resorted to self-deprecating humor in an attempt to make people feel comfortable about my size. I tried to show that I wasn't "hung up" about my height. It had a price for me, and it also gave others the idea that I must really be concerned about my height because I so willingly brought the subject up.

I think many short people share this dilemma. If you talk about your height, people may think you are too self-conscious. But if you don't address the size issue, they wonder when you are going to address the proverbial elephant in the kitchen.

You're stuck. Whether you mention your height, or you don't, people assume you are "overly self-conscious." If that weren't enough of a minefield to send any self-respecting short person scurrying under the nearest rock, we also have to contend with people's stereotypical ideas about our personalities. For a woman these include:

Cute
Sweet
Peppy
Perky
Silly
Not Serious
Feisty
Childlike/Childish
Demure
Dainty
Acquiescing

Put "short" before any of the above, and they sound familiar. For example: short and sweet.

Now, look at the following list:

Sexy
Regal
Statuesque
Serious

Stunning
Gorgeous
Distinguished
Sophisticated
Elegant
Striking
Willowy
Aristocratic

Put "tall" before any of the above and they sound familiar. For example: tall and regal.

Now put "tall" before the adjectives associated with "short" and read them. For example: tall and cute. Now do the same with "short" before the adjectives associated with being "tall." For example: short and aristocratic. It sounds much less familiar.

It is often said that in this society, it is easier to be a short woman than it is to be a short man. When I look at the adjectives associated with these statures, I see that shortness in females is associated with characteristics of women in more general terms: i.e., silly, childlike, acquiescing. The stereotypes of the short woman are compatible with the existing power structure, and so on the surface level, she appears to have an easier time dealing with a heightist culture.

I would argue, however, that beneath the surface there is often a price to pay in keeping important aspects of her submerged. I think most, if not all short women face a challenge early on in life. We must either accept people's affection based on their concept of our stature (e.g., as being compliant, powerless, childlike, silly), or risk losing that affection by acting in a way that differs from the stereotypes assigned to short women.

It often starts with a pat on the head. How childish that pat can make you feel!

Sometimes people will place a hand on top of my head and move it along an invisible line to where my height falls on their body. "You only come up to here on me!" they will exclaim.

What am I supposed to say? Somehow, I feel like they are all implying I am not as "evolved" or as complete a person as they are. That

I am not as "adult."

I know of a rambunctious seventeen-year-old student. Complaining about his behavior, his teacher told the principal, "He'll never become a real adult anyway, he's only 5 feet 2 inches tall!"

It can happen in so many different ways. Like the time I was at an accessory store with my friend Bonnie.

We were looking to buy our friend Jennifer a little bauble for her birthday. The saleswomen in the store are familiar with their customers, ours being a small town that loves to accessorize. Tidbits of conversation flowed easily as we examined the lipstick holders, earrings, and jeweled evening purses."

"Do I know the person you are buying a gift for?" the saleswoman asked.

"Yes, it's for Jennifer Katz," Bonnie replied.

"Oh, sure! Jennifer was in just the other day. She was looking at some belts. Is it her birthday, then?" she asked.

"Yep," Bonnie answered. "On Friday."

"Not the big forty yet?" the saleswoman joked.

"No," Bonnie had said, "She has at least a year or two until that one!" Bonnie and I surveyed the rack of belts, and then continued walking around the small boutique.

My eye caught a brown leather pocketbook hanging on the wall. It had a funny shape to it, sort of angled on the top, the zipper turning inward. I took the purse off the hanging nail and put it over my shoulder as I walked towards the mirror. This was just what I had in mind for a fall bag.

"Isn't it fabulous?" the saleswoman asked, smiling.

"It's great," I answered. "But I was thinking of this for me, not Jennifer."

"What a great bag!" Bonnie said. I brought it over to the counter.

"The only thing I'm wondering," I said, "is whether my wallet will fit in it." The purse was a funny shape, and the way the zipper curved down, you almost had to fit everything in on the left side on an angle.

Well let's see," the saleswoman said helpfully. She took the tissue paper out of the handbag while I took my wallet out of my purse in preparation to try the new bag out.

All of a sudden her demeanor and voice changed as if she were speaking to a five-year-old. "Why, what a big wallet you have for such a little girl!" she cooed in a singsong voice.

I froze. I was unable to come back with a quick remark like, "Ah, the better to pay you with, my dear." Instead, I quickly turned away, said I wasn't interested in the purse, and let Bonnie know that I wanted to leave the store. I was seething by the time we got into Bonnie's Suburban.

"What's wrong?" Bonnie wanted to know. She had returned to the belts on the other side of the store while I was looking at the purse and hadn't heard the exchange. I played it back to her, fuming with every word.

Bonnie, well aware that I've been working on a book about height, offered soothing comments. "That's why you need to write about this," she said. "People need to be aware of how this bias against short people keeps rearing its ugly head."

"You know, Bonnie, this kind of thing happens all the time. I don't think I fully realized just how many comments went directly to my unconscious, but still affected me. You know that store "Necessities" down the street?"

Bonnie nodded.

"Well," I began, "I love their sweaters, but I hate going in there. Every time I do, this one saleswoman pinches my cheeks and tells me I look like a little girl. And not just once. The whole time I'm trying on clothes, she's pinching my cheeks, telling me how little I am and that I look like a doll. I don't want to be a doll! Not a plastic one with a silly grin, or a china one that's fragile and breaks."

Bonnie is settling in the driver's seat, sensing that I have more to rant about.

"Just now," I continued, "if the saleswoman had said that the purse looked big for me, that would be fine. She would voice her opinion, which I could listen to or not. But what she said is so infuriating! 'What a big wallet you have for such a little girl! First of all," I ticked off, "she knows who I am. She knows I have two school-aged children. She knows that you, Jennifer and I are all in our late 30s. And yet she still feels comfortable calling me a "little girl." Ask an African American man how he feels being called "boy" by some white folks!"

My voice is getting louder now. "Second, what does that mean? Because I am short, somehow I'm not entitled to a "big" wallet? Is my height a measurement of how much economic power I am allowed? Just because I'm under 5 feet, does that mean I shouldn't carry a driver's license, credit cards, money, receipts, and all the other 'stuff' that adults carry?"

I stopped for a quick breath and then I was off again. "I should have told her yeah, a big wallet that just happens to hold enough cash to buy that purse! Somewhere else!"

BECAUSE I AM SHORT, must I stay childlike in others' eyes? Perhaps I should carry around the purse I loved as a little girl. A patent leather spring green purse that I wore proudly over my shoulder. It had a grown-up sound. S-N-A-P open. S-N-A-P close.

I put all of my essentials in the little handbag: a tiny blue comb, two quarters, a Canadian nickel, a tiny mirror, and my lucky pink rabbit's foot. How I felt like a grown-up. "Coming, mommy! Just let me get my purse!"

I'm sure no one is trying to be rude. But treating me like a child makes it difficult for me to be the real person I am, feel my own strength, determination, and passions.

Instead of feeling real, I end up feeling like a wind up doll, programmed to do very little. Pull my string and I'm supposed to smile, giggle and keep my thoughts to myself. And like the doll, never gain an ounce.

THE STEREOTYPES ASSOCIATED with short men oppose society's general view of the dominant male, and thus his struggle is much more public.

For men, tallness is equated with power, success, and attractiveness. "Tall, dark, and handsome" has a familiar ring. On the other hand, short stature in males is associated with a lack of power and success. "Short, dark and handsome" is a less familiar buzz. It's more difficult for men to conform to the attributes associated with shortness in general, as it opposes society's mandate of being the big and powerful male, commanding respect. Instead, he must strive to gain power and recognition *in spite* of his height, as an obstacle to overcome.

Like the many short women who develop eating disorders in an attempt to meet at least half of the cultural ideal (tall, thin), lots of short men try to alter more changeable aspects of their body size. Lifting weights or using bodybuilding substances to add muscle and bulk are common among short men in this society. In this way, they continue to strive for the bigness associated with maleness in our culture.

One day I was shopping at a shoe store, trying on a pair of canvas Sketchers. The manager, whose name turned out to be Kyle, was helping me find my size, and said, "These would be a good sneaker for you. The platform gives you some extra height." He smiled at me and winked, "Believe me," he said, "I'm always looking for some extra inches myself."

I told him that I really just liked the shoe, and actually didn't wear high heels much anymore. "I got tired of having sore feet," I told him.

He continued talking to me about his height and then said to me, "It's hard enough being a short man, but even harder being a short black man."

Soon the Sketchers were left in a pile and we began talking about how our shortness affected our lives in different ways. He pulled up his shirtsleeves and showed me his muscles. He told me how he had taken up weightlifting and spent huge amounts of time at the gym. He was incredibly muscular.

Kyle told me, "I'm 5 feet 6 inches tall. No one's looking at the small guy. I'm in a crowded room and I get lost. The only way I get attention is by working out; let them see my biceps. I had to figure out a way that I could get attention. Being a small guy, I was unnoticed. So I had to do something, make a physical change to get noticed. That's why I started working out and taking creatine as a supplement to pump my body up. If you're short and skinny, you're known as the little shrimp. And I got tired of being the shrimp. I said I want to be the big lobster instead."

I understood what he meant. I know well the feeling of walking into a crowded room, like at a party. I would always do a quick scan, a quick evaluation. At least 99.9 percent of the time, I was the shortest. Then I'd move on to weight: how did I compare?

I was keeping score, like at the Olympics. I'd deduct points for different aspects of our so-called performances. We all seemed to be acting in some way and evaluating each other and ourselves in another way. Through smiles I would try to hide the insecurity and jealousy.

Women in this culture compete with each other. Groups that occupy a subordinate role in society are implicitly taught to turn against each other, competing for the rewards offered to the few chosen. It is in the dominant group's best interest to keep the subordinate group in competition with factions within. In this way, the subordinate group is unable to band together as a strong force and challenge those holding power. Therefore, the status quo remains.

I imagine judges and announcers in my head:

"There's the flip. Notice how the hand gets in position just as the laugh begins and her head moves back. She leans slightly forward, then brushes her shoulder-length hair from her face and then flips it straight up and back."

"Beautiful," the other hallucinated announcer would murmur. "Did you notice at the end how just those few wisps of hair fell ever so slightly across her forehead and then slowly receded back into that luscious mane? A delight to watch. She's been practicing that move since she was a young girl. Now, the judges cannot give her a well deserving 10 because she's put on a few pounds this year. Her stomach is definitely rounder than last year, which is a shame. Still, I think she'll be able to squeak out a solid 8.5."

"Yep," the other absurd judge in my brain would add. "Her competition lies with the new woman in town. But I think this new woman is going to have to execute a truly superb performance to make up for her extreme shortness. She's thin, yes, but she is severely lacking in inches."

"You know, you have to wonder why she doesn't choose a higher heel. Couldn't she get her hands on some growth hormone? Or at least that new height-enhancing insole now on the market?" the announcer wonders.

"I agree. I think it will cost her dearly. And now, a word from our sponsors at *Sharper Image*, makers of the "PowerFlow Height-Enhancing Insoles.""

"Who wouldn't like to be taller?" the announcer in the commercial asks. "I'm 5'11, and even I notice that at parties or social situations, the tallest guy seems to have an advantage…"

FOR ME, it is the initial entrance into a room of crowded people that is the most difficult. The initial jolt.

I feel fine as I prepare to go out to a particular function. I feel okay about my appearance, and comfortable with my ability at conversation. But once I enter the room, the height thing affects me in a lot of ways. All of a sudden I am literally looking up at everyone, and they are looking down at me. This physical necessity takes on an emotional component.

Most people react to a short person with a lot of stereotypes attributed to that person based on height. They act in ways that are often offensive, yet the comments and gestures are dismissed because height prejudice is not taken seriously. The way short people are often not taken seriously.

Most always, people will comment on my being "so short." Despite a strapless black evening dress, I am still subjected to pats on the head. It's hard to feel sophisticated and sexy with pats on the head.

When approaching a bar at a function, I try squeezing my way through to order a drink. A few men will just look at me in a snide way and say, "God, we

Reprinted with permission

didn't even see you down there. Are you ever short!" Others will snicker, point, and laugh with their friends.

Just the other week I was at a Christmas party hosted by Steve's firm. I was standing with a group of six people when a new employee walked over. His name was Jon, and someone in the group introduced him to the spouses in our group. He shook everyone's hand and said "hello." When he got to me, Jon bent down to his knees with a silly grin and said, "Well, hello down there." I was mortified.

I think the hardest part about these feelings of not measuring up physically is dealing with the stereotypes that are attributed to short stature. And to being a woman.

Inside, I feel smart. I feel important. But for a long time I would keep that self undercover and play the silly, funny, flirty, cute little girl. Acting this way gives me a quick fix, but a hangover the next morning. When my internal self enters the outside world, it is as if I must continually battle with the external expectations that others have about me because of my shortness.

I have struggled with aspects of myself that didn't meet the adjectives associated with being "vertically challenged." It's hard. Hard to risk alienating others by being true to yourself.

For a long time, it was as if I were engaged in my own personal civil war. Part of me continued to be the people-pleaser. The happy-go-lucky, perky, silly girl/woman with a smile on her face. The other side was the rebellious, adventurous, intellectual, serious type, much less known to others. This was the side of me that enjoyed sitting in a coffeehouse or bar late at night discussing art, literature, and politics. A serious, articulate woman without a pasted-on smile. Only somewhat recently in my adult life have these two sides merged much more easily. The merger was a long time in the making.

I remember attending a social function with Steve. During dinner, the conversation shifted to a heated political debate about welfare reform. A man at the table looked at me and declared, "What a big mouth you have for such a little *thing*."

It was a reaction not unfamiliar. I have struggled with being taken seriously for a long time. As a high school cheerleader, I received a lot of attention and praise when climbing to the top of a pyramid. Very rarely was I given such attention for my intellect or aspirations.

Later in life, such sentiments were echoed even after I established myself professionally. When you are short, people enjoy treating you in a childlike manner. Once a colleague physically picked me up before a meeting just because "you're so little!" Another time an office manager said to me, "That's so funny, you have to stand on your tiptoes to reach the file cabinet!" The entire office staff laughed.

One worker asked if I counted as a midget. "You sure are lucky that you're thin. You must have to watch every ounce because you're so damn tiny! I bet your clients wonder if you're old enough to even be a therapist!" She walked away, but not before patting my head.

What do I do? What do I say? Do I just stand there and foolishly smile? Do I tell them that I find this kind of talk offensive? Over and over, day after day, it's hard to let these comments go by without saying anything.

But when I do say something, I'm told in a surprised tone that no one was trying to be hurtful. That I am "just so cute and little."

So often I feel stuck. As a short female, I am subjected to countless cultural biases against both my gender and my height, and yet in both instances, I am supposed to accept these biases graciously, as if they were not real prejudices, but rather benign comments.

Women in general, and short women in particular, have lived with the expectations the culture holds in demanding that females "act happy." Countless times as I am walking down the street I have been stopped by a man demanding, "Where's your smile?"

Can you imagine a woman feeling free to demand a smile from a male stranger crossing her path? How about a short woman asking a tall man, "Where's that smile?"

Just the other day I was at the airport en route to join my husband in California for a few days. I was standing at the ticket counter waiting to check in, rolling my blue suitcase along as the line slowly inched forward. Three different men felt compelled to comment about my size.

The first said, "Your suitcase is almost as big as you are!"

Then I heard, "How can someone so little have a suitcase so big?"

And finally, "I bet you could pack yourself right into that suitcase!" ("Yes, but there's no fucking air!" I wanted to yell).

I just smiled and laughed. What am I to do? When I landed in San Francisco, I collected my suitcase and proceeded to stand in the taxi line. Two businessmen got into line behind me and seemed fascinated with my luggage. First I overheard them talking to each other about my height, and then the size of my trusty Samsonite. Soon they looked directly at me and said, "How can such a small thing like you have so much to pack?"

I just don't get how it's any of their business. How does my height dictate the size of my luggage, or where I go and what I choose to take along? Can you imagine if I questioned something of theirs?

It's the kind of comment or question that an adult says to a child. That someone in a position of power might say to someone "beneath" him. These comments make me feel frustrated that people see someone short and feel so comfortable discussing his or her body and its size, as if the person was a free-for-all show.

"It's funny," my friend Bonnie said to me last month. "I don't see you as short at all. Your look, your attitude, it's just not like a short person's. I just don't think of you as being short."

She meant this as a compliment. She's heard me challenge the stereotypes associated with being short, with being female.

My heart sank. It's easier for me to hear the comments of strangers at the airport than her remark. To me, that statement implicitly meant she accepts the stereotypes associated with short stature. It reminds me of the "funny you don't look Jewish" or "you don't act gay" comments, the "you're not like them" statements.

I think being "complimented" in this way is one of the worst types of prejudice. Coated with a seemingly accepting attitude, it is deceptive, giving the person a sense of believing that he or she is not prejudiced or biased.

Bonnie had already made up her mind about how a person with a particular characteristic "should act." Declaring that the person in question "surpasses" such a conclusion and is the exception to the (judgmental) rule has some negative results.

First, it makes who I factually am invisible. To declare that an adult woman measuring 4 feet 8½ inches tall doesn't appear short is like saying a 400-pound woman isn't fat. It's not bad to be short or fat or described as such. The pain comes from the assumptions and judgments attached to a particular body size, and the discrimination that results from those attitudes.

These conclusions are culturally based and changeable over time. Think of artists such as Rubens, Rembrandt, and Renoir, who glorified the image of the large woman. Or consider Nigeria, where a big female is considered beautiful and being fat is seen as "…a sign of good health, prosperity, and allure."[62]

Put me in Japan, where my height is closer to average. Or visit Ghana, where "…a quick glance around is enough to tell the arriving visitor here that Ghana is a country designed for the abbreviated of stature."

THE PREJUDICES DIRECTED against those taller in stature led to the establishment of the "tall men's club of Ghana" where, according to member Sammy Dodoo, 6 feet 4 inches tall, "To be a tall person can be quite embarrassing, especially for a lot of younger guys. This society does everything it can to remind you that you are too tall. The result is that lots of tall people feel shy about asserting themselves."

Joseph Mensah, a founder of the club and at 6 feet 2 inches is one of its shortest members, states, "Our biggest preoccupation is to improve the social and financial well-being of our members. We can't do this until we have begun to make people feel proud of themselves."

He continues, "When kids are playing soccer, no one wants you on their team because you are so tall. When you are standing in a crowd, the short people jeer you, telling you that you are too tall, that you should get back. When boys start dating, everyone makes fun of you because of your height."[63]

SO VIEWS CHANGE depending on when and where a person is placed in a particular culture. The physical aspects of the body assume a positive or negative bias based on subjective assumptions.

Bonnie doesn't need to deny my shortness. Rather, she needs to resist the temptation to equate a person's height or weight with their worth, and to resist as well the prejudicial stereotypes associated with a characteristic.

Second, Bonnie's statement serves to separate me from a group: "You're not like those other (fill in the blank)." Being separated from a minority group membership by a person in the majority is like being given a dose of saccharin in your beverage: short-term, it may feel incredibly sweet, but long-term, it can be hazardous.

And finally, such statements are precarious. Saying I don't seem short because of certain reasons implies that tomorrow those reasons may change, and so, too, how I am perceived.

Better to see a short, assertive woman as short *and* assertive, rather than as not short because she is assertive. Better to see a fat, athletic woman as fat *and* athletic, rather than to embrace a stereotype that labels fat people as lazy and conclude, "I don't see you as fat because you are a runner."

Tara Lipinski, the fourteen-year-old 1997 U.S. National figure skater champion, wears a necklace engraved with the words "Short But Good." I wish her necklace said simply, "Short and Good." Without the qualifiers, without the surprise when a fat woman runs or a skinny person lounges in front of a television set deciding that channel surfing is an athletic pursuit.

I wish there was more space for a short person to be serious or seductive, and a tall person to be cute and silly. I want to live in a world where strangers don't pat my head, or comment on my suitcase, or laugh at me.

I want to be visible, including my shortness, which is a part of me, but doesn't define me. I don't want to be judged based on an ingrained bias against short people. I don't want to be part of a culture that attempts to physically alter the body as a way of "addressing" prejudice.

I think back to the eating disorder groups I ran. The skeletal women who dare us to look at the consequences of an unrealistic expectation of slenderness. The large women onto whom our culture projects its fears and mistrust of the body. The looks, stares, and whispers these women face on a daily basis. The unwelcome comments. The whole question of how much space one is allowed to take up in this world. The desire to be seen, really be seen, as a person, and not simply a number on the scale or the tape measure. The wish to fully express oneself and one's nature without the cultural constraints of being or acting a certain way because of one's body size.

I understand. With my legs dangling off the chair, feet barely brushing the floor, I solidly take a stand. It's not our bodies that need to be manipulated and altered. It is the continued acceptance of height and weight prejudice that must be changed.

"A comment here, a comment there, so what?" you might think. Tell that to the kid who is getting a shot every night in hopes of adding an inch to his height. Tell that to the fat woman who longs to feel the ocean wash over her body, but hasn't put on a bathing suit in years. Tell that to the anorexic in the hospital with an IV running through her vein. Tell that to me.

I LONG TO FEEL the wholeness of my soul, and the fullness of my spirit, but so often I feel like I am being shrunk instead. Like the fabric of my being, that 100 percent natural fiber has, from without and within, been carelessly cared for. It's not a simple machine wash and dry—sometimes the material needs to be handled with care, a gentler cycle, a place outside on a clothesline to soak in the sun and the scent of the breeze off the lilac bush. Some space and time to smooth out the wrinkles.

I can almost hear the ghosts of my past and the critics in my future saying, "Ellen, how can you put yourself in that category? You're not getting a shot each night, you're not suffering with anorexia."

I can remember hearing similar words as a child. "What do you have to be sad about? You have everything."

And so I tried to cover up the pain I felt, pushed it deep, deep down and covered it with the color and façade of bubble gum pink. I got caught in the thick stickiness and was unable to more forward without carrying around that stuck feeling, like gum on the bottom of the shoe. Because externally my life met the criteria of "good," I felt I was not entitled to express the pain I was in.

I remember Melissa. Oh, how I remember Melissa.

SHE WAS A YEAR OLDER than me, and one of the most beloved students in my high school. She was beautiful, with wide brown eyes in a face soft as a rose petal. Her auburn hair fell gently in waves to the thick of her back.

Melissa lived in a mansion with every manner of material wealth. One of the most popular girls in the school, we all sought her out for advice and looked to her as a role model. She excelled in her academics and was a social activist, organizing students in numerous volunteer programs to aid inner city youths.

On a hot July morning before beginning my freshman year at college, I was waiting for the train to bring me into Chicago, to my father's law firm, where I was working in the file room. A friend of mine ran up to me on the platform, her eyes red and swollen.

"Oh my God, Ellen!" she began as she hugged me. I felt her body shake in my arms.

"Julie, what is it? What's wrong?" I asked.

She looked into my eyes, which were still dry and bright, and she held my hands. "You haven't heard."

I shook my head slowly, my mind frozen and afraid. What is it?" I asked again.

"Melissa," she said. "Melissa's dead."

My heart fell. Fell down to my pelvis and on into my legs rendering them useless, as if the muscles just let go, the bones refused to stay solid.

"Oh my God," I kept saying over and over, folding my hands across my chest, suddenly cold, empty inside; no organs, just blood pumping and not knowing where to flow.

Before I could get my bearings, before I could ask what happened, what terrible accident had happened, my friend cried, "They found her early this morning. She killed herself."

"How could this be? How could this be? This girl had everything," is what the community said that whole summer, and each year after. They say it still. "She had everything."

Yet at the tender age of eighteen she put on her white graduation gown, got into her blue Corvette, and drove into the woods. She found a tree, took out a rope, and hung herself. Her long hair, I imagine, blew in the breeze long after her neck was strangled, long after her breathing had ceased.

MELISSA HAS NOW BEEN DEAD longer than she was alive. For years, I thought of Melissa every day. Even as an adult, when I was sad or in pain, I would take out my high school yearbook and look up Melissa's graduation picture. Her face has a faraway look, and she is holding a rose.

I know why I look at her picture during those times. She continues, as she did during high school, to teach me things. Looking at her, I remember and remind myself that internal pain exists regardless if the community and the culture tell you "you have everything" with the assumption that you should be happy.

Our society sets certain definitions regarding when a person should feel "content" or "happy" or what type of pain is legitimate, permissible to reveal. Our culture defines "happiness" in capitalist terms, such as through financial success. Even though the culture claims "money can't buy happiness," the enticements made through the accumulation of goods and looks promise otherwise. But if this were true, if economic success and thinness and fame bring true satisfaction, why are so many rich and famous people unhappy, struggling with eating disorders, or addicted to alcohol, drugs, or sex?

The problem is, material and financial wealth can offer an illusion that the person is or will be satisfied by the fulfillment of such goals. But desire for these things brings suffering. It brings suffering because these goals are elusive. They are impermanent; they cannot last forever. So the person who seeks happiness in such a way is forever trying to gain more wealth, more things to increase that happiness, or else he is trying to figure out how to maintain these things and thereby his state of happiness.

True happiness, true joy, cannot come from these things, despite what the culture at large may preach. Buddha's Four Noble Truths attest to the inherent problems in attempting to find happiness and inner peace by this method.[64]

So to look at the external life of a person and conclude that the person in question "should be happy, has everything, is not truly suffering or in pain" (i.e., emotional, spiritual) is a serious problem. It's the same sort of myth operating in the diet industry or in growth hormone treatment. The myth that being thinner or taller will lead to a more satisfying life, will reward the person with happiness and the removal of pain. It's a position that places the person in a cycle of looking increasingly to the external rather than the internal.

Because I am a short, thin woman who through marriage has financial wealth, economic advantage, and material comforts, I am not supposed to want or need more. But each one of us, deep down in our fabric, regardless of being wealthy or poor, thin or fat, black or white, tall or short, will feel pain. Capitalism has defined that certain conditions (appearance, socioeconomic status) override that expression of pain, but the heart, the soul, doesn't necessarily share that definition.

PICTURE YOURSELF ALONE, on an island, never having been part of a culture. Your first concerns would be food to feed the hungry stomach, water to quench the parched throat, and shelter. Even after satisfying these conditions, I can't imagine you would worry that your thighs looked fat, or spend time wishing you were taller. But you might think along these lines: Who am I? What is this world? How was it created? How am I connected to it? What is my purpose? Spiritual questions.

Living in a culture that places the material before the spiritual, the external before the internal, the assumption is often made that certain people have "no reason to be in pain." "How dare she feel dissatisfied when she is living the American dream?" This is in contrast to Bhutan, a small Buddhist kingdom nestled in the Himalayas, where when people talk of "wealth" they are referring to spiritual, not material, wealth.

The fact is, ours is a culture that doesn't want to let go of the myth that happiness can be found on the outside. We close our eyes and ears to the people who challenge this myth. Sometimes they close their own eyes and ears.

The attempt to numb, to distract from this realization, is strong. The anorexic mocks the notion that thinness brings happiness through her skeletal body, the drug addict proves that true happiness cannot be found by injecting the external.

I WANTED TO PROVE to others and to myself that I was important. I didn't want my soul to be measured by the inches of my height, or strictly by my role as suburban wife and mother. To shrink into the stereotypes associated with being a small female. But I didn't know how to begin the process of being fully me.

During childhood, my parents and doctors seemed to think that being taller would make my life happier, would improve who I was. That assumption itself made my life sadder. It translated into my belief that I had to prove my worthiness, compensate for my size, and find something that would make me seem bigger, taller, powerful. All with a smile on my face and a lightness in my heart because "Why should I complain? I have everything."

I developed my own addiction, a cycle of unhealthy relationships in which I sought to find my fabric, myself. But all in secret, because after all, who would understand when I supposedly had everything?

THERE

There, in the fog!
I know it exists,
Shrouded in the dense white mists
Opening, as if in Avalon.

I was there on the Island,
In a world that exists
Beyond my reality of what is.
A side hidden
Open
For a mere glimpse, before closing.

Take me there!
Let me walk into the mysteries
Let me dance in the clearing
Let me bathe in the tearful salt water
And let me dry in the sand
Of existence!

I belong
Where I cannot be seen
Until the sunshine of my soul
Infiltrates my clouded veins
Pumping life into the dormant dusk
Waiting for dawn.

How to clear the fog? To find what I know is there?
Enter. That is all.
Keep moving closer and closer
And closer, into the white, blanketed space
And there you are.

But there *you* are.
And I long for you to enter me.
To be my symbolic transformation penetrating
Into the passion that lies deep within the hidden layers of my heart.
To bring me to a place where I can never go with you.

Because once I enter with you,
I've already lost my direction.
But for the moment—
Ah! For the moment,
It is as if I have found my way in the mist.
I turn back, and I see the fog rolling in.
Already is the Island invisible. No sign it was there.
Foolishness! Of course it is there, how could I live if it were not?
It is merely hidden once again.
Soon, the outline will reveal itself,
Longing to be filled. With truth?
Or with a mockery of it?

Chapter Five
SELLING YOURSELF SHORT

I ALWAYS THOUGHT that
stature was inches, measurement.
What I am learning is that stature
is much, much more. It is power. It is heart. It is
spirit.

Like so many notions our culture has defined, we have mislabeled the "problem" of shortness as a lack of height and have sought the addition of physical inches in elevator shoes and growth hormone shots. But that aspect of stature is minor, much less consequential than the feeling of being authentic and being seen.

Like many women in this culture, I learned early on the importance of being attractive to men. Being "chosen" as special, singled out by a powerful man, is a sanctioned method of obtaining some fleeting experience of self-esteem, which the woman may be lacking.

We learn to diet and obssess about our weight; we are virtually competing with all of the women we know to be the prettiest, the thinnest, and the most coveted. It is one of the few ways females have learned to attain power. Female sexuality has always bestowed some sense of power on the woman.

This type of power comes with a hefty price. The woman's creativity, intellect, aspiration, and spirit are stifled. Only the magic wand of a man bestowing her as his princess offers her power and happiness. It is the stuff our fairy tales thrive upon.

What captures my attention so vividly in the popular fairy tales of today is the yearning to assert the true self that lies within the heroine. She sings:

I want adventure in the great wide somewhere, I want it more than I can tell. And for once it might be grand, to have someone understand, I want so much more than they've got planned.

"Belle" from Beauty and the Beast

In my own little corner, in my own little chair, I can be whatever I want to be. On the wings of my fancy I can fly anywhere, and the world will open its arms to me.

"In My Own Little Corner" from Cinderella

What would I give if I could live outta these waters . . .
Bright young women sick o' swimming
Ready to stand.

"Part of Your World" from The Little Mermaid

By the end of each tale all three characters have married their Prince Charmings, and that longing with which they sang at the beginning of the story has been silenced.

In her book *Revolution From Within,* Gloria Steinem states, "Several millennia worth of observers have believed that a unique and true self resides in each of us. It may be suppressed or nurtured, thwarted or developed, but it is there."[65]

What happens to these heroines who sang of such drive and strength? The desire to express her true self and power, to gain access to the wonder the world has to offer, to leave her mark, is supposedly satisfied through her marriage to the prince.

Steinem quotes from the *Gnostic Gospels:*

If you bring forth what is within you,
what you bring forth will save you.
If you do not bring forth what is within you,
what you do not bring forth will destroy you."[66]

IN ESSENCE, with each rendition of these fairy tales we reinforce the notion that the ultimate fulfillment of a girl's dream is marriage. Only when a woman is young and beautiful, about to become a bride and take on her husband's identity, is she supposed to achieve happiness. And even then, it is only in her passivity that she is admired.

Indeed, Snow White and Sleeping Beauty were in a "deathlike sleep," the spell only to be broken by the kiss of a powerful prince. Ariel, the little mermaid, literally gave up her voice in her struggle to win Prince Eric, and thereby become a human.

Today, we call it "marrying well."

RATHER THAN FOCUSING her energy to achieve a true sense of self, power, and spirit, a woman is often expected to devote a substantial amount of her time and energy to self-preoccupation. Her body (height and weight), her hair, nails, lips, makeup. Her eyebrows (do they need waxing?) and her bikini line. Her clothes.

It is no coincidence that as women gained greater economic and political power in the 1960s the "Twiggy" look was popularized. As women gained ground, they literally were told to lose inches.

It's hard to climb the corporate ladder in high heels, a miniskirt and an emaciated body. It's hard to focus on important matters when the culture teaches us to be concerned about the minutiae of the body and its appearance.

JUST THE OTHER DAY I overheard my daughter Allison and niece Katharine having the following conversation:

"Ninety percent of being a girl means caring about your looks," Allison stated in that animated, bubbly way pre-teens have perfected.

"I know," Katharine agreed, gesturing with her hand like, "ain't it the truth."

"Boys really don't have to do much. But for us, we need to worry about fashion and how our hair looks." Allison, much to my dismay, doesn't seem to be bothered by this reflection.

"It's so true," her cousin continued. "For girls, looks are everything!" They are giggling happily.

"Hey!" I said to them. "Do you know what awesome kids you are? If you only focused on how you look, you'd miss so many great things about each of you."

They look at each other with resignation. They know what's coming, have heard different versions of this from me before.

"I can't help it," I offered in protest to their silent pleas of, "leave us alone!"

"I agree with you," I told them. "I always blow dry my hair. I get manicures. I like to wear clothes that make me feel good about my body. But we live in a world that sometimes tell us that that's *all* we should care about, or at least that it's the most important part. There are so many wonderful things about each of you, and so much in this world for you to do…"

"We know, we know," they said before resuming their conversation.

I don't say it aloud to Allison or Katharine, am uncomfortable with the phrase myself, even. But in my mind I think silently, "Don't sell yourself short."

FOR A LONG TIME, that's what I did. For a long time, I didn't really feel seen.

I felt that my shortness created an image that I was supposed to embody, a cute, silly girl. Not a smart, introspective woman. My passions and need for power, meaningful work, and spiritual connections didn't disappear. Rather, they took a detour. A detour with hairpin turns and endless construction and steep cliffs with sheer drop-offs. Half the time I think I was trying to navigate the road with my eyes closed, too terrified to fully appreciate the wrong highway I was traveling.

It hit me hard a few years ago in a session with my therapist, Barbara. I realized how I feared being overlooked, ridiculed, and rendered invisible. What I feared had happened to me concretely many times, developing into my dislike of crowded places (lines, concerts, bars, public transportation).

The fear affected me both physically and emotionally. I hated the feeling of being squished between bellies, my eye level at inappropriate places. Oftentimes I had difficulty breathing as taller bodies smashed against me. Lots of times people looked down at me and laughed because I am so much shorter than they are.

How quickly feelings of inferiority and discomfort washed over me. Sometimes it felt like I would be trampled. On a crowded train, when all the seats were occupied, I often found myself standing under yet another armpit, observing another missed belt loop of a stranger's pants. Emotionally, these are the times I have felt that "otherness." That I was too different, "abnormally short."

To this day, when I see a group of teenagers looking at me, talking and laughing, I still assume they are discussing my height and laughing at my expense. I still catch myself turning around after they have passed, to see if they're looking back at me, pointing at me like the bearded lady at the circus.

And sometimes I still find myself walking on a curb, like I did as a child, wondering what it would be like to stay at that level, that height, when the curb ended. What would it be like to walk down the street like all those (taller) fifteen-year olds?

These feelings don't often come up in everyday conversation. Sometimes they are manifested in pretty silly ways. Like for years, whenever I sent birthday or anniversary cards to my parents, I sent three to five different greeting cards.

I'm sure that Hallmark appreciated my "caring to send the very best." I always told myself it was due to the numerous appropriate cards out there, and I wanted to cover all my bases: serious, humorous, decorative. For years, I didn't think too much about this practice. Sure, as I grew older and holidays like Mother's Day and Father's Day approached, things became somewhat complex if not downright factorial. Having children brought me back to math classes, to potential equations.

For example, there were my own Mother's Day cards to contend with, then the "from the both of us," which included my husband. Ditto for his side. Then you had the Grandma and Grandpa cards from each child, for each set. Enter next the "For a wonderful sister on Mother's Day," and you had to answer with each child sending a card to Aunt Judith. Which reminds you of your sister-in-law, and so back again to the "aunt" cards! All those aunt cards remind me that I am still a niece, and what better way of playing the "good niece" than by sending a card to Aunt Janice?

Thinking I've exhausted the possibilities, I run face to face in the greeting card stacks with categories I'd never even considered. "To a wonderful friend on Mother's Day," or "Because you've been like a mother to me," and even "Remembering my father on Mother's

Day!"

You'd think I'd have learned by this point, but standing at the cashier purchasing my cards, I was always amazed by the grand total. And once I'd tracked down everyone in the house to give their John Hancock on the appropriate cards and had addressed, stamped, and mailed each one, the next holiday was just around the corner. Father's Day (where uncles are involved) and Halloween (where cousins confound the issue even more). But still I went through each holiday dutifully, the way I would shop for milk, bread, apples: a given.

The past few years, however, I have been aware of a certain level of murmuring about this "habit." First, cashiers always seemed to comment upon the number of cards I had purchased. If Joe Shmo, the consumer down the aisle, had said this, I would simply have ignored him, wondering if he were as thorough as I was in recognizing the potential card recipients of a particular holiday. But you gotta figure that a cashier in a card shop has a mighty good sense about what constitutes a large card order. Still, any lingering concerns easily left my mind as I exited the store, looking forward to once again playing the good (and here come the possible combinations): daughter, daughter-in-law, mother (having my children remember to send to grandparents, aunts and uncles, cousins), sister, sister-in-law, niece, cousin, friend, and in cherished times of days gone by, granddaughter.

As life became increasingly hectic, I often got in the habit of leaving a stack of greeting cards for my husband, to be mailed from his office. Sometimes it was laziness in buying stamps. Other times, it was severe laziness in which remembering to find a mailbox seemed too taxing. In any event, Steve's secretary began making comments to him, and eventually to me personally. It became a joke around his office that my stack of cards was not just excessive, but mysterious as well.

"Who," they wondered, "could she possibly be sending so many cards to?"

Why did, say, my mother have five bright pink and red envelopes addressed to her? They wondered if my mother's birthday fell on Valentine's Day. Steve would explain that it fell over Labor Day.

"Does her father have a birthday near Father's Day?" They'd ask. Steve would tell them his birthday fell near Halloween.

"I guess I get a little carried away," I'd say. "No big deal."

So a few years ago, I was relaying this practice to my therapist, believing I was acting quite entertaining. Carrying a large plastic yellow Hallmark bag, I opened it, revealing an array of greeting cards (and hopefully matching envelopes) that I had just purchased. As usual, she allowed me to find myself humorous. When I was done sharing this story, I placed the bag on the end table and sat myself down in the chair, rearranging pillows and footstools to make myself more comfortable. Now I was ready to begin my one-hour session.

"Tell me more about the cards," Barbara requested.

Surprised, I met her gaze. "What did she want to know?" I wondered. That story was incidental, part of my transition into this "inner world." Often I'd tell her something about a radio program I'd been listening to on my drive to her office, a story that was on National Public Radio or, I must confess, and this has happened more than once (but certainly less than ten times), something from the "Dr. Laura" show. The card story had been filler.

Patiently, she waited for me to answer. Finally I asked, "What do you want to know?"

"Why do you buy all those cards?"

Thinking about it, I told her that I enjoyed it. I loved finding the perfect card.

She remarked, "But you seem to find many 'perfect' cards."

I thought about this. It was true. For my parents, children and husband, I bought numerous cards. But, I told her, for the others, I merely purchased one on their behalf.

"Do you enjoy picking out the cards?" she wondered.

Did I? In truth, I often felt it was a burden. "Not all the time," I had to admit. There were so many people to find the right card for. "But I know after I do it, I feel good."

"Tell me more," Barbara coaxed.

Shifting the pillow behind my back, flipping the hair from my face, I said, "It's just that I feel I have to cover all the bases. Like for my dad. He loves to sail, so if it's Father's Day, I like to get him at least one card with a beautiful sailboat on the ocean with sentimental words inside."

"What kind of sentimental words?" she asked.

"Oh, I don't know. Something about what a wonderful father he has always been, something hopeful about the past, present, future, that type of thing." I choked up a little bit at this point.

"What's going on for you now?" Barbara asked gently.

"I don't know. It's the same feeling I sometimes have when I read those types of cards. It sounds so silly, but I guess I get a little sad."

"Do the words of the card fit with your feelings?" Barbara questioned.

Thinking for a moment, I answered, "The words fit with the feeling a good daughter should have…sometimes I wish it were more true. But I want to reassure them. I think there was a lot in my childhood that was not spoken of, and those cards remind me of that. Sometimes I feel responsible for making my parents feel good. But that's also why I like to buy funny cards. You know, besides finding a floral card for my mom, I like to find ones that speak to our private jokes: like talking on the telephone a lot. Or for my dad, a funny card about golfing. And then I like to get a political humor card because we all like those. And then there is this sort of reinforcement that happens. My parents always tell me that I find the perfect cards. And my aunt and uncle once told my mom, 'That Ellen, she always remembers us and is the only one in the family to send us cards like that.'"

Barbara does her favorite *hmm*. It's something as a therapist I have often done. Hmm. *Hmm.* "Hmm" translates into the therapist seeing something important in all this, and she is willing to wait patiently for you, the client, to continue reflecting.

In the silence that blankets the room, I let my eyes wander to Barbara's bookshelves. Mentally, I am calculating how many of those books line my own shelves at home. Yalom's *Group Therapy*, *The Dance of Anger*, *Diagnosing and Treating Eating Disorders*, *The Diagnostic and Statistical Manual of Mental Disorders*.

I begin to realize something. There is a reason I have just chosen this moment to compare our books. "Sometimes I think I spend a lot of time trying to prove myself. To whom, I don't know, but still trying to prove myself."

"Tell me more," Barbara urged.

"I don't know. I mean, just now, I was noticing that we have a lot of the same books. That's where my attention wandered while I was telling you about the cards. I think I was trying to tell myself that I was important, smart enough, or whatever. That like you, I have my MSW, and that I have had some success in the field. That maybe I am 'good enough.'"

"And you've doubted this?" she asked.

I shrugged. "One way or another, I've always felt I had to prove myself, to be better than good, so that I wouldn't get lost in the crowd. In college, receiving an 'A' on an exam was fine, but I wanted it to be the highest 'A' in the class. If a term paper was expected to be thirty pages in length, I would often produce fifty pages. Even in dinner conversation with friends, I often feel compelled to mention a book reviewed by the *New York Times*."

"To show you're smart?" Barbara asked.

"Yeah," I replied.

"And do they already know you're smart?"

"I guess, but I feel like I'm not taken seriously. Not seen for who I really am. Maybe not so much now, but definitely when I was growing up. People saw me as the cheerleader, as a silly and boy crazy kind of gal. As little, as nice.

"I still try to be so nice. Like if a friend is in a bind with a sitter, I always offer to take her kids. Or I make a meal for a friend who is sick, or make sure I remember birthdays, anniversaries. Most of me does this because I want to, but part of me does this because I feel I have to do more than others, be nicer, be better."

Barbara looked at me and asked, "Do you feel you are enough? Just as you are, are you enough?"

My eyes begin to water. I feel a tear disengage from my eye, dropping down my cheek. I taste its salt on my lips.

"I don't know, "I whispered. "I guess if more people lacked the self-assurance that they're enough, Hallmark's stock would really be booming!" I attempted to lighten the conversation, to laugh.

Barbara smiled.

"That is, I presume, why I am buying all these damn cards. Sending only one, from me, can easily be put aside in the stack of cards sent from other well-wishers. But three or four or five from me demands that I am seen, that I am noticed. And remembering the others on the list makes me feel special, sort of a surprise, when the other nieces don't send their aunt or uncle a card."

Over the next few weeks, Barbara and I discussed these feelings. I realized that much of this overcompensation of wanting to be seen and of striving for perfection in so many areas could be traced to my height and people's reactions to my short stature.

"She's such a tiny *thing!*" I'd hear from so many people. "Why, I didn't even see you down there!"

"She's like a doll, isn't she?"

"You look so young!"

"Sylvia, can you believe this little *thing* is going to college next year? Why, you don't look more than thirteen years old! You're lucky, when you're my age you'll appreciate looking so young!" Pat, pat, pat on my head.

"My son is short; he'd love to meet someone like you, nice and little. Someone like you would make him feel taller."

"Smile, honey, be nice."

"Sylvia! She's a mother now! Can you believe this little girl now has children of her own?"

What I wanted was to be a grown woman. A woman who could openly display her passion for life and zest for learning. Instead, I most often smiled and answered "4 feet 8½ inches" to the never ending question of, "boy, you're short! How tall are you?"

I ALWAYS DID WELL in school, and had friends. But I was also, as I mentioned earlier, "the short kid with the big boobs." People saw that first, and put together various notions based on their assumptions of short (developed) kids. I quickly learned that adjusting my personality to those assumptions offered certain rewards, at least in the short run.

In sixth grade, the boys and girls would congregate in a chosen backyard after school for a nice round of chicken fights. Being the lightest in size, boys always fought to carry me on their backs. To a twelve-year-old, that became an achievement.

I also learned that adults enjoyed me cute and smiley. Being short, I was often treated as younger, with expectations that I would acquiesce to being childlike, silly, and subordinate. I learned to be quick in wit, but often used self-deprecating jokes to achieve that goal.

I watched other girls my age growing taller, looking older, and I felt trapped. I was unable to appreciate my short legs for all they allowed me to do. Quite muscular, I was a good gymnast, cheerleader, and dancer. As I entered my teens, those same legs offered me the pleasure of endurance in running. But instead of noticing and being grateful to those limbs, I stood in front of the mirror when no one was looking. I'd pinch and curse their shortness. I thought if I were only taller, I'd be happier.

THE TEENAGE YEARS are a common time for feeling hypersensitive about one's body and for being overly critical. What was difficult for me was how much of this self-consciousness was due to my height and the mixed messages I received regarding my stature.

Comments from teachers, doctors, and my parents made it difficult for me to discuss the feelings I had about my size. I was either deemed "perfect" as I was—all the while both my parents and doctors were trying to figure out what they could do to make me taller, measuring me over and over—or I was seen as the "teacher's pet" because I tried to be so very good, to be noticed and seen, to be "perfect." The attention I received revolved around my being a helper, a "good girl," which fit the expectations of girls in general and of small girls in particular.

The side of me that loved to study comparative religion, to meditate, to practice yoga, and to write—well, it seemed to be almost invisible in what others responded to in me, that silly, smiling little redhead. In response, without realizing it until years and years later, I played out these passions, yearnings, and needs through my relationships, especially through my relationships with men.

Because of the externally imposed limitations I experienced from others because of my size, and my own internalization of messages about how I should behave, what I should desire, and who I should be, I let my needs and desires play out in less than fulfilling ways.

Here's an example.

WHEN I WAS fifteen years old, I was quite involved in my synagogue's youth group. As was common in the 1970s in Reform Judaism, I was not Bat Mitzvahed. During my freshman year of high school, becoming a Bat Mitzvah was something I wanted to do.

I was already taking Hebrew in my high school, and spoke to our assistant rabbi about my desire. I explained that I wanted a low-key service with family and a few close friends. No big party, just a small celebration of my becoming an adult in the eyes of Judaism. The rabbi was agreeable, and because I babysat many Saturday evenings for his children, we decided that I would simply come an hour earlier, and he would tutor me. My bat mitzvah was an important and special event in my life, and led to a commitment to continue my Jewish studies.

Twice during high school I visited Israel, and I attended confirmation and post confirmation classes through my senior year. I loved studying Halacha (Jewish law) and looked forward to various youth group weekend retreats where, in addition to having a great time together, we sang, studied, and prayed. One day, soon after my bat mitzvah, I spoke to our head rabbi about something that I had spent a lot of time considering in recent months.

"Rabbi," I began, "I've been thinking lately that I might like to follow in your footsteps. I wondered if we could set up a time to talk."

He looked at me for a moment and then laughed. "Ellen," he said, "you can't become a rabbi!"

Now I knew in the Orthodox movement of Judaism that this was true. But the Reform movement proudly boasted female rabbis.

"But in Reform Judaism women can be rabbis, you know that," I said.

"Yes," he replied, "Women can be rabbis in Reform Judaism. That's not the problem." Then he laughed again and said, "Ellen, you can't be a rabbi because you're too short! You couldn't even reach the pulpit!" And he chuckled, and chuckled, and chuckled.

I felt as if I had been slapped across the face. Even now, as I write about it, I can feel the sting.

I think that's when my self-destructive pattern started. I didn't feel that others took me seriously, and I began to have difficulty taking myself seriously.

I didn't know how to release the bigness I felt was in me. I didn't know how to reveal my passions, my drives or my need for power and recognition. Instead, I sought to find a release of these needs and longings in external and superficial ways.

Like during my early involvement with my temple youth group.

How I longed to delve deeper into the spiritual beliefs of my religion, and to discuss and debate philosophical points of Judaism with my teachers and my peers. The rabbi's response to my question about pursuing a life as a rabbi was hurtful. Not just the obnoxiousness of his response and his willingness to joke about my height, but even more so, his dismissal of me as a person to be taken seriously; who deserved to be taken seriously.

What did I do? I allowed myself to dismiss my own passions and yearnings little by little. Without realizing what I was doing.

IN TEMPLE YOUTH GROUPS, and mine in particular, rabbi's sons hold a great deal of power. Joshua, our head rabbi's son, held power equally over the guys and the girls.

The guys loved his superb athletic abilities, his good and bad boy image, his intellect, and dry sense of humor. The girls admired all of these things plus his rugged good looks, which made him the desire of each one of us. His dark, curly hair and deep, soulful brown eyes, along with incredibly sexy lips, left us all a bit breathless. His body, lean and firm, was as graceful as it was athletic. We loved watching him play basketball and soccer. The fact that he could later shift gears and read a beautiful Hebrew text, or thoughtfully light a Havdalah candle when the Sabbath drew to a close, simply fueled the fire that was burning inside each girl.

In groups of two and three we'd whisper about him, and fantasize that we were his girlfriend. Joshua would walk into a room and something just seemed to happen. The guys sort of fell into court around him, and we girls were as ladies-in-waiting. He was power and prestige in flesh and bones. Jewish bones, the kind our grandparents prayed for.

Needless to say, everything inside of me gravitated toward Joshua and to finding his favor.

Despite being popular, I always carted around a self-esteem that was compromised. I worried about my weight. Did my jeans make me look fat? Should I untuck my shirt? Would that offer a thinner illusion? Was my hair straight enough? My lips glossed enough? My nails manicured? My height, well, clearly too short. It really didn't matter if everything else passed my inspection. There was nothing I could do about my height. Subtract ten points just for that alone.

This was the time in my life when I was reading and studying about different religions. When I was falling in love with Herman Hesse's *Siddhartha* and practicing meditation. This was the period in my life where I was visiting the Bahai Temple, despite my parents' protests. The time when I was reading about Buddhism and Hinduism and getting totally off on existentialist questions. How I had longed for my own sense of power, freedom, and adventure. I felt so full of spiritual wonder and ecstasy about life and its mysteries. But I didn't know how to express these feelings anymore. Instead, I searched for a place to put these yearnings. A place that fit more with what others expected of ("little") girls.

Certainly, the responses I received from parents, teachers, and friends throughout my childhood regarding my spiritual quest were not encouraging. My attempts to feel powerful and visible and recognized for who I was regardless of my shortness seemed to fail. But they were part of me. One way or another, these needs and longings sought, no, *demanded* expression.

What I did was nothing new. I, like many women, sought to find expression and fulfillment of these needs by being selected, chosen, by a man who is seen to have those very attributes burning inside her own soul. Just like Belle, Cinderella, and Ariel did.

Joshua chose me. I was his girlfriend. The youth group used to refer to Joshua as "The King." Needless to say, by virtue of my new elevated status, I became "The Queen."

I was smart and passionate. I believe that went unnoticed. I was simply "the little redhead, Joshua's girlfriend, his sidekick."

Through a warped osmosis, I attempted a spiritual union of sorts. Only instead of the relationship being about God and me, it was about Joshua and me.

THESE EARLY boyfriend/girlfriend relationships were central to my being. While my parents laughingly told their friends I was "boy crazy," it wasn't until adulthood that I was able to understand the seriousness of my obsession with a particular boyfriend (and there would be others).

I remember driving everyone crazy with my constant chatter

singing Joshua's praises. I ate, slept, and breathed him. I was obsessed with him, because through that relationship I felt seen, noticed, and important. To stop talking about him or being associated with him held the fear of becoming invisible once again. Even at that young age, I saw Joshua as a vessel to hold attributes of myself that felt fragile and invalidated. Not the best vessel, to be sure, but certainly better than the alternative of sinking.

In Joshua I temporarily put my spiritual longings, dreams, and the need for recognition, power, attention, and respect. My association with him made me feel taller because I put my heels on his feet, and used his power to make myself feel special. He was a mirror through which I struggled to find a favorable reflection. A taller reflection.

The attention I received for being a " little social butterfly" made it difficult for me to display other central aspects of myself. So all day, I thought about Joshua. And all night, I worried about what I could do to ensure I remained Joshua's girlfriend, "The Queen."

And when Joshua wanted to French kiss, which seemed to me rather gross, I learned to French kiss. And when Joshua wanted to un-strap my bra and feel my breasts, I let him. I had to keep my vessel, to keep myself from disappearing. I didn't realize that I was already becoming like a shadow—there, but not real. That was the only way I felt important, to be the girlfriend of the big and powerful rabbi's son.

At some point, Joshua and I broke up. I was devastated. Thinking it was due to my undying love for Joshua, I missed the fact that it was my fear of becoming invisible.

I needed a new home for the parts of myself I was unable to incorporate. I was ill equipped to build my own dwelling. It was the beginning of an addictive cycle.

I needed a powerful man who somehow held the prestige to which I aspired, but which was thwarted by society in general as well as the dynamics of my own family and my own personal limitations. So my religious longings became an obsessive crush on Joshua, who, along with his father, commanded respect, power, and spiritual leader-ship from their adoring congregation. It also served as a distraction and a source of procrastination to do the real work on myself that needed doing; namely, figuring out a healthy way to be true to myself and be seen in the world without assuming the assigned stereotypes being a short female generated.

LATER ON IN HIGH SCHOOL, I fell madly in love with Jeff. I had become involved in the theatre and dance department of our school, and found I loved the creativity and spotlight these activities offered. Jeff was also involved in theatre, especially in dance. When we first began dating, he stood about 5 feet 10 inches tall. By the time we broke up, he stood 6 feet 3 inches tall.

Jeff was the boyfriend who was forever discovering new diets and weight loss gimmicks, and encouraging me to try them as well. Never one for academics, he spent most of his time in the dance studio or rehearsing for a musical. Many days, he didn't bother to go to class.

I was a "good" student. Homework done, hand raised, fine grades. There was a part of me that wanted to be the "creative artist." I'd rather spend hours working on my *grande jetes* or jazz runs. I wanted to wear more black, less varsity cheerleading uniforms. I wanted to develop a pallor, high cheekbones, maybe a cigarette dangling from long, slender fingers. Cool. Artsy.

Jeff smoked. True Blue 100s. He had beautiful hands. I used to watch him at a store, buying a sweater with his mother's credit card. The way he held the pen to give his signature, returning the credit card to his wallet, placing it in his back jean pocket. His watch was perfectly loose on his wrist. When he'd light a cigarette, balancing it in between his middle and index finger, using his thumb to flick the ashes, I'd stare at his tanned hands. They were the hands of a tall man.

He cared mainly about two things, and though I would like to say I was one of them, I wasn't. Jeff cared about his looks, and about dancing. And the two were connected. He felt better dancing when he was thinner, and he became thinner the more he danced. He dropped out of high school his senior year to join the Joffrey Ballet in New York.

The point was, I wanted to be reckless sometimes, instead of the "good girl." For me, being short meant conforming. Like a child, I learned to follow the adult rules. The stereotypes associated with being a short girl influenced what people expected of me, and, ultimately, what I came to expect from myself.

While I often felt like an actress playing a role, I also benefited from that role. While I wasn't seen in the way I wanted to be seen, at least I was visible. I didn't realize the huge and cumulative cost of acquiescing to those expectations and denying who I truly was, and what my passions and dreams really were.

I wanted to be admired for my dancing, singing, and acting during those high school years. At school, Jeff was central to this world.

He had a group of friends from the theatre and dance department who defined the performing arts at our school. They even called themselves "The Clique." They were all very sophisticated and dramatic. My friend Mandy and I were outwardly referred to by "The Clique" as "3/4" members. I can't believe we tolerated this, but we accepted our roles.

Jeff elevated my status in the group. Sure, I wanted my creative side to be seen and to be admired, but it was easier, at least in the short run, to realize these yearnings through Jeff.

"The Clique" spent a lot of time making fun of people's appearances, and I was often teased about my height. I remember one clique member talking about my height to Jeff and telling him, "You could do so much better than Ellen. Why would you want to go out with someone who's so short?"

I experienced my connection to Jeff, with his model-like looks and dancing abilities, as permission, a validation of my right to be a part of the dance and theatre world in our school. I longed to take off to New York, like Jeff did each summer, to dance. I wanted to be independent. To "hang." To discover the underbelly of things. Instead, I worked each summer in the file room of my dad's law office, fantasizing about seeing Jeff, and starving myself so he would think I was "thin enough" when he saw me again.

In my fantasy, I would get very thin. Jeff had repeatedly told me to lose weight. To wear my hair in a French braid. How about this color lipstick? That nail polish? Critical, very critical. "You should wear clothes more like Melanie, or shoes with a bigger heel. You have very short legs, you know."

I picked somebody to love who on the one hand, I lived vicariously and creatively through, and who on the other hand, found fault with my body and let me know I was never "good enough." Never really measured up.

He suggested various ways to help me look taller and thinner. He was proud of me when I starved myself though a summer tour in Israel. He agreed with my neighbor: being short meant a lifetime of vigilance around dieting and a preoccupation with weight. In Jeff's eyes, I was a work in progress, with many imperfections that needed to be covered and molded.

Implicitly, I knew Jeff believed I would never be a work of art. But to me, he was Art. The creative, the rebel, the visible. Through him, I felt closer to those attributes that lay dormant in my "good girl" exterior, and my non-dancer's legs.

I learned about secrecy with Jeff. Though we had officially broken up, we continued to have a sexual relationship.

"Don't tell anyone, " he would say, defining the rules I despised but followed.

I continued to date the "nice" boys, with whom I felt no passion. It drove me crazy to keep my ongoing relationship with Jeff a secret. When I was with Jeff and his theatre friends, I was supposed to act like we were "just friends," despite the intimate moments we continued to share.

It was a metaphor for what our relationship became for me anyway, a place to once again feel my own power and passion, but in secret, and in an ultimately unfulfilling way. Pretending to be something I wasn't. Friend? Or lover? Protecting the image of myself that found short-term rewards but long-term consequences.

The role that demanded I laugh and smile when someone called me "a little shrimp." When someone patted me on the head in a dismissive way and declared laughingly, "OOPS! I didn't even see you down there!" The role that taught me to hide the tears when a group of kids laughed and said in whispers too loud, "Look at how short she is. Like a midget!" and giggled and pointed all the way down the corridor.

I felt important by being Jeff's girlfriend, but the rules now said no one was supposed to know. No one to bear witness. It was like the secret about myself I had carted with me for so long; so much of my authentic self was invisible to others, to the outside world.

I was hiding what in the past, I believed, people in my life had wanted me to hide: my spirit of adventure, and my need to be seen and to be taken seriously.

I MET MY HUSBAND, Steve, my freshman year of college. I was eighteen years old and he was nineteen. I loved the University of Wisconsin-Madison. It was a great college town. I enjoyed my classes, and my friends. But that didn't stop the insecurity that lay deep within my skin, like a stain on a shirt you tried to hide by the layering of a sweater.

I can remember spending sometimes two hours trying to find something to wear before going out. I'd put on jeans and sweater and tuck it in, take it out, try standing casually, more erect. I'd change my pants, my shoes, and my hair. I was trying to fit the image of what I thought I was supposed to look like, what I wanted to look like, the All-American co-ed: cool, tall and thin.

I'd French braid my hair and then, on the last twist, decide a wisp of hair was out of place. Rather than trying to ignore it, or smooth it over, I'd pull it, yank it, and make it so obviously a mess that I'd have to start all over again.

It was worse during the weeks when I'd been reading the new issue of *Cosmopolitan* or *Glamour*. I wanted to look like the models. I could never measure up. Could anyone?

And of course, Steve would get so frustrated with me. I wouldn't be ready when I said I would. I'd complain that I was "too fat." I didn't want to be in a crowded bar where people often pointed at me and laughed, where I felt too short, inferior.

I focused so much on dieting to compensate for my height. But even as my weight continued to fall, my feelings of inadequacy remained.

Steve and I were married five years later. Steve was smart, funny, and nice. He treated me like, dare I say, a princess. My friends loved him. My parents loved him. I loved him. This was what I was groomed to do. Marry a nice Jewish boy. Become a nice Jewish wife. Have nice Jewish children.

I tried to forget the hunger in me that still growled to be fed. I always felt something was missing. I just couldn't put my finger on it.

My friends and parents used to tell me, "It's just that you always wanted a challenge. You were never interested in the nice boys who liked you."

Steve wasn't the problem, I was. I was scared that if I got married, I wouldn't ever be able to develop and experience that part of me that sought independence, power, and respect in my own right. But as much as I longed for my own independence, I was too scared to own it.

In my family, my parents seemed to put a lot of the American Dream onto me. I wanted to please them, so I went along with it. A part of me wanted it. Good marriage, great kids, nice home, friends, travel. My mother used to tell me, "If there's such a thing as reincarnation, I want to come back as you."

I always felt sick when she said that. I knew the "me" she wanted to come back as was the version of me my parents wanted to see. I hated the pressure.

Deep down, I saw myself hiking the Himalayas, meditating in Buddhist monasteries, working in a soup kitchen. I pictured myself protesting on the steps of Washington. A social activist. But I didn't articulate this. I didn't understand how essential these passions were within me. The closest I came was my senior year in college, after I had become engaged.

I was running some errands after class. All of a sudden my heart started pounding and I felt a cold sweat. "Oh my God!" I thought. "I'm not ready to get married!"

I found the nearest pay phone and called my college roommate, Beth. She answered after one ring.

"I'm not ready to get married," I said evenly, trying to mask the mounting terror rising up from my stomach, catching in my throat.

"What? Where are you?" She asked.

"In front of the drugstore on State Street."

"Oh Ellen, everyone feels this panic. It's part of getting engaged. It's normal," she soothed. "Steve is terrific. You're going to have a wonderful life together."

"Okay." Click. I told myself that maybe that jumping I felt in my stomach was just gas. I didn't understand why I was so afraid. I didn't understand that I feared that getting married now, even to someone as wonderful as Steve, would cut off forever the spiritual hunger longing to be acknowledged and filled, my need for adventure.

As the wedding grew closer, Steve's job search after graduate school took him to Boston, where he fell in love with a firm. When the job was offered, Steve accepted, and after our honeymoon we moved from Chicago to Boston.

I attended the welcome dinners his firm graciously hosted. I would smile, make conversation, and laugh when I was supposed to laugh. I enjoyed the functions, really. But I knew that this was Steve's world.

He was busy at his job, traveling, and meeting a lot of interesting people. Because the decision to move to Boston had come only two months before our wedding, I had had no time to apply to graduate schools in Boston. Initially, we had planned on staying in Chicago. I took some graduate courses that would be applied when I could attend full-time the following year, but that first year left a lot of empty hours.

Away from my family for the first time, and not knowing many people in Boston, I was lonely. I was playing the part of wife, and didn't realize how much I had allowed my own inner voice that continued to cry out for recognition, independence, and adventure to be stuffed to quietness, like a mouth filled with marshmallows.

I MET KEVIN during graduate school. Six years older than me, he already held a master's degree in counseling and was now pursuing one in social work. While we were attending different graduate schools, we shared the same internship at a Boston hospital.

I was a newly married, full time student. He was a part time student, working full time at a drug rehabilitation center. When I first met him, he looked serious, a bit disheveled, intimidating, and humorless. I was not thrilled about the prospect of sharing an office with him. As I got to know him, I came to admire his seriousness, found he had a great sense of humor, and discovered he had very set opinions on almost every subject.

He wielded power. Even among our supervisors, he held power. Other interns were quick to seek his approval in the way they conducted a clinical interview. Supervisors respected his treatment plans and often batted around difficult cases with him in an attempt to formulate a working diagnosis and intervention.

Certainly, some of the attention he generated had to do with his level of experience. But even more so, Kevin just sort of commanded respect, or more accurately, a healthy dose of fear.

No one wanted to anger Kevin, who was quick to temper. Despite the lip service the other female interns and myself gave to gender equality, we colluded with cultural stereotypes and provided room for Kevin to show his power, moodiness, and demands for respect.

We female interns learned to be nice. We were taught to put others before ourselves. As a short woman, I learned this as a survival lesson. If I'm patted on the head like a dog, I learned to just smile. If by chance I was walking down the street and a man demanded, "Hey! Where's your smile?" it was somehow easier to go ahead and smile, all the while swallowing the rage.

When I felt on shaky ground, I resorted to the quick fix. The action that would get me through any hurdle was to rely first on being "little and sweet." If there was time left over, I would try to let whomever I was dealing with see that I was actually quite capable, as well.

While my mantra at the time of my internship seemed to be, "OM my goodness! Hope I'm being sweet and nice enough," Kevin's mantra was, "Don't fuck with me." He was more comfortable in the extremes, with black or white rather than with softer shades of gray. And he seemed to be admired for that.

People enjoyed his good moods immensely. He was funny, knowledgeable, and unwilling to take flak from anybody. He was elusive about his past, but we all knew something was greatly amiss in his childhood. You could tell. The way when someone asked him if he'd be with his family over Thanksgiving, he'd laugh ironically and say, "Hmph, ah, no," and walk out of the room leaving us uncomfortably silent.

Kevin was like a magnet. People seemed to orbit around him, despite his aloofness and moodiness.

I was busy trying to please everyone and being really, really, really nice. I did it so well, I wasn't about to give it up now, especially at a hospital. Especially with doctors. Especially with mostly male doctors, busy saving lives. I was nice and conscientious, volunteering for whatever needed doing.

Kevin didn't volunteer. We all understood this. Kevin was busy with his "real" job. Kevin had other, mysterious demands.

No one tiptoed around me. Rather, it was repeatedly pointed out to me by the hospital staff that I didn't look much older than most of the kids in the clinic (ha ha!).

Kevin was pure power and respect. I wished that I commanded that. I had learned early on what characteristics fit with my gender and my height. I knew all about acquiescing. I probably did it on an unconscious level by that point.

Kevin once asked me about it. He said, "I would imagine that being short plays a great role in defining who you are and what you do and how you act."

No one had ever said it like that before. No one had ever acknowledged in a serious way that being short influences your life to an enormous extent. So on the money! His words struck me the way those "magic eye" pictures strike. The *Aha!* when reality shifts and you are able to see what was always there, only blurred or obscured in some way.

I learned all of Kevin's childhood secrets, and kept them. I learned a lot of his adult secrets, too. I became one of them.

WE WOULD TAKE OUR BREAKS together over coffee. This time, I would watch Kevin's hands light his Marlboro cigarette. Kevin balancing the cigarette and flicking the ashes. Kevin rattling off this diagnosis and that.

I wanted to be a wonderful social worker. I wanted to specialize in treating eating disorders. I felt I had a lot to say about the subject. After reading *Feeding the Hungry Heart* and *Breaking Free From Compulsive Eating* by Geneen Roth, I came to understand how diets cause rather than cure weight obsession. From my personal history and my graduate studies, I felt this specialty was just right for me. But I continued to feel the frustration of being taken seriously. It wasn't lost on me that this very issue replicated the experience of many people suffering with eating disorders.

Hospitals can be intimidating. Doctors can be intimidating. I think I was worried that I wouldn't really be seen. I felt I had to work twice as hard to prove I was "good enough." Perfect grades, perfect reports, perfect, perfect, perfect! I feared if I was anything less, I didn't stand a chance.

I was performing fine as an intern, but I felt like I was performing. I still smiled so damn much. I was still ready to be the people-pleaser at the hospital, with my colleagues. And apologizing. "I'm sorry to bother you, can I ask you a quick question? I'm sorry, can I borrow a pen?"

Someone would say that they had missed the train that morning, and I would say, "I'm sorry." Another would walk into work wet from the rain, and I'd apologize for the weather. What was I so sorry about?!

I had given up dieting by this point, but I carried an uncertainty and dis-ease about myself and my place in the world. I still felt I needed permission to take up space, even if literally I didn't take up much space, and feared the comments people made about my size colored how they viewed me.

Because I internalized these comments and attitudes about my height and gender for so long, I sabotaged myself.

I REMEMBER MY FEET DANGLING above the floor at the big conference table in the hospital lounge, surrounded by physicians in their white coats. Kevin didn't feel he needed to smile at each doctor when he spoke. His feet reached the ground.

I had an affair with Kevin. That way, I realized in hindsight, I reminded myself of my secret power. I placed a huge part of myself that felt powerful, passionate, and serious, on Kevin. It was almost as if his devotion to me carried extra inches. I was somehow, in my mind, more important.

In my own secret life, all of those attributes that were hidden so the "good girl" could shine now took on a starring role. Of course, they were elusive and a mockery of any real power. In fact, they merely replicated the feeling of being invisible and resulted in grave feelings of despair.

I used to tell my therapist that I felt like I couldn't make a choice between Steve and Kevin; that that would be like making a choice between cutting off my left leg or my right leg. It wasn't until much later that I was able to see the reason why I chose this metaphor. Both Steve and Kevin represented the parts of myself that I was unable to integrate.

Steve represented the part of my life that sought stability and unconditional love, while Kevin was the part of me that yearned for adventure, that served as a container for my hidden passions, and offered a place for me to try to prove that I am "good enough, special enough."

I wanted to stand on both legs, but hobbled when I sided with only one. I didn't know how to incorporate both within me, and the distress and pain often brought about thoughts of Melissa. Thoughts of suicide.

It wasn't so much that I wanted to die as that I didn't want to live in a way that felt artificial or inauthentic. If I left Steve, I left what I loved unconditionally, and being loved unconditionally. I left the stability that was my life. But if I left Kevin, I feared I would lose the fire that burned within my soul, but which I concealed from my world.

The relationship with Kevin, by definition, was a secret, mirroring the secret self that sought adventure, power, and stature. These qualities were simply finding another hiding place.

THE INTENSE GUILT I experienced in having an affair also mimicked the guilt I had in acknowledging that those hidden attributes were crucial to me, and were not going to disappear. For so long and by so many, I was told what a charmed life I led. I am grateful to the many wonderful people and things in my life. But I felt guilty that that wasn't enough.

Too many loved ones at the wheel drove much of my life while I played the dutiful passenger. I didn't want to rock the boat (or car) by yelling, "STOP! We're using *your* map and not mine!"

Everyone important in my life thought that I should happily continue following the safe AAA road map that highlights the directions, the "spontaneously planned" detours. I wanted to get behind the wheel, roll the windows down, feel the wind on my face, and live. Turn left when most cars were turning right. Stop at a beautiful vista. Take time to say "this is my life." Without the apologies.

Being the "bad girl" gave me a taste of power. And being in an illicit relationship, at least I had heard the alarm bell I sounded, and had to take my predicament and myself seriously.

When I smiled and played the "good girl" in other areas of my life, my secret reminded me that the outside world wasn't seeing the "real me." The me I didn't know how to reveal but was scared to death of losing.

It was really a coward's way of dealing with pressing life issues, but I guess at that time I didn't know I was so afraid of being me. For so long, I was trying to be whom I thought others wanted me to be. I was scared to see what was underneath.

EVENTUALLY, I GOT ON with my marriage and my life. I specialized in treating eating disorders. An interesting choice in and of itself.

On the one hand, most therapists who pick this specialty have recovered from an eating disorder. While I clearly had disordered eating during high school and college, I had never had any treatment in my recovery. Therefore, when other clinicians talked about their own painful history, I felt that somehow my story wasn't "serious enough" to be included among the clinicians with a "personal history."

I always believed that my height played a huge role in my poor body image and feelings of "otherness," which people with eating disorders so often discussed. Much of eating issues center on paradoxes of which I knew well.

Eating disorders can be viewed as a plea to be seen, even while the patient grows thinner and more invisible. For a long time, our culture viewed eating disorders affecting girls simply as enthusiastic dieting, instead of the serious and potentially fatal illness that it is. These women were striving to reveal their power and control, despite becoming increasingly weaker and out of control. They demanded space in the world, while increasingly requiring less and less physical space. They were willing to risk death rather than live in a world in which they felt unheard, unseen, and unable to live an authentic life.

I could buy that. Intrinsically, my soul understood that. I identified with these dilemmas.

When someone would ask me what kind of work I did, I would find myself emphasizing the serious nature of eating disorders. There were simply too many jokes attempting to trivialize these disorders, whose victims are 90–95 percent women. I was trying to be seen as serious myself after years of feeling that despite my accomplishments, I was dismissed as "silly," as "little."

I adhered to a feminist approach in understanding eating disorders and the political components in its development and treatment. The stereotypes, rewards, and punishments assigned to thin, fat, tall, and short affect so many people in enormous ways. In my work as a therapist with this population, the axiom that "the personal is political and the political is personal" was played out daily.

AFTER A TIME, WRITING became a central part of my life. My kids were in grade school now, and that left me with ample time (if there is such a thing). I had been involved with meditation and ashrams during this period, and I realized I was going back to whence I came. Back to my spiritual self, my own words and my own power. It was like being a young teenager again, when I used to write near the gardens of the Bahai Temple, and contemplate life. It was a time when, step-by-step, I saw myself in a different way, and so too, then, did others.

I became less likely to follow the stereotypes of gender and stature I had perfected so (unhappily) well in the past. I was more independent, outspoken, and political. Friends and family became familiar with my weekends away to study with a Zen master on a meditation retreat. Me, Miss Social Butterfly, remembered how much I loved to be alone. I saw myself, and was seen then by others, as more serious and introspective.

I used to write in a coffee house. I think it spoke to my desire to have my once private self (the part that was serious, a spiritual seeker, and powerful) become more public. Sure, I would laugh and hang with others, but much of my time was spent in solitary pursuits.

Now I really did give up days with friends to metaphorically get behind the wheel and be the driver of my own life. I also played out this "new me" concretely.

I BOUGHT A MITSUBISHI Montero. People would always comment on what a big truck it was for "someone so little." I would smile and call it my "in your face car." And I meant it in the nicest of ways.

Being in my car was the first time in my life where I enjoyed a view from the top. A bird's eye view. I could decide to be "nice" and let a car in front of me. Or I could plow right on down, establish no eye contact, offer no smile, and feel (almost) no guilt.

In my car (where I still had to worry because the mandatory air bags put someone my size at dangerous risk), I would disappear for a day. Now I could feel the wind on my face as I drove to wherever my fancy desired. I felt adventurous, free, and happy.

Even the Mitsubishi dealer couldn't rain on my parade. Let me explain.

I HAD READ NEWSPAPER ARTICLES documenting the deaths of short people and children who were killed when their air bags inflated. Story after story demonstrated how children and short adults (under 5 feet 4 inches) were put at risk by airbags designed to protect the average man measuring 5 feet 10 inches, weighing about 165 pounds, and not wearing a seatbelt. Sure, it outraged me in theory that once again short men and most females (measuring average in height or below) were being discriminated against by a law that pretty much renders them invisible, yet puts them at grave risk. But really, I preferred to live in denial about my personal safety. It was easier to be outraged but passive.

My mother didn't see it that way. She reminded me weekly that I should see what could be done about my airbags. She reiterated what I had seen repeatedly in the newspapers, that a simple fender bender could deploy the airbags and in what would have been an accident in which maybe a cut or bruise should have resulted, the driver or passenger had died.

Finally I decided I should take action. First, I called my Mitsubishi dealer to see if they could disconnect my airbags. I was told that airbags were mandatory in the new cars, and could not be disconnected. Then I asked if they could call their headquarters, because they were already instructing that children under twelve sit in the back due to the many deaths that had occurred as a result of airbags killing children who were sitting in front.

"Yes," I was told by a man in service, "You should make sure any child under twelve sits in the back."

"Yes, I know. My kids sit in the back. But I am the size of a twelve year old. So my airbags are putting me at risk. Shouldn't I have the right to disconnect them for my safety?"

"Oh, don't worry. If you're an adult, it's fine."

"Well, how can that be? I know twelve year olds who are bigger than I am."

The man at the service desk told me, "I think it has to do with their bones. They are not as tough as adults' bones. So you are fine."

"I don't think so," I replied as I rolled my eyes. "I'd like to talk to someone who can help me understand my legal rights concerning the airbags. I don't want them in my car."

"Oh!" the man said. "You need them. They can save you in a car crash."

"That's what I'm trying to tell you. They can save some people. Taller people. But they can actually kill a shorter person even in a crash that should not have been fatal! Can you please find out what my options are? I am 4 feet 8½ inches tall, and I weigh less than 100 pounds. My concern is that my size makes airbags a danger rather than a safety."

The service man said he would call me back. A half hour later, he called with great confidence. "I spoke with our headquarters. They told me to tell you that with your height and your weight, you should definitely sit in the back to avoid the dangers of airbags."

I couldn't believe his answer. "But I keep telling you, I am an adult! I am the mother! I have to drive my car! I have carpool! I can't drive and sit in the back seat!"

"Well, you're right. Of course you can't." Silence. "Then it's very important that you sit as far away from the wheel as possible. Put your seat back as far as you can. That way you will be much safer."

"How can I do that?!" I asked, exasperated. "If I put my seat back all the way, I can't reach the gas or brake pedals. That's not very safe now, is it?!"

I hung up the phone, furious. Denial was a much more comfortable place to be. Now I felt my mother's concern inside me. That, and the shock that I was mandated by law to have a safety device that could kill short people.

A few weeks later I had to bring my car in for a tune-up. While I was waiting for my car, I began talking with some of the servicemen. I told them about my frustration with the whole airbag situation. I mentioned that I had received a form that allowed some people the right to have their airbags disconnected, and that my height qualified. That as soon as I received the documentation that I was allowed to have my airbags disconnected, I would bring my car back in.

"No way," I was told. "Even if you have a letter saying you can disconnect them. We won't do it. We can't because of legal issues."

"Like what?" I asked.

"Like, let's say you get in a car accident and you're injured or killed. What if there is a lawsuit saying that if your airbags weren't disconnected you would have been okay? No dealer wants the legal responsibility. No one will do it."

We talked for a while, my anger fading to disbelief and from disbelief back to anger. The guys in service were nice. One of them told me that his wife is 5 feet 3 inches tall, and he worries about the airbags with her size. He called the Department of Motor Vehicles for me, to see if they knew where I could get my airbags disconnected. They said no. They didn't know anyone who would do it because of legal issues. He then called the Police Department. Again, no luck. He told me, "You know, it won't matter that you have permission to turn your airbags off. No one will do it. Even if you're willing to sign a paper giving permission to disconnect those airbags, no one wants the liability issue. Everyone is worried it wouldn't stand up in court."

I told him I had read about people going to Canada to pay someone there to disconnect the airbags. I told him I thought this whole thing was absolutely ridiculous, because my rights as a short person were absolutely being violated and no one seemed to give a damn. I told him I was writing a book on being short, and that if I got killed because of an airbag it would make a great promotional splash, but who was going to raise my children?

Then he did the kindest thing. He called over a younger service-man and said," I need you to pull down that wire in the front…" and continued to give him directions. Without explicitly saying what he was really saying.

The young service man looked surprised and said," Are you telling me to disconnect the airbags?"

"No, no, no, no. I'm just saying that if in the process that wire is just hanging, leave it." The man looked perplexed, and then looked over at me. I smiled. He left and was back in a second. "All done."

"That's it?" I asked, surprised. For all the refusals to disconnect airbags, I pictured it involving a lot of mechanics.

"That's it," the older man said. "But your airbag light will always be on now. You can just ignore that."

I told him what a gift he had given me, and how much I appreciated it. The man said he was glad to do it, just make sure I don't let the dealer know what was done. I assured him I wouldn't. I drove confidently away. Over the next few weeks, I thought about the incident. About the layers of meaning. How easily a law designed to protect people can hurt people.

Then, a few weeks later, I had to bring my car back to the dealership because of a problem with the battery. I dropped it off and got a ride home. An hour or so later, the same serviceman who had given instructions to disconnect my airbags called me, very upset. He told me that his boss had seen the red light indicating the airbags were disconnected and demanded to know if it had been done in their shop. His boss had threatened to fire him if he found the serviceman lying. The serviceman confessed that he had disconnected my airbags, and his boss promptly informed him that they must be reconnected immediately. Which, of course, he did.

The thing was, the service guy sounded angry with me. I reminded him how grateful I had been when he had the bags disconnected, but that it was his offering, and not my asking. I was really furious. How could this be so difficult? Why was this so difficult to see? I spent the next few months driving with my airbags reconnected. I couldn't find anyone willing to disconnect them.

Then one day I was at the beach with my family. A man came up to me and said, "Don't you have a Montero?"

"Yeah," I said. "How did you know that? "

He introduced himself to me as Roger, and said he worked at the Mitsubishi dealership. "I remember the day we disconnected your airbags, and I heard about how later they reconnected them. I always felt badly for you. Did you ever find someone to disconnect them?"

"No," I said. "And my mother is not too happy."

We talked about the many places I had called in an attempt to get them disconnected, all to no avail. Then he asked if he could see my car.

I took him to the parking lot and he said, "Do you mind if I have a look?" He looked around for a minute or two and then said, "Yep, I can do this if you want."

"Really?" I asked. "You don't mind?"

"Not at all. Actually, I think it's insane that you should have to worry about your airbags. I would be glad to disconnect them for you. You just have to be sure not to let anyone at the dealership know I did this."

"Absolutely," I said, gratefully. It took him two seconds. That's it. And he wouldn't let me pay him for it.

I told him how kind he was. He told me he was glad to do it. Just to make sure when I bring my car in that I always write a note saying DO NOT RECONNECT MY AIRBAGS and if they asked, to tell them I had had my airbags disconnected on my own. And that is how they have stayed.

THROUGH MY DAILY INTERACTIONS, be it in a car dealership or socially, I was becoming more mindful of how my shortness affected me and more aware of trying to be more "me" and less of a stereotypical version of a short female. These were good years, ones in which I felt the civil war within me had signed a truce.

For so long I had struggled with being serious rather than frivolous. (I saw myself as serious, but felt I had to portray the image others expected of me). Now I was listening to and trusting my own rhythms and desires.

Writing felt like a high. After a day of writing, before picking up the kids from school, I would roll the windows down in my car with the radio blaring. It was like the feeling of falling in love, where you can't contain the joy, the rush. I guess I was falling in love with myself.

It wasn't only in the written word that I was taking more chances. I began trusting my own voice, talking with others about my experience being short, and others offered to me their own stories about themselves or a loved one.

Like the elderly gentleman in Starbucks who shared with me a story he'd never forgotten, when his short stepdaughter was nine years old.

Her homework assignment asked her to respond to the question, "What do you want most in this world?" The girl had written, "To be tall."

The second question was, "What do you want least in this world?"

The girl had responded, "To be short."

Certainly the NIH consent form reinforced these cultural biases with the explanation it offered to the child about why she was being considered as a subject in that experiment: "Your parents have brought you to the National Institutes of Health because you are shorter than most children your age."

IT SOUNDS LIKE THIS STORY would have an easy ending, then. But change is not always linear. The closer I got to living my own truth, the closer I came to my own power and voice, the more scared I became. On an unconscious level, I sabotaged myself yet again.

Germaine Greer, the great feminist writer, maintains that the fear of freedom is strong within us.

Old habits die hard.

A SUCCESSFUL WRITER befriended me. I had been taking one of his writing courses, offered in Boston. Carl offered to look at some of my writing after class. I was thrilled. He had written several bestsellers. He wielded power, respect, and was recognized nationally and internationally. And he was really, really tall.

As our friendship grew, the power I was realizing through my own writing and reflection took a detour. All of a sudden I felt my power by becoming Carl's "special friend."

I liked the fact that I knew the plot of his next book and watched him write it, chapter by chapter. I didn't like that when we talked, in the privacy of his renovated Beacon Hill townhouse, he would pick me up and set me on the granite kitchen countertops so we could see "eye to eye."

I felt as inanimate as a coffee cup being picked up and moved at will, only to be left on the counter, turning cold. Do I jump down (they were high counters) or, like a child, lift my arms to this new friend, old enough to be my father, and will him to carry me down?

Other times, he liked to stand up straight and tall on his toes, towering over me so his height was overwhelming. He'd flex his stomach, arm, and shoulder muscles, wanting to be admired for his physical dominance. Still other times he would put me in front of him and walk me to a mirror with his arms around my waist and look at the reflection of our height and size difference.

I surprised myself by my responses. Instead of pointing out that such behaviors made me uncomfortable, I played the old "silly and nice" role. Sure, sometimes I voiced an opinion about these instances, or set them in the climate of what I was writing about, but it felt so familiar to allow this man to set the rules.

While his successes continued—along with the fame and notoriety—I found myself feeling powerful and successful through his phone calls and "lunch dates."

I watched him open his mail. I think Carl liked to have a witness to his fan letters, royalty checks, and articles and reviews touting his success. I spent a lot of my time stroking his ego.

I wrote, but I was often distracted. I carried around this secret, this belief that I was special because this man, this successful and powerful writer, had chosen me as his special confidante. Again, I thought it elevated me, if only in a most elusive way. It was again my "secret" that gave me power and importance. But it was still unseen.

It was as if my aspirations of being a writer took second place to being a special person in the life of an already established writer. Another chance to prove to someone that I was "good enough, funny enough, witty enough, pretty enough." The antidote to the countless remarks ridiculing my height. The antidote to the ever-present smile that wanted a rest. A chance to feel "cool" in a world in which I felt I was supposed to be bubbly. A metaphorical trade in which I give up my blue jean jacket embroidered on the back with Disney characters for a deeply faded indigo jacket with no embroidery whatsoever.

I realized that I was really scared. Scared of my own voice. Scared of what would change in my life if I really did "let myself go" in a public sense, rather than in secret. Of what it would mean to write it, read it, and live it everyday. To let the power, spirit, and stature seep through my veins and make my short bones strong and hardy. To stand by my words and become fully me, fully alive.

Maybe much easier to stay in the box that I, with the help of others, had created for myself. The box with walls built of stereotypes, with a lid offering reward for conformity to those expectations. To only come out of the box for little (not always healthy) excursions.

It was like Pandora's box. If I let myself out, God! What might happen? What would need to shift in my life? How would my marriage change? What would my family think? How would my friendships change?

And if I truly tapped into my own power and stature, I could no longer use the success and power of other men, tall men, successful men, to distract me from my own feelings of insecurity and inadequacy. Once I left the box that allowed me to act one way in public and another in secret, that was it. I would be box-less. I would have to stand on my own two feet, short legs and all.

It was a final attempt to stand on the (taller) legs of men who wielded power and offered an elusive sense of power by being the special companion. The ironic thing is that I spent a great deal of time helping *them* feel good about their lives and accomplishments.

To BE HONEST, I don't think it was a huge breakthrough or insight that led me away from this self-destructive cycle as much as it was sheer exhaustion.

I wanted to simplify my life. I was tired. I wanted to give up the opposites that kept me in the box, and that kept me from being a big person despite having a little body.

I missed the drives in my car after a great writing day. I even missed the not so good writing days. At least they were based on *my* writing, and not somebody else's.

My own power got lost in favor of being just another adoring female ready to lap up the power dripping off Carl's writer body, as a sampling taste of what it might feel like.

I wanted to feel real. By that, I mean being out with friends and feeling good and strong because of who I really was, rather than to whom I was secretly connected. Being fully present.

It's embarrassing for me to admit how many Saturday evenings Steve and I spent with other couples at dinner when I would excuse myself to use the bathroom. Alone in the stall, I would lean against the tiled wall and whisper Carl's name as if to acknowledge and confirm the pieces of myself that I felt were hidden during my typical social evenings out.

Frankly, I was bored by the minutiae that was suburbia. I often found myself sitting with the women on one side of the table and the men on the other. The conversations were like re-reruns of the Saturday night before. The women would discuss which summer camps the children planned to attend, and the current gossip around town. The men would compare cell phones and discuss the quickest routes into Boston during morning rush hour, or the stock market.

At these times I would find myself ordering another glass of wine, and in my own way distancing myself from this group and my life. Those were the times I most looked forward to my trips into Boston, the pulse of the city shared with Carl. My hair long and loose, my jean jacket for cool more than warmth, my day unaccounted for. And you know what? I finally became frustrated with the whole thing.

Maybe I needed to spend time with some new friends; shake up my world a little bit. Stop living the life my parents wanted so much for me to live. I needed to take responsibility for living my life in a way that was fulfilling for me.

I no longer wanted to be in a box that was wrapped up so nicely on the outside while I was suffocating on the inside. I no longer wanted to taste a facsimile of power in secret, and then scurry back to safety like a mouse finding refuge in its little hole. I wanted to be myself.

I'm a grownup, despite being the height of a child, and it was time I began acting like one.

WITHOUT THOSE POINTS of distraction, I'm simply left with paper, pen, and me. I can write the way the way I feel, or I can not. I can feel my own strength and power, or not.

I used to see a speck of sand on a powerful man and think somehow he held the whole beach. Then I realized *I* was the beach, a fleck of my sand had simply flown away, and I had set off on a wild goose chase.

I no longer look at my love of adventure as an option. I need to take my needs and myself seriously. If I feel the need for a good long walk, a space to meditate, a day to get lost in the city, I need to satisfy those needs directly. No longer will I give up time and energy satisfying those needs through osmosis—spending time with men in similar pursuits.

THE BUDDHIST MANTRA of compassion reads: "Om Mani Padme

Hum." The jewel of the lotus lies within.

We all have a lotus in our heart, an organ that pumps just as readily if you are 4 feet 8½ inches short or 6 feet 4 inches tall. Experiencing the wisdom, joy, and power within keeps you from searching endlessly on the outside for that which no one else can give you.

I realized that only through speaking my own truth could my yearning for true stature be satisfied. Only by engaging in the activities that nourished me could I stay healthy and strong. Only through standing on my own accomplishments and failures could I feel alive and counted and real.

No longer would I sell myself short and hide behind the perceived power of a man, or play along with stereotypes about my size and my gender. Only then could I truly grow. Not through extra inches, but on the inside. Where it really counts.

On Being

Chapter Six
LEAP OF FAITH

I try to imagine who I would be if I had lived all my life here at this Temple by the river. I wonder what I would want if I had grown up without ads telling me my heart's desires: to be thinner, richer, sexier, look better, smell better, be all that I can be, have a faster car, a brighter smile, lighter hair, whiter whites, hurry now, don't miss out, take advantage of this special offer. If instead I had spent twenty-four years absorbing the silent weight of the mountains, the constant pull of the river, the sound of hot white light burning into black rocks.

JAMIE ZEPPA
Beyond the Sky and the Earth: A Journey into Bhutan

I USED TO have this dream over and over. It started around college. Sometimes I would have the dream every few months. Other times, it might not visit me for over a year. Always, it was the same.

I am dancing. Dressed in my leotards and tights, I am dancing, feeling the pulse of the music within my body. And then I go to leap. In dance classes, from high school through today, I can do a full split leap. But in my dream, as I go to leap, I cannot lift my feet or body at all. It is as if weights have been attached to my shoes, or my feet have stepped into crazy glue on the floor and will not budge. It is terrifying for me to watch. My arms are in position. My body is prepared, my focus is set, but I can't for the life of me get off the floor. I want to soar through the air, and I can't leave the ground.

When I would awaken from this dream, I always felt exhausted and defeated and anxious. Over the past few years when this dream would visit, I spent a lot of waking time reflecting upon its multiple meanings. Though I hated the dream, I embraced it as well. It started to feel like a "good hurt," like when someone massages a sore neck muscle and the pain feels good.

I knew that this dream offered an important message for me, and that I could learn something from its many re-runs. I knew it wasn't only about a fear of not accomplishing goals, of being unable to perform to certain standards, or free-floating anxiety. It held, for me, a spiritual dimension. I think I feared my soul, my spirit, was grounded in the same way, trapped in that box of conformity and expectations.

We live in a culture that focuses on the external, on appearance and economic success. There is very little focus on the internal, on spiritual questioning or spiritual paths. And while religion plays an important role in our society, too many organized religions have unfortunately become more concerned with the externals and trappings of religion than with religion itself. Christmas has become a time of heightened consumerism, and Bar and Bat Mitzvahs have turned into glitzy $50,000 parties. Religion has become yet another label that serves to identify and then separate us into groups, and away from each other.

I think my dream was really a wake-up call; your soul wants to rise up and soar into the expansive space of Earth and sky, timeless, suspended. How are you going to set it free?

I think this dream had its origins in my childhood, during the time I was experimenting with meditation, studying comparative religion, and writing. Instead of following those passions, I learned to not rock the boat. I learned that where I grew up, girls were rewarded for looking pretty and smiling. By behaving nicely, appropriately.

That was when my internal self, my spiritual self, felt large and split wide open. When the adults in my life relabeled these passions as rebellious and tried to tame and quiet them. It was a time when my external self, my physical body, was focused upon. I was too small, too short, each measurement confirmed. And the doctors and my parents tried with great effort to make me bigger. Meanwhile, my spiritual body, pregnant and growing with life energy, was deemed inappropriate, and the implicit message was to make it smaller.

That's what I think my leaping dream was about. To leap, the physical body must be strong, strong enough to glide through the air and defy the forces of gravity if only for a split second; to allow the soul that moment in time where it is suspended between Earth and heaven and cannot be touched by anyone. That leap breaks the rules of gravity. That leap is the merging of the physical and spiritual bodies.

I surprise people when I leap. The height I reach, the split extension of my legs, my arms in flight.

I think this dream expressed my fear that I won't reach my height. Not in the concrete measurement of inches, but in the immeasurable yearnings of my heart and soul. That the years of stereotypes, jokes, teasing, and expectations around my shortness, and my own internalization of those messages, would ground me, immobilize me.

How I feared living a life where I kept my heart, soul, and passions locked deep inside, hidden and boxed like a majestic tiger confined to a tiny cage in a zoo. Back and forth she paces, humiliated at the claustrophobic space that constricts her movements as well as her nature and spirit, while people look on and point.

How I feared being ready to leap, and not being able to move.

Summer 1998

I think unconsciously,
I understood what this dream
represented. I don't think I fully understood this
dream in a way that demanded action on my part,
though, until my husband and I went to the Museum of Science in Boston and its IMAX theatre. The *Everest* film was showing, and it changed my life.

Jon Krakauer's *Into Thin Air*, in which he recorded his experience climbing Mount Everest and the disaster that unfolded in May of 1996, had fascinated Steve and me. What would lead someone to risk everything to stand on the summit? What was it about, this wanting to stand on the highest point on Earth? To enter such an inhospitable place, not fit for humans, where the altitude can render each breath a tortuous feat, where any breath could easily become one's last? And yet the beauty of it all, the wonder and the awe.

When Steve and I picked a warm July evening to see the *Everest* IMAX movie, I was excited. I wanted to see the photography. Did the images I had in my mind reflect what Everest was really like? Steve had commented to me while purchasing our tickets that I was like a kid at a circus. I just felt energized and full of anticipation. So I guess I shouldn't have been surprised by what happened as we were waiting in line to enter the auditorium.

I noticed a little table with some applications and a few pens. The sign on the table read, "Do you want to travel to Nepal?" and instructed you to fill out an application to receive a travel brochure for further information. I picked up an application. "Yes," I thought. "I absolutely do want to go to Nepal."

"Look Steve," I said. "Wouldn't it be great to go there?"

He looked at the application and said, "Sure, fill it out," as he walked forward with the line.

"Really? Could we really go to Nepal?"

Steve smiled and said, "Yeah, why not? When the kids are in college, it would be really neat to think about taking a trip like that."

The line started to move into the auditorium. We picked out our seats (stadium style seating, so I didn't have to obsess over who might sit in front of me and block my view) as I kept up my banter.

"No, no. I mean now. Why can't we think about going to Nepal this year?"

The lights began to dim, and Steve looked ready to end the conversation. I couldn't let the question go. The advertisement over the application box had said, "Do you want to travel to Nepal?" The "yes" in my head had come so immediately to me, so clear and definite. My almost visceral response surprised me in an unsurprising way.

Like returning to my childhood home as an adult and falling into my childlike quirks without even realizing it, opening up a particular cabinet to look for the Salerno butter cookies my mother always bought when I was a kid, even though I don't like them anymore. Or sitting in the same corner of the family room couch with the mauve pillow on my lap. Moving back into the familiar. The actions only surprise because they still come so naturally after all these years of not doing them.

That's what the Nepal prospect did to me. Of course I wanted to go to Nepal. My whole life I wanted to go to a place—call it India, Nepal, Tibet—where the land, culture, and religion captured my yearnings, piqued my curiosity, and made my heart skip a beat.

I remember, as a child, those long driving trips with my family.

How I used to look out the window for my "perfect spot." In my mind, the "perfect spot" was a place in the woods or forest where a large patch of meadow would reveal itself by a stream or a flowing river or a brook. My fantasy was that I would live in the forest as a spiritual seeker. I would live simply (forget that we were driving from Chicago to Disney World, and that I had a zillion car activities to keep me busy). I would eat berries, bathe in the stream, and meditate. I used to get sad because I assumed all the seekers had already sought, found, and established religions. I thought in modern times such as these, there were no more seekers.

I don't recall having conversations about spirituality with my family, my friends, or their families. I remember a lot of talk about religious events and celebrations. About Christmas dinners, Passover Seders, bar mitzvahs and communions. I thought that maybe I was weird. I wished that I had lived during a different time in history, when, I figured, the questions I was asking weren't already answered. I didn't know people were still asking unanswered questions. Religious school at my synagogue seemed to have an answer for everything. Except the Holocaust. There was never an answer for that. Everything else, it seemed, had an answer, a reason.

More than anything, I loved the story of the Buddha, which I was introduced to through Herman Hesse's *Siddhartha*. I would read it almost every year, from middle school on up. Siddhartha was my hero. He had left the comforts of his home, his parents, his religion, his wealth, and his status as a Brahmin. People adored him. He left that, too. He wanted to seek enlightenment, and believed he had to leave home to find his own, true, spiritual path. His best friend, Govinda, followed him.

In his travels, Siddhartha tasted the extremes of life. For a time he lived with the ascetics in the forest, and learned to deny his physical needs and his physical body. He found that this was not the way. For a time he lived as a merchant, took a lover, and experienced the appetites of the flesh. He found that this, too, was not the way. During his wanderings, he met Guatama (the Buddha), with whom Govinda became a disciple. Despite feeling awe in Guatama's presence and acknowledging that he would never learn better teachings, Siddhartha left this enlightened master to forge on to discover the Truth for himself, which is, in fact, part of the Buddha dharma, and which, in the book, he did. He found the middle way.

Buddha himself, at the time of his death, reminded his disciples, "Be a lamp unto yourself." And a popular saying today is "Don't be a Buddhist, be a Buddha." In other words, find the Buddha nature within you and trust yourself.

It was just part of my psyche, my karma, my quirk. I gravitated toward this philosophy.

The historical Buddha, born Siddhartha Gautama and called Shakyamuni Buddha, was born 2,500 years ago in Nepal.

I REALIZED I WAS READY to go. Nepal was *now*. It was one hundred percent where my heart was.

For me, Nepal was like a magnet drawing the deepest part of me out into the open. I wanted to travel in the remoteness and beauty of the land graced with gods and goddesses and other deities. I wanted to wander the streets that blended Hinduism and Buddhism as easily as sugar mixed with water. I wanted to see the prayer flags hanging from the temples and monasteries, the monks with shaved heads and maroon and saffron robes. I wanted to witness a spiritual life that seeped like tea leaves in water, permeating the culture, the day to day business of living and dying. I wanted to dare myself, push myself.

What would it be like to lose myself in a city like Kathmandu? To trek through the mountains? What would it be like to dress strictly for the elements and the rigors of such a trip? What would it be like to leave behind the "little black dress" and sandals so typically thrown into my suitcase? I wanted to spend the days trekking, putting one foot in front of the other.

That's it. I just wanted to be in the moment. I wanted to fully walk like the title of the great Vietnamese Zen Master Thich Nhat Hanh's book, *Peace In Every Step*. I wanted to watch the sun melt behind a mountain in shades and hues I've never seen. I wanted to hear the chanting of the devout. I wanted to spin a prayer wheel. I wanted to see a different way of life, another option.

I wanted to go, in some ways, where I wasn't supposed to go. Where I wouldn't "typically" go. If I was ready to begin challenging the stereotypes associated with being a short female, with being a suburban mom, I was also ready to prove to myself that I was strong and adventurous and a seeker.

I was often my own worst enemy, sabotaging my efforts to be taken seriously by falling back into the attributes I had internalized: being silly, acting powerless, playing "cute." I wanted to challenge myself physically and emotionally.

Maybe there was a part of me that wanted to jump-start the process of chipping away at the stereotypes that kept me in the box. Maybe I needed that at a time when I was trying to shed expectations the way you peel off layers on a hike. A "thank you, you served me well for a time, but I no longer need your protection."

"Not when the kids are in college, what about now?" I asked Steve.

The screen came to life and the movie began before Steve had a chance to answer.

We were both mesmerized by the movie. The images captured on the film challenged my view of the world. The landscape broke apart my heart in ways that brought tears to my eyes.

The colors that danced through Kathmandu, across the red, blue, yellow, green, and white prayer flags waving mantras in the wind. The blessings offered from the monasteries before the climbers set off for their arduous journey. The skyline of the Himalayas, their snow peaks impossibly brilliant against the open sky. The vastness of snow blanketing the mountain that looked as if it covered the entire Earth. The crevasses that prove the unending snow is but a dangerous illusion. The Khumba Icefall, where ordinary human beings climb ladders across the icefall and their passage looks, to me, extraordinary.

The stark blue sky and brilliant golden sun hovering like a jewel in the horizon, setting off sparkles like diamonds in the snow. The watercolor shades of dusk and dawn and the fullness of the moon in the jet-black sky lighting up the night like recessed lighting in a world of no electricity. The perfect day suddenly turning unforgiving, uncaring, with blackened clouds and fierce winds and blinding snow. Stark, hard, cold rocks where the snow has blown free, their jagged edges falling down into nothingness where it seems no bottom exists. Freezing, freezing cold, with humans trying to survive in a part of the world where perhaps they ought not to be.

The altitude can kill, and often does. One out of ten climbers who attempt Everest will die on the mountain. And yet each year, try they will. The challenge calls to them, the desire to stand on top of the world pushes them where most people could never imagine wanting to go. And in the film, the cost of this desire is seen clearly, as corpses frozen in the snow.

After the movie I stuffed the application into my purse, and we went across the street to eat. I picked at my shepherd's pie as I listened to Steve talk about the *Everest* film. I listened, but all I kept thinking about was how much I wanted to, *needed to* travel to Nepal. For Steve, it seemed like an interesting proposition to consider a good ten years in the future.

I passed on dessert. I could hardly keep my heart from jumping out of my skin. The last thing I needed was a sweet concoction trying to digest in what had become a constant drum beating through my heart. I knew I couldn't let my heart keep pounding like this for ten years.

I fell asleep during the car ride home. I don't remember thinking about or dreaming of anything.

By August, the travel brochure for Nepal arrived. I took it out of the mailbox and ran inside to open the large white envelope the way a lovesick teenager opens a letter her boyfriend sent from overnight camp.

The brochure was all that I had imagined. The cover revealed hearty men and women bundled in warm gear, the snow-capped Himalayas peaking out from behind as they celebrated their ascent, arms up in victory. Trekking poles and water bottles were strewn beside them, and mani stones, carved prayer rocks inscribed with the Buddhist mantra of compassion, were stacked up like a sacred offering, as if bearing witness to their achievement.

Opening the brochure, I was face to face with more photographs: this one a lush green terraced rice field, that one a sandy dirt path nestled between green shrubs, leading steeply up a mountain, the Himalayan range outlining the journey. One tiny photograph showed a small Nepalese boy, probably less than seven years old. Another was a snapshot of Namache Bazaar, a prosperous Sherpa market town where each weekend Nepalese and Tibetans sell their wares, and climbers from all over travel through en route to Mount Everest or Ama Dablam or some other glorious Himalayan peak. And the ever-watching eyes of Buddha, a constant on each of the sacred Buddhist shrines called stupas, highlighted the brochure.

I read the brochure cover to cover. It was clear to me that of the two trips offered, only one seemed plausible for the two of us: "The Royal Nepal Lodge to Lodge," a sixteen day trip, including air travel time. The other trip, "Everest: The Sherpa Homeland," consisted of the same amount of time, but was much more strenuous, taking the trekker to thirteen thousand feet at Mount Everest and camping the whole way.

The Royal Nepal trip seemed to be an easier trip, though still demanding, and allowed the visitor an opportunity to explore many aspects of the country. The first few days were devoted to exploring Kathmandu with its wonderful, eclectic mix of Hindu and Buddhist cultures. Then we would leave Kathmandu for Pokhara, where we would begin a five-day trek through the Annapurnas, staying in small lodges with no electricity or heat, but which did have bathrooms. Next, we would continue viewing the beautiful countryside with a two-day whitewater rafting drip down the Seti River, which eventually flows into the sacred Ganges River in India. Following this adventure, we would make our way to the Royal Chitwan National Park, where we would stay in bungalows in the jungle and spend two days on an elephant safari. And finally, we would return to Kathmandu for another day or two of sightseeing before our long flight home.

When Steve came home from work, I excitedly showed him the brochure. "I'm so there!" I shouted gleefully, dancing around the kitchen.

Steve agreed that it looked very cool. When I pointed to the dates the trip was offered and suggested March, he was less enthusiastic. "Ellen, it's a big trip. We're going to have to really take our time in thinking about this. I'm not so sure this is the time to go."

He promised to read the whole brochure, and I promised to try to be patient.

That week we flew with our children to Chicago and then drove to Michiana, a small village on Lake Michigan where my parents owned a summer cottage. I spent all of my childhood summers there, and many weekends and holidays there as well. My kids loved to visit each summer and had a blast with their grandparents, aunts, uncles, and cousins. While packing, I had thrown the Nepal brochure into my suitcase. One evening, I took it out to show my parents, my sister, and her husband.

"Are you crazy?" my mom asked.

"Are you nuts?" my dad added.

"It's like one of the poorest countries in the world," my sister offered.

"What would possess you to want to go there?" My brother-in-law, Dave, wondered aloud.

"Look at these pictures!" I exclaimed, pointing to the brochure. "Doesn't it look amazing?! It's incredible to think we could really go there!"

"Steve, how do you feel about all of this, or do you even have a choice?" Dave asked.

"I think it would be really neat," Steve began. "I'd love to do it someday. I used to love whitewater rafting, and I did some rock climbing during prep school. My cousin, Alan, used to go on African safaris. Remember seeing his slides, Ellen?"

I nodded yes.

"I just don't know if now is the time," Steve said.

"What about the kids?" my parents asked.

"Lupe would stay with them," I volunteered. Lupe is our sitter/angel. She has grown children of her own and has helped take care of my kids since Allison was only two and I was pregnant with Matt. She knows everything about my kids, from how Matt likes his grilled cheese cut to Allison's favorite pajamas. She knows their doctors, teachers, and friends. She is so wonderful; she puts Mary Poppins to shame.

"Lupe would be great with them," I said easily.

"Do you know what kind of diseases they have there?" my mom asked.

"I'd get shots," I shot off.

"Do you know while you're hiking you'll have to go to the bathroom in the woods?" Dave chimed in.

"I'll develop strong leg and calf muscles," I challenged.

"Do you realize it'll take like two or three days on an airplane just to get there?" my sister asked.

"I'll rack up lots of frequent flier points." I replied feeling ever more confident with my answers.

"I don't know, Steve," my sister said only half jokingly. "I think she really means to go."

"Wait, wait, wait!" Dave jumped in. "What about showers? Ellen, you take like two or three showers a day, and in all the years I've known you, I've never seen you let your hair dry without a blow dryer."

I agreed that could be a problem.

My mother looked like she couldn't tell if I was kidding or not, like if she could be relieved that I wasn't serious about going to Nepal after all.

"I'll braid it while it's wet," I said.

My mother's face fell.

"Ellen, there's snakes and filth," my mother said. "My hair dresser went to India and there were dead bodies all over the street. He just took one look around and went right back to the airport and left. He couldn't stay. And Arthur Goldberg went to Nepal, remember, Joe? He went to base camp at Mount Everest like fifteen years ago. Oh, I remember him telling us how sick he got. He says he's never been the same since. He still has health problems from that trip."

"Really? What happened to him? What kind of disease did he get? I asked.

"Oh, I don't know, but he swears he's never been the same."

The conversation shifted. I put the brochure away. When we returned to Boston, I was busy getting the kids ready for a new school year, and their schedules set. It wasn't until the end of September that I sat down with Steve to talk with him about the trip.

"No, Ellen. There's no way I can just take two weeks off from work, not now."

We had some angry words. I knew how much I needed this trip. How I didn't want to play out my need for adventure and my passions through a relationship with Carl, or to stuff it away all together.

The next day, I called Steve at work. I told him that I feared our lives were going in two very different directions. That I didn't want to end up like so many people I saw around me who never seemed to venture beyond our small town, unless it was to Boca in the winter. That if it was because he had no desire to go to Nepal, that was fine. But that wasn't what I was hearing. I was hearing, "I want to go, but I can't, because it's not the right time."

"I don't want to wake up when I'm seventy years old and realize I have lists and lists of things I wanted to do but never did because it was never the right time!" I lamented.

I think what I was also doing was telling my family and Steve, for the first time in my life, that I couldn't conform anymore to the Stepford picture of the suburban mother and wife. That I had to release my own voice and act on my dreams. That I was strong, both physically and emotionally, and that I could handle such a trip even by myself.

"Ellen, I have responsibilities. I just can't pick up and leave," Steve said, trying to keep a level voice.

I was exasperated. "Steve, every year we go to the islands for a week. The kids are fine; no one asks any questions or challenges us about going away. You love vacations. This is only one extra week!"

"I can't talk about this now," Steve said, sounding angry.

"I just think you should think about why you're saying this. Is it because you don't want to go? Because that I can understand. But if it's because you don't think you should or could be away from the office for two weeks, then I have a problem with that. When we talked about the possibility of celebrating Allison's Bat Mitzvah in Israel, we would have been gone for two weeks. Why did we bother considering that kind of trip if you couldn't be away from the office for two weeks?" I accused.

"That's different, Ellen. If we were going to Israel for Allison's Bat Mitzvah, that would be different," Steve insisted.

"If that's really what you think, then we have bigger problems than going or not going to Nepal. I didn't realize how far apart we've drifted. I think we have some real problems. I think I've spent my whole life with you doing it your way. Not in the little things, maybe, but in living the life you want me to lead; living where you want to live for your job, and your leisure. Well, damn it! I'm sick of playing Mrs.-Wife-of-the successful-Mr. Frankel!" I hung up.

The phone rang. I didn't answer. The phone rang again. I still didn't answer. The phone rang again. I listened to Steve's voice on the answering machine.

"Ellen, pick up the phone." Silence. "Pick up the phone, Ellen," he said evenly. "C'mon, pick up the phone, Ellen, please. Don't do this, just pick up the phone." Silence. "Okay, fine. Don't pick up." Click.

"Shit," I thought. "I should've picked up."

The phone rang again. I picked up the receiver on the first ring. Without thinking, years of built up frustration poured from my throat into my vocal chords, producing words I didn't expect. Words I didn't want to hear.

"I'm not happy, you don't understand!" I cried. "I can't live like this anymore. I feel like I'm suffocating. Like I'm living a pretend life. I'm just pretending. I can't stand the suburbs. I feel like I'm swimming against the tide. I isolate myself more and more each day. You go into work every day, in the city. You do work you love with people you like. You travel. My life mimics Sisyphus, just rolling that boulder up all day so someone can push it down at night and I start all over the next morning. Laundry, cooking, cleaning, carpooling."

I'm crying by now. "I love being a mother, but I'm not only a mother! I'm not just your wife!"

"Ellen, please calm down," Steve pleaded.

"I can't! I won't!" I yelled. I don't want to tell him everything about Carl yet, about how scared I am, about how I'm in over my head and feel like I'm drowning.

"Steve, I can't live like this. I don't think you understand at all." I was sobbing by this point. I was surprised though, when Steve told me he was leaving work to come home so we could talk. He had never done that before. I continued to cry.

An hour later, I heard the garage door open. It was noon. Neither of us ate lunch. We went upstairs in the bedroom and talked. The bright sun streamed through the skylights, making the room look light, mocking the heaviness of the mood.

I told Steve that it wasn't that I didn't want the life I was living; I just had to put my mark on it as well. "I can be happy living my life with you, but I can't ignore anymore the things that are important to me. I get crazy living in a small town, seeing the same people everywhere, every day. Where the talk at the Temple is the theme of a Bat

Mitzvah, like one person basing the party on fashion designers. Every table will be the name of a designer! About people having their Bat Mitzvah celebrations at FAO Schwarz. And my lack of involvement in the Temple is questioned! My going off to meditation retreats is seen as 'strange,' or like a lost soul who hasn't settled down and found herself yet.

"I want to see the world. I start feeling like somehow there is something wrong with me for wanting more. Not something more, but something *different.* People are always saying to me how lucky I am. How I have everything, and why am I looking for something more? Why am I dissatisfied?

"I don't want a fancier car, or a bigger house, or a bigger diamond. I want to be myself, and I want my life to be an expression of that. I'm fine with being alone, but I can't always let my only public expression be the character of the stereotypical suburban housewife." I looked at Steve, at his face. I noticed that his beard had some streaks of gray. When had that happened, I wondered?

"But I know all of that about you. I think it's great that you have all of those interests, all of that dedication," Steve soothed.

"But I need to express myself, Steve. It's like I live in two different worlds. The safe, prescribed world of suburban mom, and a private world where my passions are boundless. I need to find healthy ways of expressing those needs." I hesitate for a moment before beginning again. "And what you said the other week to me is true. I have been spending too much time with Carl."

Steve was understandably angry. He cast his eyes downward, clenched his jaw. "I thought you were going to stop hanging out with him."

"I know. I was. I want to. I don't want to escape from myself, or distract myself from my life anymore. But I don't know how to express my needs. Why is it that only men are encouraged to be powerful? I want to feel powerful, too. I want recognition for my accomplishments besides being a wife and mother. I don't want to learn to play golf and sit over lunch at the country club listening to endless diet conversations. I have a life I want to lead. I'm scared that if I don't start living the life I envision, I'll just waste away behind a pasted smile."

"Listen, Ellen. I do understand. I really do." Steve's jaws were no longer clenched. He looked into my eyes. "But why can't we just wait a few years? In my business, it's hard to be gone for two weeks at a time. Companies are going public, I have clients to visit, and I just can't be away from the office for two weeks straight,"

I watched the little specks of dust floating through the stream of light. "But companies will always be going public; it doesn't stop. You're a director. If you've reached that level and still don't feel you can leave, what's the point? Is work your entire life? And I don't understand why, when we thought about going to Israel for Allison's Bat Mitzvah, you didn't blink about taking off two weeks."

"Well, because. That's just different. Everyone would understand why."

I cut him off. "That's just what I'm talking about! I'm not playing by those rules anymore. You think it's justifiable to miss work for Israel, but not for Nepal. That's not fair."

"Well it would have been hard to leave for two weeks to go to Israel, too," Steve countered.

"But you would have done it. And no one in our lives would question that kind of trip. It's on the invisible list of what is acceptable."

"Yeah, I guess. But do you understand what I'm saying? Two weeks straight away from the office is just not very doable. And in Nepal, my office wouldn't even be able to reach me in an emergency," Steve said.

I was getting angry now. "Oh, it's doable, all right. And the fact that you don't think so is exactly why you need to go to Nepal! You think you're indispensable. Well, I love you, but I'm the first person to say you are dispensable. So am I. God forbid if you were killed in a car accident tomorrow. Your firm would still go on. Somebody would cover your companies and report on their earnings and tell your clients to buy or sell. The kids and I would be devastated, but somehow we would learn to survive. There is no perfect time for anything, and none of us will be here forever. We can all be replaced in some way. What we think are emergencies are only our egos hanging on to the illusion of our importance.

"I think we *both* need Nepal. I need Nepal because my heart is already there, and I have to catch it. And you need Nepal because you have to see that your life is more than your career. It would be great to go there together. It would be challenging and adventurous and beautiful."

"I know that. But I really have to think about it."

"Fine, Steve, but listen. I'll go to Nepal myself. Like I keep saying, if you don't want to go because Nepal is not for you, I'm okay with that. But it's when you've been saying that you'd like to go but then give me these obstacles and excuses, that's what I'm responding to. That's what scares me.

"I want to live my life in a more real way now. Not tomorrow, not when the kids are in college. Not when we've put things off because we're being 'responsible,' and end up old, bitter, and resentful. I know I'm changing a lot, but that's part of it, too. I want you to share some things that are important to me now."

"I'll think about all of this," Steve promised.

Steve went back to work. By the time he returned for dinner the clouds had rolled in. We were busy with the kids, and didn't talk much about what had transpired that afternoon.

"Are you thinking about it?" I asked Steve as he left for work at 6:00 A.M. the next day.

"Yes, I'm thinking it over," he replied.

NEPAL HAD BECOME, for both of us, a symbol.

For me, it was about pushing for a new way of relating to each other, for finding room in our marriage for both of our needs. It was also, for me, a way of expressing my commitment to acknowledge my needs and passions in healthy ways rather than through powerful men living out those passions, or by trying to ignore or suppress those needs altogether, which was like trying to sink a floating toy boat in the bathtub.

I think that for Steve, Nepal was about meeting me 50/50. Also, as a long-standing and committed Dead Head who lately showed his faithfulness to Jerry by wearing only Garcia ties to work, I think Nepal held out the option of once again embracing that younger, more adventurous and carefree side of himself.

I tried not to call him at work; I didn't want to create more pressure than I already had. But all day I felt like I was waiting for a vote that would affect our future in ways unknown.

That afternoon as I was driving into my garage, I saw a beautiful bouquet of roses had been delivered. First my heart jumped, but then I froze. "Oh no," I thought. "These are probably from Steve, wanting to pacify me, saying he loves me and that one day, we'll travel to Nepal."

I brought the flowers inside, and set the red roses on the kitchen counter. I pulled the small envelope from the arrangement and held it in my hands. I wanted to open it, and dreaded opening it, at the same time.

I slid my hand under the lip of the envelope and pulled out the little card. On it was written, "Here's to balance. Love, Steve."

I held that card to my heart. All of a sudden those roses seemed to blossom and burst before my eyes. I quickly dialed Steve's work number. He answered right away.

"Do you mean it?" I asked.

"Yep, I mean it."

"I love you, Steve."

"I love you, Ellen. But one thing I've been wondering. How many shots do we really need for the trip?"

"I think like ten."

"Ouch!" He laughed.

I still have that card. I put it in the photo album filled with photographs from Nepal and memorabilia from our trip.

"Here's to balance." These were the perfect words. To me, they meant "yes" to Nepal, and to so much more.

SOON AFTER, WE BEGAN making preparations for our trip in earnest. The travel company we were working with sent us packets filled with itineraries, medical information, maps, and lists and lists of items recommended for the trip. Steve's first order of business was to upgrade our seats to business class for the long flight from LA to Thailand. I was all for roughing it, but welcomed this decision.

Lupe was excited for us, and assured us the kids would be fine. Allison and Matt thought it sounded "neat," but like a long time away, and were appalled by the thought of having ten shots "just to take a vacation."

When Allison and Matt heard our friends express surprise to us about our upcoming trip, we would use those conversations as a reminder to them to follow their dreams despite what others may think. I would say, "Listen to what others have to say, think about it, and listen to your voice inside. What does your heart tell you?"

A lot of friends thought it was great that we were going, though most said it was not a trip for them. "We'll live vicariously through your pictures!" they'd offer.

I remember vividly a dinner we had with our friends Amy and Adam. We brought along the brochure, and they encouraged us to talk about the trip. It was such a gift. We kept laughing about how it felt like when we were pregnant. Sharing the news, and then counting down the months, talking about all of the preparations.

Still, a few others thought we weren't being very responsible because of our kids. We'd hear, "That's really the kind of trip you should take when they're in college. It's too long for you to be away, and you'll be so far. It's really a dangerous place to go."

I would point out to Steve later that such comments were interesting to me. The same people who voiced that opinion had left their kids for a week or ten days to go to Israel, or to the islands. Those places were considered "safe" places, safe by being "within the norm" places. Or they felt fine about sending their young kids to overnight camp for four weeks, eight weeks. When I chose to do something different than the norm, projections of all sorts came out.

I didn't mind rocking the boat. It was only when I sat frozen in the boat that I got seasick.

I became adroit at pointing out to people that you could get killed driving to the grocery store. That you couldn't live your life in fear. Rather than feeling irresponsible about leaving my kids to go to Nepal, I saw it as offering them a gift. I wanted them to grow up knowing that it was okay—no, *more* than okay, *wonderful*—to stretch themselves to live in the direction of their dreams.

As we prepared for our trip, I watched with admiration as my children asked about Nepal, about the culture, and where it was on the map and how the people there lived.

"What kind of money do they use?" my son would ask.

"Will you see a yak?" my daughter wondered.

"Will you talk to the monks?" they wanted to know. "Will you bring us back a Buddha?"

I was amazed by how open and curious and supportive our children were about our trip. They told their friends. They told their teachers. They made us promise to take slides as well as photographs, so we could come to their classrooms and do a slide show.

Steve was amused by the many times men approached him saying, "I hear you and Ellen are going to Nepal. You'll be trekking?" Steve would answer yes, along with a whitewater rafting trip and an elephant safari.

Someone would slap him on the back and say, "Wow, it sounds awesome. How'd you get Ellen to agree to that? You sure are going to owe her big time. Guess you'll have to take her to Aruba, at the Hyatt, on your next vacation. Wine and dine her. Make up for taking her to Nepal."

Steve would laugh and say, "No, no, no! You have it all wrong. This is her idea, not mine!"

"You see, Steve," I would say to him when he would tell me these stories, "it's expectations. People think this trip is a 'guy' thing. It's great for me because I can publicly challenge those stereotypes while I get to enjoy the trip of a lifetime!"

Steve and I had great fun getting ready for the trip over the next five months. We had "dates" in which we would meet at the doctor's office for shots. We were given every possible medication to bring on our trip in case of illness. We learned how to tell the difference between bacterial diarrhea and your ordinary "run" of the mill variety. We learned about the possible side effects of our anti-malarial medication. We had medicines to cover strep throat, sinus infection, yeast infection, conjunctivitis, allergies, nausea, and inflammation. At night, before falling asleep, we'd play a new game. "Name an illness, I'll tell you the prescription." We both agreed we'd never prepared for a trip quite like this before.

We had fun going to Eastern Mountain Sports (EMS) for gear and other hiking essentials. Steve and I would take walks together in our hiking boots to wear them in. It was so freeing.

Under other circumstances, I don't think I would have walked out in public wearing baggy jeans, a turtleneck sweater, hiking boots, a ski jacket, and a hat. Those kinds of clothes made me look and feel even shorter and too unfashionable. I look better in tapered, tight jeans, cowboy boots, a tank top with a V-neck pullover and a leather coat with no hat, even if it's cold. But you know what? I never felt more comfortable! I was warm and cozy. I felt like I had a proper excuse to dress how I was dressing. (I didn't yet know that I didn't *need* an excuse.)

I wasn't covering up or trying to disguise my shortness with tailored clothes or fashionable footwear. Instead, I felt real.

STEVE AND I anxiously and excitedly waited for February to end, thankful for the fewer days of that short month. We began reading the Nepal news on the Internet each morning, and tried not to think about the mysterious disease that had become rampant in the remote western villages, killing hundreds of people each day.

We called the Centers for Disease Control and the U.S. State Department. They assured us that the rampant spread of unknown diseases was a common occurrence in Nepal, and tended to stay in the remote parts of the country, which, though only a hundred miles from where we would be, was at least a three-day journey through mountains and passes, making us "safe enough."

We packed our duffel bags. We unpacked, repacked, and waited some more. And then March 17th arrived.

Somewhere near Japan...March 18, 1999

WE LEFT yesterday. Dropped the kids off at school and said our good-byes. We had a relaxing breakfast of pancakes and hazelnut decaf at our favorite coffee shop, and then off we went to the airport.

I awoke early that morning. Anticipation. My shower felt great. I figured it was the last time for the next two weeks that I could carelessly let the water wash over my face, into my mouth.

I've been told repeatedly to keep my mouth closed while showering in Nepal. Visitors may be vigilant about not drinking the water, or not putting ice cubes in their sodas, but the shower gets them. The trickle creeps into their mouths while washing, practically invisibly, and then the tummy trouble and diarrhea sets in. A woman from Nepal advised me over the telephone last week, "If you sing in the shower, start humming instead."

I dried my hair, wondering what it will feel like on our adventure to not bother with such things. Without electricity, my hair will simply have to dry on its own, in whatever fashion it chooses. Just as I am trying to let go of my ego, it seems I will have to let in a natural wave I have resisted for years.

Lipstick. My daughter, Allison, teases. "Mommy, you said you're not bringing or wearing any makeup on your trip." She's right, and it feels wonderful and freeing. But to me, lipstick is not *really* makeup. It fits into another category all together. Even if I have a fever and the flu, lipstick makes me feel at least a degree lower on the thermometer.

"I can't let go of the lipstick," I tell her matter-of-factly.

She rolls her eyes as she leaves the bathroom to finish dressing for school. My budding feminist. I think I'll buy her a copy of *The Beauty Myth,* by Naomi Wolf. Wolf wears lipstick.

After nine and a half hours of traveling, we are still in the states. Our plane to Osaka and then on to Bangkok has been delayed. We call the kids.

"Where are you?" they ask excitedly. "Can you see Mount Everest?" I tell them that we are still in the United States. In Los Angeles.

"Oh," they answer, sounding less enthusiastic. "Is it really sunny and hot?" they ask hopefully.

"No, it's cloudy and in the fifties," I answer.

"That's what it is in Boston," they tell me.

During the flight from Boston to LA, I had read *From Heaven Lake,* by Vikram Seth. My brother had sent it to me a few months ago as a preparation gift for our trip. I had been saving it to read during our two and a half day journey through the skies. The book is an account of Seth's travels from China to Nepal via Tibet. I accompanied him in mind and spirit through Turfan, Urumgu, Liuyuan, Dunhuang, Nanhu, Germu, Nagu, Llasa, Shigaste, Nilamu, Shangmu, Lamasangu, and finally Kathmandu and then to New Delhi, all the while I am still on a domestic flight somewhere over Nevada.

I am very comfortable. I have on khaki hiking pants, hiking socks and Teva sandals. I am wearing a blue-cropped T-shirt and a gray zip sweatshirt. These are what I would call my "short clothes."

Without the security of tight, tapered jeans with at least a slight heel, I often feel like I am back in middle school. Looking too short and frumpy. Until I began preparing for this trip, I wouldn't have been caught dead in jeans and sneakers. Jeans and a flat loafer (without socks) or sandals were okay.

It sounds crazy, but my body felt different to me with these peculiar rules. Sneakers and shorts were fine. Tapered jeans, ankle length with sandals, were okay. But a pair of jeans with socks and, say, a pair of running shoes put me back to my most insecure years, when I "fell short" as I compared myself to my peers.

My friends in junior high school and in high school looked great in that casual jean and sneaker combo. They had long legs with jeans that hugged them just so, and cropped sweaters that hung perfectly. My legs felt short and stubby. In sneakers I felt extra frumpy and ungraceful. My sweaters, though cropped, fell longer on me, and I would constantly try rolling or tucking the bottom of the sweater underneath, so it would hit me the same place my friends' sweaters hit them. I would have bulges on my arms because the sleeves were too long. My jeans were often cuffed once, twice, sometimes three times, so they felt too wide to me.

When tucking shirts into my jeans, I spent what seemed like hours doing what I called "fluffing." I wanted the shirt to fall casually, evenly, around my waist and tucked into my jeans. I wanted to look thin. If I looked thin, I wanted to look thinner. I'd fluff the shirt out a little on my left, then on my right, bringing it just over the belt in front. Oops! Then the left side hiked out a bit too far. Fix the left, adjust the right. Look from each angle. I know I'm too short, but do I look thin enough? Casual enough, acceptable enough?

Getting ready for Nepal offered another chance. An excuse to wear jeans with sneakers and pants with hiking boots. I didn't care how I looked, but simply enjoyed the feeling. Ah! The comfort!

I'd look in the mirror and say to myself, "Yeah, you do look shorter in these clothes." And then I'd notice also how unbelievably comfortable and cozy they were.

I'd leave my house in them. Help at the children's school in them. Go to the grocery store in them. I noticed, too, that I felt stronger and heartier in them.

The extra fold-down seats in my Mitsubishi Montero could sometimes be stubborn. When I am dressed in my Enzo loafers and Liz Claiborne petites, I find it inconvenient to hoist myself into the back of the truck to fix the problem. When I am in my baggy jeans, hiking boots, and sweatshirt, I'm kind of into it. With my hands pressing on the floor of the trunk, I hike my behind in, swirl around, and begin to investigate. Is the latch caught? Something jammed?

I pretend I am in Arizona, driving through the Painted Desert, when my car makes a coughing sound and falls ill. Do I use my cell phone or my Triple AAA card? I probably couldn't even get any reception out there. No problem. That tactic would be for Ellen with manicured nails and heels, wearing jeans that don't offer much freedom of movement. Ellen in hiking boots and baggy pants fixes the problem herself with calm and ingenuity.

Okay, okay, I know I am only at the Stop-and-Shop with a cartload of groceries and dry cleaning hanging in the back, but it's the *feel*.

Evening on the Osaka to Bangkok flight

STEVE HAS EXCITEDLY been
explaining the joys of upgrading.
A seasoned business traveler, he has upgraded
our seats to business class for the twenty-two
hour flight to Thailand. He raves about how wonderful the food and service will be, about the warm towels and the soft blankets. The movie choices. But mostly, on our Boston to LA flight, where we flew coach, he tells me about the leg room.

It's funny, because people assume that if you are short, leg room on a plane is not a problem. That's not really the case. Since my feet don't reach the ground, they grow tired and uncomfortable. There is no place to let them rest.

I try to sit with my legs crossed, which offers some temporary relief, but the muscles feel cramped if I sit this way too long, and my knees jab into the arm rests. I watch Steve, who can't be too comfortable either. While his feet are most definitely on the ground, they are cramped.

Steve enthusiastically tells me about his Nirvana, the business class we will soon be in. "They have these foot rests from the seat in front of you. You just pull it out, and your feet can rest there. The seats are so roomy, you'll feel great."

We finally arrive in business class flying Thai Air. I feel like this is a mini-pilgrimage, a preparation for our entry to Nepal. Steve has been extolling the sheer ecstasy of this upgrade. I feel as though perhaps I should have brought an offering.

On the plane, we walk up a flight of stairs to our seats. Beautiful flight attendants in traditional Thai dress greet us. Everything looks like the Thai Air commercials I have seen on CNN during the Larry King breaks.

Steve looks pleased. Like somehow he is solely responsible for business class itself.

We take our seats, settling into the soft, lilac cushions with matching blanket, pillow, and tray. Without a sound, Steve pulls out the footrest in front of him, pushes his seat back and produces a satisfied sigh. I smile, and pull out my footrest.

"There must be some mistake!" I think to myself. I adjust the footrest up, down. Try again. My feet don't reach the footrest!

It's not fair. I want the benefits of the footrest, too! Reclining my seat merely exacerbates the impossible reach.

"Never mind," I think. "Be one with the moment."

I revert to my cross-legged position and take it as a sign that I should meditate.

LATER, I LOOK AROUND the plane trying to figure out who else may be part of our twelve-person group in Nepal. A few women catch my eye. Dressed in long gauze skirts and Tevas, they had what I always wanted, what I called the "Cambridge Look." Tall, thin, artsy.

Already I find my "Inner Middle School Child" begin to emerge. Suddenly my comfortable, freeing clothes make me feel inadequate, short, a child.

"Okay, Ellen," I think. "Embrace this moment and these feelings. Whether those women are on this trip or not, they have already given you a gift; a deeper look into the baggage you didn't check through. About your fears of not "measuring up.""

I had to remind myself that these feelings were purely my own mind and its projections. I hadn't even spoken to these women. There was no reason to think we wouldn't get along or like each other. I didn't even know if they were in our travel group. They simply triggered in me the comparisons I used to make so often, between the girls who looked "perfect" (tall, thin) and me, who felt childlike and inadequate.

I was surprised by how quickly my confidence could become weakened. My own projections created my reality, and I was learning that it was up to me, that *I* needed to be responsible for my own head games.

I was an adult now, no longer a child shopping with my mother and being told to walk next to a short girl to see if I was taller, if I had won that match. It was time to stop comparing, stop assessing, and stop obsessing.

BECAUSE MY KNEE was giving me some trouble this month, the doctor had advised anti-inflammatory drugs and no exercise during the past few weeks. Our travel brochure reminded me to be in tip-top physical shape for our adventurous trip.

I ponder whether the turbulence that kept me awake half of the night counts as a workout. My legs, arms, chest, and neck are bobbing up and down, jiggling and wiggling back and forth. It's actually not an unpleasant feeling, as my body is quite stiff from sitting. I'm beginning to classify this as an aerobic activity after all.

Surely I will be able to make it through our trek with flying colors. I want to feel that hearty feeling in my hiking boots and in my soul, not the "too short" feeling of someone who wonders if they are enough.

Sitting at the airport in Osaka

STEVE AND I are talking with
and listening to the many people on the plane.
Because of the earlier flight delay, the crew
wants to make up lost time, so we will not be able to get off the plane and stretch our legs in the airport before our Bangkok departure. We talk to a couple who look to be in their fifties, on their way to Vietnam

and Thailand. They sound like they have been everywhere, and plan to visit Nepal next year.

A semi-aloof, rugged guy dressed primarily in denim listens at close range, waiting to answer any question directed toward him. He answers quietly, so that you have to focus on him carefully to hear his reply. It turns out that he is going to Kathmandu and then to Tibet to climb Mount Everest with a group of other rugged men dispersed in coach. He is an ER doctor, and will be the physician on their two-and-a-half-month expedition. (I don't know it then, but we will run into his group a handful of times in Kathmandu and chat with them. Some of the women will develop little crushes on some of the climbers, to whom we give made-up names. Not until we have returned home will we realize that this was Dave Hahn's group, filming a documentary for PBS as they searched for English mountaineer George Mallory's body on Everest).

When people on the plane ask Steve and me our plans, we share with them our itinerary. "Wonderful," is the reply. "But it's a short trip, huh? A little sampling," they add.

The relativity of life is displayed even before we have finished our flying journey. At home, in our safe, suburban neighborhood, we look adventurous. Friends remark how incredible it is that Steve is taking off two whole weeks of work to go to Nepal, that they couldn't/wouldn't do that. Friends tell us we are "rugged." They say they will live vicariously through us, because "we'd never do it." They promise to be there for the slide show. We feel excited, a little nervous, and adventurous.

On the plane, we feel like toddlers allowed to roam the park under the illusion of freedom without noticing the protective white picket fence. We are still excited, a little nervous, and adventurous. It's just that it depends on whom you surround yourself with.

At home, we have become "risk-takers, adventurers." Here, "they" are the risk-takers and adventurers, spending two and a half months in an attempt to reach the summit of Mount Everest. Compared to them, we are pretty tame.

It's like the airport in Japan that I didn't get to see. I wondered how much lower the drinking fountains and countertops might be to accommodate a population shorter on average than Americans. Around Asian people, my height fits in more readily. I am "less short" and more the "norm."

It's all relative: short, tall, adventurous, tame. The challenge is in looking at the circumstance from varying angles, and not getting caught in using the external for the internal, the subjective as the objective.

I SLEEP ONLY an hour or two despite the endless night. We fly continually away from day until I feel like I'm living in the Antarctic during the winter solstice.

Because of the direction of travel and the time changes, we lost Thursday. It simply didn't exist, but in my mind it had to be Thursday and both my body clock and Nike watch said it was 6:00 A.M. Still, darkness enveloped the sky like the color of a Hershey chocolate bar.

Then, seemingly out of nowhere, activity suddenly began. Lights were turned on, shades pulled up, and the flight attendants in their splendid dress wheeled food carts down the aisle.

A cold salad of delicately sliced cucumbers, a cherry tomato, and sprouts came first. I figured in Japan and Thailand, this was a healthful way to begin the day. I was hungry and I ate. The next course was chicken in noodles followed by chocolate truffles. I declined; the smell of chicken at 6:00 A.M was at best, unappealing.

I had moved a few rows in front of Steve during the night to spread out on the empty seats. When I returned to my original seat, I asked if he had eaten the chicken.

"Yes," he said, "it was delicious."

"Ugh!" I retorted. "I asked them to take it away. How can they serve chicken and noodles for breakfast?"

Steve laughed and said, "Ellen, that wasn't breakfast, it was a very late dinner! You're still on Boston time. They're trying to get your sleep and your meals on the new time schedule!"

Of course. You have to change your mind. It's that simple, as simple as changing your watch.

To be willing to say, "this is how it's been and now, this is how it will be." I'm still hungry for Cheerios, but the confusion around my "breakfast" is now a metaphor for me on this trip. Is the *situation* problematic? Or are the preconceived thoughts and expectations I have brought to a particular situation problematic?

What is right? What is wrong? Whose rules do we play by, and when is it only a simple matter of changing your watch, so to speak, adopting a new perspective, keeping an open mind?

On flight from Bangkok to Kathmandu

THE FLIGHT IS only three hours and forty-five minutes. Compared to the amount of time we have already spent on planes, this seems absurdly short, like a little sprint.

By now we have met the others on our trip, which does not include the "Cambridge-like" women. Embarrassingly enough, I am still slightly relieved. They could have easily adorned the cover of a magazine like *Outdoors,* or graced the EMS or REI catalogues. They are probably very cool and fit.

How dare I make these judgments so automatically in the exact way I am fighting against others making judgments about me based on my height! I still have a lot of work to do in breaking away from stereotypes that try to define me, or that I let define others.

Our group seems great, a good mix of people and ages. We are all tired, and excited.

I am looking out the window with about fifty minutes left of our trip when I mention to Steve that the weather looks like it's really clouding up. White puffy clouds seem to have rolled in out of nowhere, dotting the blue horizon for as far as the eye can see.

Steve looks out and laughs at me. "Those aren't clouds, Ellen. Those are mountains."

I look out the window again. The clouds are practically level with the plane. "Those can't be mountains. They're at the same level as us."

"Can you say 'Himalayas'?" Steve asks, snidely.

"You've got to be kidding!" I counter. "They just rose out of nowhere. But you must be right. No, you can't be right. It's too much, too incredible."

I continue staring out the window while Steve rummages through his backpack for his camera. "You're going to take pictures of clouds?"

I ask.

"No," Steve answers evenly, "I'm going to take a picture of the Himalayas."

He starts to click away and I look out again, beginning to believe him.

We are on the side of the plane that has a perfect view. The pilot begins to speak, directing the passengers to look out the window for their first glimpse of Mount Everest. The passengers flock to the right side of the plane, over our seats.

I believe Steve.

WE LAND IN Kathmandu, and the phrase that best expresses my thoughts are the words of Dorothy in the Wizard of Oz: "Toto, I have a feeling we're not in Kansas anymore."

The sounds, sights, and smells overwhelm. After the long line at immigration, we enter a large baggage area to collect our suitcases; suitcases we have not seen since Boston, and fear we may never see again.

Nepalese men wait by the stacks of canvas duffels. I am surprised. Most of the men are short in stature. In this crowded airport, I don't strain to look up, or feel claustrophobic with my body feeling vulnerable or crunched. I can look around without straining my neck.

Steve, I notice, looks like he has doubled in height. In broken English, men ask to help with our bags and can we spare some rupees? Crowds of men, crowds of people pushing. But I can see what is going on.

One young Nepalese man insists on helping us, and won't take no for an answer. He wants to get our bags and drive us to Kathmandu, to take us to our hotel and then take us sightseeing. We try to explain that we are part of a tour group, that we have to wait for a specific driver, that we have a Sherpa who is coming for us. This seems inconsequential to him.

"We get your bags," he keeps insisting. He indiscriminately pulls off two random duffel bags from a huge pile of luggage and says, "Okay, c'mon. We go now."

I don't worry that I will get lost or that I will be trampled. My head is at the same level as other heads; I can see into the eyes of Nepalese women, can look right into the marking of their "third eye" of wisdom, painted in red in between the brows. Though the air is thick, I can breathe.

"Hey!" Steve yells as the man starts carrying the luggage and pushing us forward through the crowd. "Hey, wait!" Steve yells again. "Those aren't even our bags."

Eventually we find our bags, the rest of our group, and our Sherpa, Tenzing. We pile into a small bus, and talk until the streets of Kathmandu render us silent.

Water buffalo line the streets along with worn, colorfully painted city buses with deities hanging from the rear view mirror where Americans hang air fresheners. The overcrowded buses spew out filthy black smog that fills the streets as people hang their faces out the windows. Three-wheeled vehicles that look like a cross between a car and a motorcycle with people squeezed inside dart in and out of taxis, around bicycles, water buffalo, motorcycles, and pedestrians.

There are no traffic lights. With each turn you assume you're going to crash, but you don't. There are no traffic lanes. Just a cacophony of blowing horns that sounds like a bad junior high school marching band.

And I love it. Driving down the crowded, dirty streets of Kathmandu, you can't tell what is being built and what is being torn down; everything, it seems, is in a state of flux, but it's anyone's guess in which direction it is going.

Men are building with their bare hands—short, strong men; there is no machinery aiding, no construction truck parked out front. Instead, shirtless men stand at different levels of the building, passing bricks and materials to each other in a well-orchestrated line. Some buildings stand half-finished and you can understand. How could they possibly finish building it or tearing it down by hand? There it sits, like the puzzle on my basement card table that I gave up on after I realized how many blue pieces there were, all looking the same.

We check into the hotel room, shower, and go out to explore. The streets are colorful: women dressed in traditional saris, the colors an endless sea of delight flowing in the breeze, goats wandering about, assortments of fruits and vegetables in baskets that dot the streets, or fill the little carts attached to wooden bicycles. One person might be selling only carrots, another only onions. The smell of exotic spices fills the air, and adds flavor to the street as they line the road in boxes.

We are all in our Tevas, and I notice how many Nepalese men and women are barefoot. As we continue walking, marveling at the beauty amidst the pollution and the noise, we see a horrible sight. So horrible, in fact, that at first I do not believe it is real, like it is happening in slow motion.

There is a motorcycle accident. I shouldn't be surprised. I have already seen how the driving is here. Few people wear helmets, and the women, in keeping with tradition and the constraints of their saris, ride on motorcycles with their legs together on one side of the bike, barely holding on to the driver.

In this case, the passenger of the motorcycle has fallen off, with no helmet, and we are watching him being dragged down the streets of Kathmandu as he is caught on the bike.

"He's dead," Kurt, a man on our trip, said. "He's got to be dead already."

I started to shake, and thought I was going to vomit. I held on to Steve and kept saying, "Oh my God, oh my God."

The way an accident is handled in Kathmandu is that a group of people begins running and yelling for help. Then more and more people join and run down the streets and call for help. This can go on for blocks, for miles.

Finally, it was clear to me the man was dead. He never moved. Not a muscle.

LATER THAT NIGHT, in the hotel, I was filled with so much emotion. I felt strong, but vulnerable, too. I held the image of the dead man being dragged through the street. I felt very far from home, from my kids, from my life.

I held on to Steve, thinking about how fragile life was, and how all we had was this moment. And the next moment, and, hopefully, a long string of moments that would make up our lives. But really, all you knew for sure was this moment.

BEFORE WE BEGAN our trek in the Annapurnas we explored Kathmandu. When we went to visit Boudhanath stupa, the largest stupa in Nepal, I felt as though everything in my life was bringing me to that moment.

People I grew up with often talked about the indescribable feelings they experienced when they visited the Wailing Wall (the Western Wall) in Jerusalem. I guess Boudhanath was that for me. The minute I saw the shrine I felt a release, a letting go, and a feeling like I was no longer swimming against the tide, but was now being carried along the current of a holy river.

Stupas are sacred Buddhist monuments that symbolize the enlightened mind and the path to its realization. They are often filled with sacred images, writings, mantras or the relics of holy beings. Boudhanath is beautiful, with colorful prayer flags reaching from its top out diagonally to the bottom. It is built in the form of a mandala, a circular symbol of the universe often used in Buddhist meditation, with three tiers surrounding the huge dome.

The stupa is symbolic of the five elements. The base symbolizes earth; the dome, water; the spire, fire; the crescent atop the spire, light; the flame shape topping the spire, ether. From each side of the stupa, "Buddha Eyes" are watching, the ever-present, omnipresent eyes of wisdom and compassion.

The entire circumference of the stupa consists of a low wall of prayer wheels circling the base. Tibetan pilgrims, monks, nuns, and tourists alike spin these prayer wheels, walking clockwise around the stupa, spinning blessings into the wind.

Buddhist teachings say you accumulate merit by spinning the wheels. I just know that I had the feeling I could stay forever in this place, and that I could walk around and spin those prayer wheels for as long as my time on Earth lasts. I felt like I was home.

Spinning those prayer wheels, listening to the chanting of monks from the monastery across from the stupa, walking beside the monks with their maroon and saffron robes, with water buffalo scattered about, and flames of butter lamps and smells of burning incense, it is here I felt I belonged. Whether I lived here before in a past life, or my soul simply knew this was a place for me to feel the essence of my spirit today, I felt whole.

I didn't want to leave this place, but I also knew, in some way, I never would leave. In some way that place, that feeling of holiness, was inside me already, always.

I knew the mantra on the prayer wheel read *Om Mani Padme Hum.* The Jewel is in the Lotus. In other words, the Buddha is within our own heart and soul. So of course I would never really leave this place, and it would never leave me.

THE TRIP ITSELF was everything we had hoped it would be. Even the frightening eight-hour bus ride we were forced to take along high mountain passes when our internal flight to Pokhara was cancelled.

Driving from Kathmandu to Pokhara to begin our trek in the dead of night was a terrifying experience. The high mountain roads were merely narrow dirt paths seven thousand feet high with nothing on the sides to keep the bus from falling off into nowhere—which often, they do.

With no electricity to light the black night, our driver would simply blast the horn when he suspected another bus was rounding the hairpin turn. Then they played chicken, and somehow, miraculously, one bus would squeeze past the other.

I should have known it would be a dangerous journey when the driver insisted he had to go to his home first, before starting off for Pokhara, to change his shoes, to light incense and to chant some prayers.

Tenzing, for his part, did what he could to prepare us for the bus when we, as a group, opted for a long bus ride rather than take the chance that our domestic flight to Pokhara would be cancelled again the next day. Tenzing bought us beer. Lots of beer. San Miguel beer, which he encouraged us to "drink up." As the ride grew more dangerous, we drank up.

We were grateful when our driver periodically stopped the bus to light more incense and chant a prayer. We now saw that we needed all the help we could get.

For my part, without meaning to, I taught the entire group Yiddish. It came so naturally to me that I would just blurt it out. Each scary turn brought an "*Oy gevault.*" When I would look out the window at how our bus was just barely on the so-called road that offered a sheer drop, I would say, "I'm *plotzing* here." The best was hearing my friend Patsy, on the bus, repeating these phrases in her southern drawl.

That bus ride bonded the group together in a special way that continued through our trek, our rafting, and our safari. When our trip was over, three of the people in the group were staying on for an eight-day extension trip offered through the travel company. They would be trekking in the Khumba region to Tengboche Monastery, situated at thirteen thousand feet at Mount Everest. As Steve and I returned to the airport in Kathmandu, ready for our departure, I remember saying to him that I should just stay. "How can we come all the way to Nepal and not see Mount Everest?" I asked.

We had been a little disappointed by the often dusty conditions during this dry season, which rendered the snow-peaked mountains of the Annapurnas only visible in the early morning hours. The vivid colors of white-capped mountains set against clear blue sky outlined so beautifully in our brochure were apparently taken in October, after the monsoon season, when the air is most clear, and the views never-ending—until March, when a lot of the views end.

My heart wasn't ready to leave, but my body was. Steve and I had spent the last few days fantasizing about eating fresh fruits and vegetables again (because of unclean water, tourists are warned not to eat fresh produce), about eating our favorite Caesar salad at The Lyceum restaurant in Salem. We looked forward to using tap water instead of boiled bottled water to brush our teeth. But my heart, I knew, wasn't finished in Nepal.

I thought it best at this point to leave those thoughts to myself. I knew how blessed I was to have been here in Nepal with Steve at this time. I knew I needed to practice The Four Noble Truths taught by Buddha, the second being that desire is the root of suffering.

"Desire less," I thought to myself. "Be grateful for what is."

I boarded the plane and took a last breath of the wonderful, sticky air that is Nepal, and gulped it into my being.

THE PLANE LOOKED OPULENT to Steve and me. After days without electricity, we were offered little headlights over each seat, lights I previously never thought twice about. Each seat had an individual movie monitor. There was fresh fruit and champagne and drinking water you didn't have to boil. There was a lavatory with a toilet.

As we were enjoying these comforts, I found myself thinking back to the porters and Sherpas who had accompanied us on our trek.

All were under 5 feet 2 inches. Some were closer to my height.

These men were stronger than the biggest men in our group. They had so much strength and agility. They seemed to skip over rocks effortlessly, even while carrying our duffels and gear. While we were all gasping by the end of the day, these men barely broke a sweat, despite the loads they were carrying.

I had taken a picture of Steve with the porters. Steve, who is average in height in the States, towered over them.

The women of Nepal are short like me. I bet none of them have entertained the wish to be taller. How relative height is, how subjective cultural ideals are.

I thought about how some of Nepal's larger hotels have recently started selling Diet Coke. This is for the tourists from the West. You can't find diet products anywhere else in the country. Why would you? Dieting is unheard of.

The cultures of the East and of the West have so many differences, yet I felt I belonged with both of them. I knew that part of my work, part of my growth, involved bridging those worlds.

The external worlds where I had traveled, but also the internal worlds within myself that were so often at odds. My small physical body and my large spiritual body, my conformity to the stereotypes of a short female, and my rejection of those same stereotypes. My public self, and my private self. Suburban wife, mother, and spiritual seeker, writer, adventurer.

One of the phrases you hear over and over in Nepal is "What to do?" A sort of resignation that what will be, will be. One way or another, it will work itself out in some way.

I thought I'd sit with that for a while. Rather than swimming against the tide, or being carried away effortlessly in the current, I'd just sort of float, and see what happened.

I WAS HAPPY with what happened. In a way, Steve and I brought Nepal back home.

We had a party where we showed our slides of Nepal, and over seventy people came to the little coffee house to celebrate our trip and the culture of Nepal. Some people mentioned friends they knew who were contemplating trips to Nepal, to India. Could they call us for some advice? Others asked if I could recommend a good introductory book on Buddhism. Teachers asked us to show our slides in the classrooms.

I loved doing these things. They were my passion, and I felt free to reveal that passion in public. I think my excitement for Nepal and the East was contagious.

"What to do?" Enjoy the blessings. People who didn't know where Nepal was on a map now knew a lot of its history and culture. I was enjoying floating in this river, because it felt so relaxed and so right.

I wanted to incorporate more of Buddhism in my everyday life, to develop a daily practice on my spiritual path. I had wished that some of the many Buddhist meditation centers in Cambridge were closer to my home. Because so many of the meditation sittings were at dawn or at dusk, and the centers were forty-five minutes away without traffic and double that with, it was not possible to get there when my kids needed me to get them to and from school, to make dinner.

"What to do?" I tried to make that work—my life at home—my spiritual practice, and I continued to meditate and read books on Buddhism and study the teachings. I often told Steve that spending time reading those books felt like taking a warm blanket out of the dryer and wrapping myself up in its softness.

I missed the monks and the chanting, the stupas and the smells of Nepal.

ONE EVENING I went to a local museum that was hosting an opening for an exhibit from India. One of the reasons I had recently joined the Peabody Essex Museum was because of this exhibit and the Tibetan exhibit scheduled for the following month, which included treasures on loan from the Dalai Lama.

I had read that a group of Tibetan monks from the Drepung Loseling Monastery would be at the opening to perform their chanting, and that this performance would be open to members on a special night. On the night of the India exhibit, I was enjoying talking with one of the curators of the museum. I asked about the Tibetan monks who would be there next month, and we discussed the plans for the opening. Then, without really thinking, I asked where all of the monks would be staying for their four-day visit.

"That's a problem for us," she explained. "The monks really like to all stay together when they travel, if it's possible, and right now we are unable to accommodate that wish."

"Oh. Well, they can stay at my home," I offered.

"Really?" The curator looked surprised. "That's so gracious of you, to open your home like that."

"It would be an honor," I explained.

"But do you have the room to house eight monks?" I assured her that I did. Looking over the dates, I told her that for part of their stay, my husband and I were taking the kids on vacation in New Hampshire. "But that's not until the last day and a half. They'll be familiar enough with my house that they'd be fine on their own."

We agreed to speak by telephone the following day.

That night, Steve called from his business trip in California. He asked me what was new, how the kids were. We were just about to hang up when I hollered into the phone, "Wait, Steve. I forgot to tell you. I think we may have eight Tibetan monks staying at our house next month. Well, for four days. "

There was a brief moment of silence on the other end. "Cool," Steve said.

I WAS TOLD that the monks would have a driver, Stephanie, who was from the States and would help take care of them at my house. One of the employees at the museum accompanied me to the grocery store in preparation for their visit. My cart was filled with black tea, granola, figs, and nuts. Then I baked for them all of my mother's favorite recipes. Jewish recipes. It felt good.

Steve and I listened to their glorious chanting at the Tibetan exhibit opening at the museum. I loved seeing their colorful robes and hearing the loud horns and cymbals. All of it seemed on the one hand foreign, and on the other hand so very familiar.

It was strange piling half of the monks into my Montero afterwards, the other half in Steve's Land Rover, for the short drive to our home. I tried to remember all of their names. There was Venerable Ngawang Tashi, Venerable Tashi Sonam, Venerable Thubeten Gunden, Venerable Ngawang Stultrum, Venerable Paldan Thinlay, Venerable Yeshi Sherab, Venerable Choying Gyaltso, and Venerable Tsultrim

Gyaltso. They all had olive skin and dark hair and deep brown eyes. They liked the big cars. They put on the radio and opened the sun-roof.

Our kids had decided to sleep at friends' overnight, to offer more space for the monks. They would return in the morning to spend time with all of us. After the monks had decided which rooms and beds they would occupy, they asked Stephanie and me if there was a washing machine. They were very pleased when I nodded yes, and quickly, one by one, they handed us their robes.

I laughed with Stephanie as I loaded eight maroon and saffron robes into my Maytag.

"I'm guessing permanent press even with the knowledge that all is impermanent," I said as I turned the machine on.

Then I held up my Tide laundry detergent like I was making a commercial, pointing to the opened washing machine full of monk's robes. I smiled into the imagined camera, held up the detergent, and said, "Tide. For all your monastic needs."

SOME OF THE MONKS spoke no English; others spoke some, and a few spoke English quite well. Because my family and I spoke no Tibet-an other than the greeting "Tashi Deleck," we relied on what English the monks spoke and on smiles.

As they relaxed at night, a handful of the monks were eating pret-zels while watching the NBA playoffs on the big screen TV. I laughed and smiled at them. "You guys are no different than having my father visit, except that you're not drinking a Miller Lite," I thought to my-self.

Tashi, the monk who was the chant master and leader of the group, quickly settled himself at our computer and spent the next few hours e-mailing. I felt I was receiving the opportunity to sample a taste of the East, and the monks were clearly enjoying sampling a taste of the West.

I watched the monks pointing at the images racing across the TV screen, the fast-paced commercials with wild graphics and product names. What did they think? They did a lot of laughing and pointing. I was all at once acutely aware of how busy our culture seemed.

"Don't you want to meditate?" I wanted to ask. One of them

picked up the remote control, pressed the button and eventually began channel surfing. He stopped at MTV. "Oh God," I thought.

That night, before going to bed, I asked Stephanie what time the monks would be up in the morning. "When should I start breakfast?"

"Oh," she said. "This is vacation for them. When they are at home, in India, in the monastery, they are up anywhere from 3:00, 4:00, 5:00 in the morning. Here, they like to sleep in. Maybe 9:00, 10:00 in the morning."

I was surprised. What to do? Lose my expectations.

The next morning, I awoke at 5:00 A.M. The house was still. I couldn't fall back asleep. I kept thinking, "I have a house full of monks, and I'm the one up at dawn!"

I didn't want to wake the house, so I took all of my clothes and toiletries and went to my health club, where I showered, dried my hair, and dressed. I slipped back into the still sleeping house.

When I heard people begin to stir, I began preparing breakfast. Bagels and cream cheese, hoppel poppel (my mother always makes it. It's like an egg casserole with salami, onions, tomatoes and green peppers. Most of these monks did eat meat) and my mother's famous sour cream coffee cake.

Steve and I sat with Stephanie and the group of monks in the kitchen over breakfast and tea, with the monks telling me the meal was delicious. Those who didn't speak English would point to the food and rub their stomachs with a smile.

"My mother," I would say to them, pointing to the food and holding my heart.

The monks enjoyed looking at our pictures from Nepal, and smiled at the prayer flags I had hanging in the yard since our return from Nepal.

They were eager to meet the children. Their passion, besides following the eightfold path to enlightenment, seemed to be basketball. They would rush out to our driveway and play in their robes, the balls swooshing in the net, against the garage, in the bushes.

They made quite a sight on our block. Cars and neighbors would watch, drive around the block, and check their mailboxes again. The monks would wave. "Hello," they would call out.

When the kids and their friends came home, it was like having eight doting uncles. The kids fell into the monks' open arms and hearts immediately.

They played basketball together. Allison and her best friend, Taylor, taught two of the monks how to play four square, and they played for over an hour, the monks totally into the moment and the joy of just playing. Matt was being pitched to, raced with, and cuddled by other monks. Some monks circled the yard and the house quietly chanting and praying.

At one point the monks had wanted to move the basketball net over, because they felt badly that the ball would often land in my geraniums. Steve had told them of course, no problem. A few of the monks moved over the heavy pole and net and looked down to where the base had stood. They began talking rapidly in Tibetan, and a few of the other monks walked over, looked down, and joined them in discussion. After a few minutes, the monks went to move the base, with the pole and net, back to where it had originally stood.

Steve intervened and said, "No, it's fine, you can keep it there."

Tashi, the monk who spoke the most English, put his hand on Steve's shoulder and pointed down to where some slugs lay. Apparently, they had made their home under the base of the basketball hoop. Tashi explained that if they left the pole where they had moved it, the slugs would lose their home and would die. They must therefore move the basketball net back immediately.

OVER THE NEXT FEW DAYS we went for walks, to the ocean, and out for Thai food. Tashi liked to tell me about the many times the Dalai Lama had summoned him to chant. Other monks talked about their escape from an occupied Tibet, about their homeland they so deeply missed, about the family they will never see. When we went to the beach, I was not surprised to see some of the monks write FREE TIBET in the sand, and then watch as the tide slowly washed their words away.

A day into the monks' visit, Matt would eat a meal only if he were sitting on one of the monk's laps. Allison and Tashi took pictures of each other with the digital camera. Tashi gave us his e-mail address. He loved going online. East meets West.

It felt so right, these wonderful monks in our house. At one point, on the evening before we were to leave for New Hampshire, I said to Tashi that I wished my children could hear him chant, especially that incredibly low note that he sang. "Can you just show them quickly what your voice can do?"

"One moment," Tashi said. He returned a few minutes later. "We want to do a short blessing and chant over your house and for your family."

I was honored. I gathered Steve and the kids as the monks went about rearranging my living room.

It was early evening, and the soft light of the sky bathed the room in warmth. Steve, the kids and I sat where the monks pointed, and we watched them arrange themselves in a semi-circle, some sitting, some standing. They offered a twenty-minute chant that was otherworldly in its beauty, tone, and spirit. My kids didn't move a muscle. The phone rang; it was ignored.

Afterwards, I stood up holding my heart, and poured out my gratitude. Tashi said it was they who wanted to thank us. They presented Steve, the kids, and me with special Tibetan gifts: A colorful Thangha wall hanging in blues, oranges and purples, Buddha in the center surrounded by threads of burgundy and gold; thin white kata scarves draped over our shoulders, as is custom when showing respect; "Free Tibet" T-shirts.

After the monks presented us with these gifts, I said to Tashi, "I'm sad that we won't see each other again." I knew they would soon be back in India.

Tashi laughed his deep laugh, his eyes sparkling and piercing as always, like he could see straight into your heart, and said, "But Ellen, we will meet again!"

THE FOLLOWING WEEK we enjoyed looking at the pictures taken with the monks. The kids loved to talk about the things we did with them and the places we went. I was happy to have had that time with them, to watch my children talking and playing with these monks. I would marvel to myself at how it seemed so natural that my house be full of monks and chanting. Of how right it felt to talk with them about Nepal, and Buddhism.

It was with this spirit that when August returned and we were again in Michiana, that I was inspired to initiate a little road trip for Steve and myself.

"The Dalai Lama is going to be in Bloomington, Indiana this week," I began. "Why don't we leave the kids with everybody here, and drive the four hours to hear his public address tomorrow?"

My family thought it sounded like a great idea. I also had an aunt, uncle, and cousin in Bloomington we could visit, and with whom we could stay overnight.

Steve and I went to see the Dalai Lama, driving down the two-lane highway with cornfields to our right, listening to John Mellencamp the whole way. We ended up in the third row of a ten thousand-person stadium. To our right was a small section of seats roped off. At one point, Steve and I turned around to see a group of monks walking to this special section. All of a sudden Steve grabbed my arm and said, "Look, Ellen! It's Tashi!"

" It couldn't be," I said. Hadn't Tashi already returned to India? I turned around and saw that Steve was right. Just then, Tashi looked over and broke out in a big grin.

I ran over to him and hugged him, and then realized that maybe you weren't supposed to hug a monk, especially in public before the Dalai Lama was ready to speak.

Tashi hugged me back, and put his arm on Steve's shoulder. "Where are the children?" he asked.

"At home," I said. "Tashi," I continued, "when you said back in my living room that we would meet again, I figured you meant in another lifetime. I didn't figure on meeting you again two months later in the Midwest!"

Tashi smiled and laughed. "You still have my e-mail?' he asked.

The next day we sent some more great pictures to his e-mail address: my kids in his lap, his robe enveloping them, action shots of their basketball romps.

THE FOLLOWING JUNE, I went with my dear friend Shelley to Washington, D.C. for five days to enjoy the Smithsonian Tibetan Cultural Festival, where the Dalai Lama would be speaking. Shelley and I would also be part of a march to the Chinese Embassy to protest the occupation of Tibet. I had special tickets for a smaller talk with the

Dalai Lama for one evening as well, and there were many wonderful performances and speakers scheduled throughout the days.

One afternoon, as Shelley and I were walking through the National Mall about to enter a performance, I heard a voice that I knew well, a tone so low and full of vibration, it had to be. I pulled Shelley inside a tent where a group of monks were chanting for a large audience. "Shelley! I know that voice. It has to be Tashi."

When Tashi turned around, I saw his radiant eyes. After the performance we went around to the back of the tent. The monks were in a special section roped off from the public. I asked a man who was working with them if I could speak with Tashi. A few minutes later Tashi came out and saw me, and that same, wonderful grin appeared on his face.

We embraced, and I said what I seemed to say to this man a lot. "I can't believe we meet again!"

I introduced him to Shelley, and we had someone in the crowd take a picture of the three of us. We talked for a few minutes. He said he would be chanting for the Dalai Lama at the public address the next day.

Before saying good-bye, Tashi asked, "Do you still have my e-mail address?"

Shelley and I smiled at the huge monitors all over the National Mall set up for the Dalai Lama's public address the next morning. Throughout the chanting, Tashi's face would cover the many screens. I thought of him playing basketball at my home, eating my mother's hoppel poppel recipe, and cutting Matt's food at the Thai restaurant.

"Do you have my e-mail address?" It's the wanting to connect, East to West, heart to heart. I felt blessed as I watched the direction in which my life was unfolding.

It was during this time that I realized I no longer had that dream, the dream where I tried to leap and couldn't get off the ground.

That dream hadn't been only about my own fears and doubts in expressing my full stature and myself in this lifetime. It was also about taking that leap of faith and entering a vast, expansive, opening space.

Chapter Seven

Dwarfed by Everest

Mount Everest stands 29,028 feet

I GUESS IT STARTED soon after Steve and I returned from Nepal. The high lasted a nice, long time. Having the monks at our home, seeing the Dalai Lama speak, and running into Tashi again. It all seemed so easy, so right. Like a continuation of the door that was opened when we flew East. Flew to Asia.

Still, at night, before falling asleep, I'd think about those photographs in the brochure. The ones of the snow-capped mountains masquerading as skyscrapers that were obviously taken in October, after the monsoon season, when the air was not dusty.

I wanted to go back, to hook up with another trek, to challenge myself. I still wanted Everest.

Then one day a friend came by with a new CD. "You have to hear this," she said, and put on the *Everest* CD, which was the music that had accompanied the IMAX film.

Talk about your rerun! The first track sounded with a beautiful voice you could feel filling up the Tibetan Plateau, a voice that could move prayer flags to flap without a breeze. Each piece felt so complete, so full of life, the instruments exploding out of my CD player.

I felt like I had heard the cries of my children and had no choice but to go to them. I told Steve about the CD that night.

"It sounds great. Let's order it online from Amazon."

" Okay," I thought, "he's missed the point."

I tried to clarify. "Fine, fine. But what I'm telling you is that I think I need to go back."

"Oh Ellen, don't start…"

WE ORDERED THE CD. When it arrived a few days later, I was hooked. I couldn't get enough of it.

Everything within me was shaken awake when I heard its melodies, the few chanting voices. I started having fantasies—though I preferred to call them visions—of me trekking toward Everest, putting one foot in front of the other, this time in the snow. Leaving my footprints, my boot prints.

I wanted the cold to sting my face, and to listen to the *Everest* CD and just keep walking onward, upward. I wanted to stand in the shadows of this mountain of mountains, where everyone in its presence is dwarfed.

Whether a man stands 6 feet 4 inches, whether a woman wears a perfect size six, regardless of one's successes or failures, hopes or fears, we are all rendered small by the undeniable greatness of this solid peak. Yet at the same time we are part of that peak, part of that timeless movement and flow of the Earth and its forces, the Earth and its cycles.

A FEW DAYS LATER I told Steve that I was still thinking about going back.

"Ellen, I can't leave work like that again. Not this soon after our last trip."

I froze for a minute. When I thought about going back, I only envisioned *myself* going back.

"I know," I began. "I don't expect you to go. I don't think this is your kind of trip. But I really think I want to do the Everest trip. If not this year, then next year. I know I'd have to do a lot of training."

"It's really too soon to be talking about such a big trip again. There's a lot to consider," Steve said, ending the conversation.

THE WEEKS WENT BY, and Everest continued to grow from an embryo to a fetus within me. I felt its movement, its little kicks at my belly. It had a life force all of its own.

"I just want to listen to that CD while I trek toward Everest," I told my friend Shelley. She understood. She had left her husband and kids for three and a half weeks the year before to visit Nepal, and to reach Everest base camp from the Tibetan side.

"I know," she soothed. "Just one foot in front of the other, nothing else."

One evening while Steve was out of town I rented the IMAX film *Everest,* which was by then out on video. I waited until my kids went to sleep for the evening, and then I settled into my denim couch to watch the movie. I hadn't seen it since that time over a year ago, at the Science Museum. So much of the movie now looked familiar to me, a place I had already been.

The main reason I had wanted to watch the film was because I had become so familiar with the soundtrack. I hadn't focused on the music consciously the first time I had seen the film. Now I wanted to see how the images fit with that wonderful music. Already in my mind I pictured how that one crescendo must celebrate the safe crossing of the Khumba Icefall. How the slow, sad melodies toward the end must surely chronicle the disaster when so many climbers, including Scott Fisher and Rob Hall, died in the storm.

The film mesmerized me. I was cognizant of the music, of how the sounds were pieced together to tell a story where words simply would not suffice. The story went beyond words to touch that humanity in all of us, and the holiness in each one of us.

I was so involved in what I was watching that I didn't hear the garage door open or Steve walk into the house. Rather, I felt a presence and looked up to find my husband standing beside the couch, hands on his hips.

"Oh!" I said, startled. "I didn't hear you come in. What are you doing home so early?"

"I caught an earlier flight. Go," he said.

"What?"

"Go. You want to go back so badly. Go."

"Oh Steve, thank you! If I can just look into it. I'll talk to Brian at the travel company. It's already November. I'll see what trips are being offered for October." I gave him a great big hug. "Do you want to finish watching with me?"

"Nah. I'm going up to change. I'm exhausted. You finish watching."

And I did.

OVER THE NEXT FEW DAYS I spoke with two of the three people who had been on our trip last year and had joined the Everest extension. I wanted to get a better feel for the trip, how strenuous, the weather, and so forth.

Andrew told me, "Remember how we thought we were really roughing it in those little lodges?"

"Yeah."

"Okay, so picture that in comparison to the Everest Trek, and we were living high at the Ritz."

"But you loved it?"

"It was spectacular." Andrew went on to tell me that a lot of people on the trek had problems. "It's a steep climb, it can get really cold and the altitude can do a number on you."

He very generously added, "I remember you trekking on our trip. You had a lot of strength and endurance. I think you should go. I think you'll do fine. Just remember to drink a lot of water and to go slowly. The main thing is not to get dehydrated. Remember, there are no showers and you're in tents for eight nights. You get pretty dirty."

We talked about different items to bring on the trip.

"Oh, and one more piece of advice," Andrew offered. "Try to take a dump in the morning. When the ground is frozen. That way you can avoid the stench that builds up in the latrine. That, or try to be the first one to use it when they dig a fresh hole."

Ah.

My friend Patsy, with her southern drawl, told me to "go for it."

"The reason I had problems was because I let myself get dehydrated," she said. "Plus, I was out of shape. I was having trouble on the trek I did with y'all. Y'all remember how much slower I was. You'll do great. I wish I were going back. You're not going to believe the views. Oh! But watch out for the dogs. They bark all night and then the yaks get angry and their bells start ringing. Bring ear plugs."

"Are the views like the brochure?" I asked, hopefully.

"Better than the brochure," Patsy said.

"I'm going to call Brian tomorrow," I told Steve that evening. "Have him send me another brochure with the new travel dates. See what's going on for next October."

The following day I spoke with Brian at the travel company. We talked about the March trip he had helped Steve and me with, all of the details he had taken care of that proved so helpful. All of the unexpected problems that occur in Nepal that you can't anticipate—about which you can only adopt a *laissez-faire* attitude and the Nepali refrain, "What to do?"

I told him how much I wanted to go back to Nepal, on the trip they called "Everest: The Sherpa Homeland." I explained that Steve would not be going, just me. I told him that I wanted to go in October, "so I can enjoy views like in the brochure. It was too dusty in March," I explained.

"You know, Ellen," Brian started. "With the Everest trip, the best views aren't only in October. Because you'll be at a higher altitude, you'll be above any dust or smog. And really, for this trip March is a better time because you get the views and the temperature is often a few degrees warmer. And trust me, when you're out there sleeping in your little tent in the cold, you'll want every degree of warmth you can get!"

March. That was only four months away! The plan was to go next year! I was ready, but was Steve? Were the kids? Was my body?

"We have a few spaces left on the March trip. March 18th."

"Wow! That's exactly one year and one day to the date of our last trip! I'd have to talk to Steve."

"Why don't I just put your name down, save you a spot? You can send me a deposit that can always be refunded."

That sounded reasonable. I decided not to call Steve at work, but rather wait for him to come home and hope the stock market was up. Really high. That all his companies reported great earnings and that he would be in an incredibly good mood.

"Guess what?" I said to Steve before he was barely in the house, before I had even remembered to check CNN to see what the Dow Jones or Nasdaq had done. I had been sitting on this piece of news since noon and it was already 6:00 P.M. I couldn't contain it any longer. "I can go to Everest in March! In four months!"

He smiled, threw up his hands, kissed my lips, and said, "I guess my wife is going to Everest this spring."

And that was that.

MY PARENTS, OF COURSE, were another story. They had come around about the other trip; my mother had even sent me books on Kathmandu and other traveling materials. But this was different. This was Everest. Alone, without Steve.

Steve picked up the other phone while I spoke with my mom. "Hey," he said. "She doesn't need me on this trip, trust me. I slowed her down on our last trek."

Over the next month my parents questioned my decision, but supported my actions 110 percent. That meant a lot to me. They'd send me newspaper clippings about Nepal. They were always willing to listen to me about the trip. But they worried about me sleeping in a tent by myself. When Brian called to tell me of another woman who would be traveling without her husband and wanted to share a tent, I agreed, and my mother seemed reassured.

I would listen to my parents sharing with me how they had been telling their friends of my plans. They seemed impressed.

"I can't believe I have a daughter getting ready to trek at Everest," my dad would say to me on the phone. At one point he said to me, "You know, you are one crazy gal."

I told him that that was the nicest compliment he could give me. This was the side of me I had so much wanted my parents to see in me when I was a child. That passion for adventure—me, as a spiritual seeker. As someone strong and hearty, regardless of being short. Of not simply complementing someone else, but standing on my own.

CHRISTINA HAD BEEN TO NEPAL a few years back, and wanted to return for the Everest trip. Brian gave us each other's phone numbers and e-mail addresses. She lived out in California, and over the next few months we spoke to each other often.

We talked about gear, about leaving our husbands and children at home. About workout schedules. About if we were going to have our periods on the trip. About how excited we were. About what our friends thought of our going. About what it would be like to not shower, about how cold it would be at night.

I learned that Christina was focused on weight. That despite being tall and thin, she was hoping she'd lose even more weight on the trip. Somewhere in each of our conversations, she would estimate how many calories we were likely to burn each day on the trip. I'd either ignore it, or mention again how I used to treat eating disorders, had struggled in the past with my own eating issues, how I wanted to be strong and healthy for the trip and not focus on appearance, on weight. How for me this trip had a lot to do with my spiritual yearnings. Still, in each conversation Christina talked about losing weight and hoping there would be "cute guys" on the trip.

The thought of my own tent sounded more and more appealing, even with howling winds and wild barking dogs. Christina and I would also be sharing a hotel room at the Bangkok airport, en route to Nepal, and at Kathmandu. While the security of being with another person on such a big journey offered some reassurance, the more we spoke, the more I wondered whether I should break off these plans now, and be on my own.

Other than a few comments to Steve, I tried to keep my misgivings to myself. I focused instead on the trip, on the itinerary. The flight would be the same: Boston to LA, LA to Bangkok with a quick hour in Japan, a night in the Amari Airport Hotel in Bangkok, and then the flight from Bangkok to Kathmandu. It sounded almost easy now. Like the last trip, we would spend a few days in Kathmandu. I couldn't wait to be back there, to walk those wild streets and smell those smells and spin the prayer wheels at Boudhnath Stupa.

For this trek we would fly into Lukla, a tiny mountain airstrip where we would spend a night acclimating to the higher altitude. From there we would follow old mountain paths into the land of the Sherpas, Buddhists who live in the shadow of Everest—or as they refer to the mountain, Chomolungma, which is commonly translated as "Mother Goddess of the World."

Using porters and yaks, our first day we would cross bridges over the Dudh Kosi River (Milk River, named for its glacial silt) to Phakding. The following day, we would climb to 11,270 feet to Namche Bazaar, where we would have to tackle "Namche Hill," a steep climb up a forested hillside. With an additional day to acclimate, we would explore this bustling, prosperous Sherpa market town. From Namache, we would trek toward our destination of Tengboche Monastery, which is considered the religious heart of the region.

Tengboche has the largest and most active monastery in the Khumba region. From this vantage, we would be able to see breathtaking panoramic views of the magnificent Himalayan peaks, including Everest, Nuptse, Lhotse, Ama Dablam ("Goddess Charm Box"), Kanlega ("Snow Horse Saddle"), and Thamserku. It is on that trekking day, I have already decided in my mind, from Namche to Tengboche, where I would listen to my *Everest* CD.

On our trek down we would go through Khumjung, and view the skull of the yeti in the Khumjung Monastery. It was this monastery that was highlighted in the IMAX film, when Jamling Tenzing Norgay spoke of his father's and Sir Edmund Hillary's first successful ascent of Mount Everest in 1953. As he basked in rows of lit butter lamps, he spoke of his feelings in attempting to climb Mount Everest with IMAX photographer and climber David Breashears.

I couldn't believe that I would soon be standing in that same space. That what captured my heart and spirit in that IMAX theatre only a year ago was now a reality for the second time. How following a dream could be as easy as putting one foot in front of the other, setting it in motion, with determination and love.

So when worries about the cold or getting along with Christina popped into my head, I tried to keep an open, loose mind. "What to do?" I was determined to meet each challenge mindfully, awake, and with as much wisdom and compassion as I could find.

Lofty goals, I know, but I was trying to make my life, each and every aspect, my spiritual practice.

STEVE ACCOMPANIED ME to EMS as I purchased the warmer clothes I would need. So many times Steve and I had called Brian last year with this question or that. Do we need a sleeping bag? What about special gloves? Parkas? He would answer, "For the lodge-to-lodge trip you probably don't have to worry about those things. You won't get too cold. Those items are really for the Everest trip, where it can get really bitter and you're tenting." Well, now it *was* the Everest trip, and I wanted to be prepared for "bitter."

I bought a warm, bright yellow ski jacket that could roll into my backpack easily. I had a matching Patagonia pullover, a hat that covered my head, neck, and most of my face. I bought lined gloves.

Steve was great, helping me to prepare, fully involved yet with no burning desire to join me. It felt right. It felt good. He patiently, over three months' time, helped me find a sleeping bag that would meet my requirements.

I needed a synthetic bag with a -20 rating for someone under 5 feet 4 inches. It seemed that the colder rating the bag had, the less availability there was for a shorter person. Most really warm bags were made for someone around 6 feet.

"Do you mean to tell me that short people don't go camping in the cold?" I mused with the salesclerks at camping store after camping store.

The reply was always the same. "We would have to special order one. It could take up to six months. You could have one custom made, that might take quicker, but it will be pretty pricey."

Eventually I took to calling camping stores across the country in search of an appropriate bag. Many times it was suggested to me that I just buy a "shorter" long bag geared for a person "only" 5 feet 8 inches and stuff my clothes on the bottom so I won't lose that much warmth. Most of the conversations went something like this:

"I don't think I'll be packing enough clothes to stuff that size bag," I would say to the faceless voice on the other end.

"Well, you won't really need that much to stuff it."

"I keep telling you, I'm very short, and with a long sleeping bag, I'll lose too much warmth."

"Nah, you'll be fine, really. It's a great bag."

"No, I'm telling you I need a short bag, one for 5 feet 4 inches and under. I'm 4 feet 8½ inches tall."

"Wow! You really are short! You need a much smaller bag. Like the ones for 5 feet 4 inches and under."

"Yes," I would try to explain patiently. "That's what I've been trying to find, but no one seems to carry them in stock."

"Let me check again on what we have." After a few minutes on hold, the salesclerk would return to the phone with an enthusiastic "Found it! We have a great little bag made for a person 5 feet 4 inches and under."

Relief! "Is it a -20 degree bag?" I would ask, by this time my fingers crossed for good luck.

"Oh, no. It's a +20 degree bag, but I'm sure that should be warm enough."

"No," I would insist. "I need a -20 bag."

"C'mon. Do you really sleep that cold?"

"I'm going to thirteen thousand feet at Everest," I tell him. "And I don't want to freeze every night."

"Oh yeah, you need a -20 bag. Sorry, I can't help you. The only bags for that temperature in stock are for people in the 6 foot range."

Finally, a month before my trip, I found a synthetic -20 bag for someone 5 feet 4 inches and under in a Seattle REI store. I spent the next month trying to figure out how to roll that sleeping bag back into its compression sack.

I knew it had to fit; it had come inside the bag initially. But I'd be damned if I could get it back in that sack.

The sleeping bag was warm, all right, but all that warmth carried a bulky price. My kids would come home to find me sweating, wrestling with the sleeping bag half in, half out. I couldn't manage to get the sleeping bag in the sack with unlimited time in a nice, toasty house. How was I going to get the bag in the sack at 5:30 in the morning in the middle of the Himalayas, in the freezing cold in a matter of minutes before the trek took off?

I was determined. This was the "new me," up for a challenge, ready to tackle problems head on, strong, competent. I called my brother-in-law, an avid outdoorsman. "Please, Jeff, you've got to come over and fight with my sleeping bag."

He did, and the sleeping bag won.

"Ellen, I can't get this bag in. If I can't, with my strength, no way are you going to be able to. You should have gotten a down sleeping bag, they're warm and not bulky and much easier to pack."

"I know, but I can't. If the down bag got wet from rain or snow, I would freeze the rest of my trip."

Jeff nodded in agreement. I was secretly impressed with my newfound knowledge of camping equipment and gear. I'd never gone camping or been in a tent in my life.

"Ellen, you should just tip the porters well, and they'll figure out a way to stuff the sleeping bag in the compression sack."

I said no, that's not what this trip was going to be about for me. Jeff wished me good luck and left.

The next day, as I was once again trying to tackle the problem, I had the grand idea to sit on the part of the sleeping bag that wouldn't be stuffed in, and use my weight to somehow push the bag in and pull up the sack at the same time. I was pulling on the straps when I fell on my butt on the hardwood floor, the sack slipping out from under my legs.

I caught a glimpse of myself in the mirror. "I've always tipped well," I thought, but then made a quick trip to EMS before I lost my resolve and reverted to old ways.

Much to my relief, none of the salespeople were able to stuff the bag in, either. I had them order me a bigger compression sack, and enjoyed the feeling of competence that began washing over me.

The new compression sack was delivered. This time I was able to fit the bag into the compression sack.

I was proud of myself. I decided this would serve as a metaphor for me: I wasn't going to try to fit myself into places and situations that tried to stuff me into stereotypes and expectations that were confining and crushing, and stifling to who I was.

I asked the kids if they wanted to see how well mom could now fit her sleeping bag into the compression sack. They rolled their eyes.

"Aw, c'mon. Humor me," I said. I took the bag out of the sack, but before I could even begin to roll the sleeping bag up, Allison and Matt had unzipped the bag and cuddled inside.

"It's so cozy," Matt said.

"It's so warm!" Allison shouted.

I jumped in with them and told them I was going to roll them all up and take them with me.

They shook their heads. "No way! I'm not sleeping outside in the freezing cold," Allison informed me, and Matt nodded in agreement.

I told them that I'd take pictures of them instead, and that I'd carry them in my heart, all the way up to Tengboche, and I hugged them and kissed them and breathed in their skin.

THE DAYS WERE MOVING quickly by, and before long, it was March. Christina and I spoke at least a few times a week. Then one day she began speaking more openly about marital problems she had, in the past, alluded to.

About how her husband had finally confessed last spring to a five year affair. How he only told her after she confessed to having her own affair because for so long she had felt his rejection. How despite these revelations, she was continuing with her lover, and she assumed her husband was probably still having his fling as well. "But we're doing some marriage counseling right now, and things are going well," she had added.

Christina seemed energized by these confessions, like she was filling me in on the latest update of a favorite soap opera. I knew she was probably experiencing a great deal of pain as well, but I just didn't want to hear that much about it. This was what I wanted to get away from. This trip was about letting go of my own past mistakes, my own addictive relationships that I wanted to replace in healthy, adaptive ways. The trip was for letting go, and opening up.

"Oh! I can't talk right now," Christina said. "My older daughter just walked into the room. Oh well! I can fill you in on all the details on the plane, and we have two whole weeks ahead of us. Bye for now!"

"Oh no," I thought. "What to do?"

I certainly didn't want to spend the trip discussing her marital problems or my own history. But I didn't want to be rude, either. I thought of the stack of books I had been collecting for the trip, to occupy myself on the plane. I thought of them adding useless weight to my backpack if I couldn't even take them out because Christina wanted to talk throughout the flight, during the trek.

Over the next few days, I devised a plan. If Christina seemed bent on sharing this part of her life, I would listen. How could I not, when I'd been there, too? But I would try to set a boundary around the conversation. I'd say something like, "Christina, we can talk about our lives back home on the plane and stuff, but once we get to Nepal, let's leave it all on Thai Air, because Nepal will fly by in a second and before we know it, we'll be back home, and all those problems and people will be waiting for us when we get there." So that was my plan.

I PACKED AND UNPACKED my duffel bag (my new motto was "don't over pack, it will kill the yak") alone, while Steve relaxed, watching me as he lay on the bed, arms crossed behind his head. Then I would lie beside him in bed and we'd talk, or hold each other, or make love. It sounds sweet, but the other part of our nights was my annoying habit of sharing my fears with him at 2:00 A.M.

"Steve, are you up?"

No answer.

"Steve," I'd say again, nudging him, "are you up?"

"What," he'd mumble, pulling the covers more closely around his neck.

"I have to pee, and I'm too cold and tired to get out of bed. If I'm too cold in a warm, heated house, with a warm blanket and my own bathroom a few steps away with a fine, Western toilet and indoor plumbing, how the hell am I going to sleep outside in a tent covered with snow? How am I going to get out of my sleeping bag, go outside into the freezing cold, and pee?"

"You wanted to go on this trip, Ellen," he'd say, falling back to sleep.

I'd get up, hurry to the bathroom, and sit down on the toilet and pee. Flush. Then I'd scurry back to the comfort of my bed, my husband, my blankets.

In the morning, when I'd take my kids to school, I'd ask them, "How cold do you think it is outside? Do you think I could sleep in this?" I had a one-track mind.

IT WAS STRANGE, repacking for the last time the night before I was to leave. I lay in bed hoping I would fall asleep quickly. I wanted morning to come. I was ready to go.

In the morning I once again luxuriated in my shower, sang with my mouth wide open, not worrying about the water dripping into my mouth. I tried to remember to appreciate brushing my teeth with tap water straight out of the faucet, a pleasure I had been so happy to enjoy again after our last trip, but quickly learned to take for granted.

The strangest part was getting out of the car at the airport and hugging and saying good-bye to the most important people in the world to me. I waved good-bye to Steve, Allison, and Matt until I couldn't see them anymore, until the Land Rover disappeared into the flow of traffic exiting the airport.

I took a deep breath, then picked up my duffel and walked into the airport. After checking my baggage, I realized this was it. This was the beginning of my adventure. "Ellen's Excellent Adventure." I was independent, confident, and free.

The first thing I did was go directly to the pay phone and use my AT&T calling card.

"Hello," Steve answered from his cell phone.

"Hi! It's me. What's new? How are the kids?"

"They're fine, Ellen. Kids, yell hello to mom…"

"Hi mom!" they yelled into the phone.

"So where are you?" I asked.

"C'mon, Ellen, we haven't even left the airport yet! Now go and have a wonderful trip. Don't worry. We all love you. I love you."

"I love you, too."

Click.

March 18, 2000

I AM ON THE PLANE to LA, the
first leg of my journey. The plane is
half empty (or half full? Perhaps a Zen koan), and
very quiet. There are no restless children; I don't
believe there are any children on this plane at all. No mothers reading to their kids, no juice bottles, just a few adults scattered about, here and there.

I sit alone, in a "premier" window seat. At first there was a young man on the aisle seat. Maybe a college student. He settled into his seat, gave me a nod and a smile, and then opened the first page of his Tom Clancy novel.

A few moments later the flight attendant announced that there were many empty seats and that everyone should feel free to move to any open row. He glanced back to a seat in an empty row behind us. He seemed unsure if he should say something to me. Perhaps offer an apology or an explanation. He pointed his finger to where he contemplated moving and said, "I guess there will be more room."

I smiled and nodded and he departed.

I felt a little lonely. It felt funny. Not good or bad, just funny.

Odd, really. I'm on the plane without my kids or my husband. There will be no one expecting me in LA. I will just be staying in a hotel near the airport until my flight to Bangkok leaves the next morning. Each day will bring me further and further away from my home, across the world.

I keep thinking, "Oh my God! I've lost my wedding ring," as my fingers brush against each other and I feel only the emptiness of skin. Then I remember, of course, my ring is home safe and sound in my dresser drawer. No point in wearing a diamond ring on a trek in which I need to hike across rocks and my hands will swell and get banged. I wear only my trusty Nike watch, which offers me two time zones, and a power bracelet for safe passage that my good friend, Susan, gave me for my trip.

So it's odd. I travel alone, sit alone, with no conversation, no visual markings of my marriage, kids. Just me, on the plane, beginning my journey.

So it's good, really. I start without the attachments I use to define my world and myself: wife, mother, social worker, writer. I am simply on a plane to LA, the woman in seat 14A.

My backpack is heavy and my Teva sandals hang down from the front, clipped to a strap. It was easier than sticking them inside my pack, and I might want to change into them later. (I am wearing my hiking boots because packing them in a duffel that may or may not make it to Nepal seemed too much of a risk).

I feel like a stranger to myself that I'd like to get to know. No one knows me, and I feel I am just getting used to myself. I am dressed in jeans and hiking boots, sweatshirt and ponytail. I noticed how in the airport, I even surprised myself with a different sort of walk. All of a sudden I found myself walking with an ease of step I hadn't known before. A casualness, almost like a drifter who has all the time in the world to check things out and go where the spirit moves.

I sit on this plane alone and try to convince myself that this is real. I am going to Nepal; I will be in the shadows of Everest.

The boundaries that up to now have defined me are slowly being broken down. I am me, but in a different way.

I am on the plane, looking out the window, and the man who was on the aisle has moved. Alone, but not lonely, attached, but letting go, stepping slowly into an outer and inner journey that will just as surely fill me as show me glimpses of the true emptiness of nature.

It is this that I pray.

Sunday, 6:00 A.M. in LA

LAST NIGHT, I settled into
my hotel. I looked out the window
into the rooms of another hotel. I was excited,
dizzy with anticipation, and also savoring the travel
time, like the way you feel all warm and cozy under the blankets before
falling asleep for the night.

I now knew my AT&T calling card number by heart. I called Steve again, called some friends and my parents. After a shower, I changed for dinner. I had been craving a good steak and a cold beer. But before I ventured downstairs to the hotel's restaurant, I lost a battle that had been waging in my mind for hours.

I wanted to call Carl to say good-bye. I knew I shouldn't. We had stopped spending time together, though we had been in touch a handful of times via telephone. I knew it was a bad idea to call, and I certainly didn't look forward to the chance that Steve would find Carl's number on the phone bill, especially as I had promised to end all contact, including phone. But the force to call was overwhelming.

It was like an addiction. Cold turkey was the solution. Any time Carl called me, or I called Carl, it was too easy to slip back into that deep, unending hole where there was no bottom, no landing.

I had even hung a copy of my favorite poem, *Autobiography In Five Short Chapters,* by Portia Nelson, in my office at home as a friend, a sponsor:

I

I walk down the street.
There is a deep hole in the sidewalk.
I fall in
I am lost...I am helpless
It isn't my fault.
It takes forever to find a way out.

II

I walk down the same street.
There is a deep hole in the sidewalk.
I pretend I don't see it.
I fall in again.
I can't believe I am in the same place.
But it isn't my fault.
It still takes a long time to get out.

III

I walk down the same street.
There is a deep hole in the sidewalk.
I see it is there
I still fall in…it's a habit.
My eyes are open.
I know where I am.
It is my fault.
I get out immediately.

IV

I walk down the same street.
There is a deep hole in the sidewalk.
I walk around it.

V

I walk down another street.

BUT STILL, I called.

We spoke easily, seemingly carefree, about my trip, about his work, about times we've shared. Forty–five minutes later, we hung up.

I felt bad. I wasn't going to talk with him anymore. Steve deserved so much better. Wasn't it time I took full responsibility for my actions and followed through on my promises? To Steve and to myself? Everest was so close.

I think I wasn't sure if I could contain the passion welling up within. Owning all that I, myself, had set into motion. To really feel my own sense of power and strength and spirit. That's when I looked to place it with Carl, to sort of hold it for me, maybe as a way of displacing the feeling that I'm scared to own, scared to realize has to do one hundred percent with me, and no one else.

Like writing. I think the times I had spent with Carl were like the early years of my desire to write. Then, I had spent time being a "writer" by reading books about writing. Now that's all fine and good if you're writing, too. But if it's a way of holding back the fear of writing and letting loose, of simply dancing around the world you long to enter, that can become a problem.

That's what Carl became for me. An escape, in a way, from being fully in the world I wanted to create for myself. I wanted to be a writer, but instead, I became part of Carl's writing world, part of his tools of the trade. I think I wanted him to write me into his world, and what I needed to do now was to erase and delete him from the world I was carving out for myself.

I think Carl also served as a quick fix to help me feel "good enough." It occurred to me that when I would visit my parents, I'd throw one of his books into my suitcase, like a trophy I presented to myself. I think I would kid myself into the belief that I must be "good enough" if a famous writer like Carl wanted to spend time with me. It was almost like carrying secret inches to my parents in an attempt to prove my worth.

I was tired of hiding behind the façade of a bubbly, silly little female. Now I was tired of hiding behind a powerful man as well.

I DIDN'T BEAT MYSELF UP about the call. I tried, yet again, to learn from it, to understand why it was coming up now. To sit with the fact that while I was mad that I had called, I still enjoyed, as always, our talk. That this was still a difficult relationship to let go of, and it was clearly teaching me important lessons about who I was, what I wanted, and what I was afraid to have.

It was only through letting go that I could embrace the life I envisioned. It was only by seeing clearly the reasons for my mistakes and learning from the pain I caused others and myself that I could grow more fully. Out of pain, there is growth.

I DRIFTED OFF to sleep, waking up often and early because of the three-hour time difference. At 5:00 A.M. I finally got up, did a little repacking, some stretching, and a short meditation.

So many thoughts crossed my mind. I was still struck by the insecure ones. Like how I reacted on the trip to Nepal last year, when I wondered if our group would be full of tall, thin, beautiful, earthy women and whether I would be able to hold on to feeling good about myself or end up feeling inadequate.

I tried to let these thoughts pass without judgment. These thoughts are my "monkey mind," the busy mind that spins and spins. The mind that internalizes cultural pressures as "truths" rather than projections, as reality rather than illusion.

I tried to allow my mind to pass through the clouds and the fog without judgment. They are simply there, and there is nothing to be done but to notice their existence and let them pass.

Like the plane, the mind will soon enter the clearness and ex-pansiveness of the open blue sky. The limitless nature. As clouds came along, I tried to let my mind pass through, with awareness that the mind is always, in its essence, endless and clear and bright.

It occurred to me that meditation must be for the mind what a massage is for the body. Meditation offers a break in which you allow your mind to ease, to let go of all that it holds, all that it doesn't need.

I ended my meditation with a prayer that during the trip I would stay in the moment, or at least the minute. In my mind, I pictured the clarity and starkness I imagined was on the summit of Mount Everest.

I SHOWERED, organized my "stuff" and then prepared to go the airport to meet Christina and check in for our flight to Bangkok.

As I brought my duffel down to the lobby and stood in line to check out of the hotel, the man standing in front of me looked at me and laughed. "How can someone so little have such a big piece of lug-gage?"

I looked him in the eyes and said, "It's gear. I'm on my way to Mount Everest."

8:00 A.M. Waiting outside the LA airport international terminal for Thai Air to open

It's been going on for months now, the respect and admiration Everest receives. And I, venturing into the majesty of her peak, soak up its reflection.

Men—tall men, big men—suddenly admire me, speak to me in a respectful manner. People take me seriously.

It's not why I'm going to Everest. Or maybe it's part of it. I feel strong, confident, and powerful going on this trek. Spiritually, it is where my home is. Emotionally, it is my quest.

Perhaps, difficult though it is to write, I like to be seen as powerful, solid, the way the top of the world is. Men are encouraged to seek power, to garner respect. Women are taught to look for relationship, connections. But don't men need to connect? To be in relation? And don't women hunger for power, for respect?

There is something about discussing gear that appeals to me. Put me with the likes of David Breashears, and I know basically nothing. But for the average suburbanite, I'm learning quite a bit. I'd rather complain about my -20 sleeping bag not fitting into its compression sack than discuss the latest hemline.

I like walking into EMS. I can look around casually, gathering things I need. But when I need help and a salesman approaches, I admit I like the effect. They make assumptions; we all do. It's the package thing.

"You're looking for a hiking boot. Just for some light walking?"

"No," I reply. "For trekking. I need something sturdier than that." I reject the fashionable light hiking sneaker/shoe he is holding. When I tell him I am going to Nepal, he cannot do enough for me; he brings out every sturdy hiking boot he has in a size five.

Suddenly, I am more important in his eyes. Other salesclerks offer their suggestions, tell me how much they have dreamed of trekking in Nepal. I feel accepted. I don't feel superfluous.

I'd like to be treated with respect even if I wasn't going to Nepal.

Even if I was buying a light hiking shoe for easy strolling.

It's funny, I think. People always ask me how high I am going on Everest. "Oh, just a little ways, " I say. "To thirteen thousand feet, to Tengboche Monastery."

"Wow!" is the typical response. "That's still high. Is that base camp?"

"No, base camp is another four thousand vertical feet up."

"Oh," they say. "But you're not going to base camp, huh? Maybe next time. Still, thirteen thousand feet is really up there."

I told my therapist, Barbara, about this. I told her that it's like points for going higher and higher. It's like my height: 4 feet 8½ inches, or do I round it up to an even 4 feet 9 inches? Does that extra half-inch lie mean anything? Prove anything?

At thirteen thousand feet, I receive respect. But I think the higher I ventured, the more power and respect I'd receive.

In the Nepal travel books, there is a discrepancy concerning the altitude at which Tengboche is situated. Some place it at twelve thousand eight hundred, while others reference it to be an even thirteen thousand feet. I opt for the larger, more powerful number. It's hard to let go of the quest to prove myself worthy. It's hard to stop trying to compensate for my height.

My therapist told me, "Ellen, this trip to Nepal and this trek to Everest for you is not about going higher, but about going deeper."

I agreed. I also continued to adopt the even thirteen thousand-foot altitude.

I SWITCHED FROM DANCE to the gym these past few months. I had wanted to cross-train, and get stronger for my trip.

It's funny. In dance, there is strength in the turns, the leaps, the arabesques. But it is also a strength that says, "View my body and its effortless grace." It feels sometimes like too much performance and show. A frail thinness and ease of movement that is, in reality, pure effort, power, and strength.

I don't want to conform to the ballet positions: first, second, third, fourth, and fifth. I don't want to raise my arms and twirl for the imaginary audience. I don't want to be using my muscle and energy and pretend that it doesn't burn, that it is effortless. It's too much a metaphor for my life.

There's something about a Stairmaster, boring though it may be. I'm climbing, climbing, climbing, to nowhere. Where is there to go? What is the point? It's not so different from life.

Where am I always rushing to? Running toward? Climbing to nowhere isn't bad. It makes me patient and strong. The elliptical trainers are also nice. I close my eyes and I'm cross-country skiing, or trekking.

I like that I have this trip as my focus. It centers me, not just in the gym but also in my everyday life. I am working out for endurance and strength. Preparing my physical body to follow in the direction of my soul, which always seems one step ahead.

And I admit, there is something about the admiration and awe others offer when they know for what you are training. So I appreciate their questions; their curiosity has taught me to be a better listener. What is someone else's passion? What lights her fire? I like to find out, ask questions.

One fiftyish man on the treadmill tells me about the time he climbed Machu Picchu, of his love for Peru. Another new gym friend tells me she loves archaeology, and shares with me her dream to actually go out on a dig.

I met an older woman in the coffee shop where I like to write. Sophie told me how she has always loved painting, and for years has dreamed about renting a small studio near the ocean to concentrate on her work, to really take herself seriously as an artist. I was thrilled when she told me, a few months later, that she had just signed a lease for a studio overlooking Marblehead Harbor.

These conversations are energizing.

PEOPLE WOULD OFTEN ask me, "Why do you want to go to Everest so much?' I think I need to go near the highest point on Earth to feel both my smallest and my biggest.

Everyone is dwarfed by Everest, and yet we are all part of that mountain, that eternal. My soul will dance higher than I'll ever climb.

And Mount Everest, ever beautiful, ever aloof, won't give a damn who you are—how tall you are or short you are or how fat or thin you are. It will simply stand, a projection of so many hearts.

I walked around the LA airport, killing time before meeting Christina. All night Tom Petty's "Room at the Top" had been playing in my mind. He sings about having a room at the top of the world, and I just kept singing it over and over. So I finally gave in, found a music store and bought the CD. I thought I might like to listen to the song as I trekked closer to Everest.

After some fresh fruit (again, I wouldn't enjoy that for sixteen days) and a soft, doughy bagel, I set out to find Christina at the Thai Airline counter, where we had agreed to meet. We had sent each other pictures of ourselves, so when I was coming down the stairs, I spotted her right away.

Christina was about 5 feet 6 inches tall and thin, with shoulder length brown hair, big round brown eyes framed by long lashes, and a tiny, delicate nose. I moved toward her and she threw down the sweatshirt she was carrying and her backpack and gave me a big hug.

We beamed at each other. We were so excited, we felt like "we'd already known each other for years!"

Because we were flying business class, we were able to use the Red Carpet Club. We loved the plushness, the freedom, and the independence. Christina ordered a glass of wine to celebrate. I ordered a Coke. We had a few hours before our flight. We talked about the trip, about packing, about medications we had brought, about our families. We filled out the forms that were given to us about who we were, and next of kin, and tried not to think about the need for such a contact card. We were laughing.

After a while, I joined Christina in a glass of wine. She began talking about her marriage, about the affairs, how she had slept with her lover, Jack, this past week. When Christina kept asking if I could possibly understand her actions, her dilemma, I told her about Kevin. About Carl. About how the relationships had torn me apart, torn Steve apart.

She looked relieved that we had this in common, and I think in some ways, I was, too. Carl certainly wasn't someone I wanted to focus on or talk about during the trip, but it served me well to acknowledge my history.

She had heard of Carl, had known some of his book titles. I told her I had called him last night. That I wanted to work toward letting go more and more. To end the infrequent contact we now had to no contact at all.

She shared with me her analysis of why Jack, her lover, played such an important role in her life. That even though her husband, Paul, now thinks she has stopped seeing Jack, she hasn't, and she won't. "I deserve to have Jack in my life," she said. "I married too young, and Paul was much older. He had already spread his wings, and he had his own affair for five fucking years! I deserve to have Jack when I need him. I don't think Jack will leave his wife, and I don't really care either way. I don't even feel really guilty. Why should I? It's my turn."

I told her that I was glad Steve knew of my mistakes now. That the relationships had never been about him, or a question of my love for him, but about my own internal wars, my own questions about self worth, the expression of needs I felt I wasn't supposed to have or show. A vehicle to feel my passions, but in secret, because I was afraid to show them in public.

I told Christina about how the whole thing had torn me apart. How sometimes I'd cry so hard I had no tears left. About driving to the ocean and imagining swimming out over the waves as far as I could and then drowning into oblivion.

I told her that the bottom line for me was that as much as I now understood my actions, I hurt Steve, and I needed to win back his trust. "I imagine what it would be like," I told Christina, "if the tables were turned. If Steve had betrayed me and then said, 'I don't doubt my love for you, I'm just trying to make peace with myself.' I couldn't handle that. I don't know how Steve did."

We boarded the plane. We laughed at how we sounded like a made-for-TV movie. Two women en route to Everest, talking about affairs. I told her my plan, which now sounded reasonable for both of us.

"Once we get to Nepal, no Jack, no Carl. Let's enjoy every second of Nepal without bringing everyone along," I suggested.

Christina agreed. We spent our time on the plane reading, watching movies, eating, and talking.

Christina drank a lot. "I like the buzz," she'd say. She also put on makeup a lot. A powder here, some eyeliner there. A lot of quick checks in the mirror.

She worried about bowel movements. "I hate feeling bloated," she would explain. "Traveling can really do a number on your system. I packed lots of laxatives. You can have one any time you need one."

I told her "no thanks." I had suspected she might have an eating disorder from our phone conversations. Now I assumed she was abusing laxatives. Over the course of the flight, I tried to ask her about it.

Sometimes when she stood up to use the bathroom or to stretch, she'd put her hands on her flat stomach and say, "Oh, no! It looks like I'm bloated already. I feel fat. Time for another laxative."

I felt on the one hand, I should encourage her to talk about her weight concerns (objectively, she was tall and thin), but I didn't want to. I just wanted *my* time, *my* trip. But of course, this was part of my trip.

WE STAYED OVERNIGHT in Bangkok, and got up early the next morning for the last leg of the trip. We didn't sleep much at the hotel, what with the excitement and the time changes. Christina had taken laxatives before she went to bed, and was in the bathroom a lot of the night.

I kept thinking about Bangkok last year, with Steve. About how on the way home, our overnight in the Amari hotel seemed so glamorous compared to our accommodations in Nepal. We had had a romantic evening together. I remember late at night turning on CNN, which we hadn't seen for over two weeks, and staring into the terrified faces of refugees from Kosovo already a week into a crisis we hadn't known about.

Christina and I walked around the airport, picking up souvenirs from the many gift stores. The airport was lined with beautiful orchids. We found ourselves in a bookstore.

"Do they have them here?"

"Hmm? I answered nonchalantly, not willing to admit even to myself what I was looking for.

"C'mon, you know you were looking for Carl's books! Do you see any? Let's find one. I don't think I know what he looks like," Christina said. We scanned the book covers, which look different from the American editions.

"There's a lot of John Grisham," Christina observed.

"Yep, don't know him personally. Oh, here's one." I picked the book up and turned it over to find Carl's face staring at me. I handed the book over to Christina.

"Oh, wow! He's a lot older than us, isn't he?"

"Yeah," I said, putting the book back on the shelf. I shook myself awake. "Let's get out of here."

We left the bookstore and waited in the lounge to board our flight to Kathmandu. There we met the other five people who would make up our trekking group.

This time I knew to get a seat on the right side on the plane. This time, when it looked like high clouds rolling in from nowhere off in the horizon, I leaned over to the other people in our group and said proudly, "The Himalayas."

Kathmandu March 21, 2000

WE ARRIVED IN Kathmandu today. The city actually feels slightly less chaotic than last year. Because of new emission laws enacted in Kathmandu this past year, the exhaust from the buses is not jet black.

Christina was tired and wanted to rest in our Everest Hotel room. I was learning quickly that she felt tired a lot. "I was here a few years ago," she said. "I'm in no hurry to see the city; it will be here tomorrow."

While Christina rested, I went out with the other five people on our trip to explore Kathmandu.

The country was still filthy and colorful. A small mountain of garbage and debris housed an enormous rat. A dead pig and a dead cow drifted lazily down a polluted, almost dry river, the monsoon season long past.

Bright saris dotted the streets, the women's long black hair pulled to one side. Horns beeping, motorcycles roaring, weaving in and out, dodging around the crowded city buses, around scooters. The different horn sounds filled the air and still reminded me of a poorly practiced school band, trying to tune their instruments.

Ripe, full vegetables are piled on the curbs. Nepalese men and women sell stacks of long green onions neatly tied with rope. Bicycles are parked on the side of the road filled with cauliflower, bananas, and carrots. On the sidewalk are baskets of woven rope full of colorful spices.

We try to take pictures of everything, to capture this scene, this person, that radish. Some Nepalese let us take their pictures, others refuse. Faces of people hang out over tops of windows and over roofs.

An old man, skinny as a rail with dark, weathered skin, piles bricks on top of a roof. Children, barefoot with snotty noses, run up to us asking for rupees.

The sounds, sights and smells of Nepal are mesmerizing, frightening, and electric.

6:00 P.M.

WE MET WITH our Sherpa, Pasang, in the hotel lobby. He will be with us for the entire trip, through Kathmandu, to Lukla, and for the trek.

He is a handsome man with a dimpled chin, a wife, and two children—a ten-year-old son and an eleven-year-old daughter. He lives in Namache Bazaar, one of the places we will be camping at for two days on our trek in order to acclimate to the higher altitude, and to explore.

His wife owns a teashop there, and his children go to boarding school in Kathmandu. He sees them twice a year. Namache is close to Tibet, a seven-day walk that takes you over a seventeen thousand foot pass.

Pasang has summitted Everest two times, in 1995 and again in 1997. This April, he will join an American environmental expedition. The goal of this expedition is to clean the South Col, which has become littered with debris and old oxygen canisters. Sherpas and porters will be paid $25 for every tank they bring down the mountain. In a country where the average annual income is approximately $200, this is quite a hefty sum.

Pasang will also be in charge of one of the climbers on the expedition who hopes to set a record by becoming the oldest man to summit. Pasang hopes to summit again. "You get much more money, bigger tip, if you can summit and help clients be successful reaching the top. I need the money to pay for my children's education."

Our Sherpa explained how he always uses supplemental oxygen. The last time he summitted, he was able to stay on the top of Everest for one hour. The weather that May 21st had been perfect. Only the day before, others on an expedition had to turn back close to the summit because of deteriorating weather conditions. Pasang had left advanced base camp at 11:00 P.M. and summitted at 8:00 A.M.

His wife is worried. Many Sherpanis are widows, their husbands dead on the mountain.

I badger Steve about what time he will be home after a meeting. It makes you stop and think. Sherpas get paid well on these expeditions; wives sit home and wait.

IT WAS CLEAR TO ME that Christina and I were not going to travel well together, but "what to do?" I didn't know if I should try to work with the situation, or bow out.

Christina worried aloud about her bowel movements, about feeling bloated. About how she wanted to lose more weight on this trip. She commented upon every guy she found attractive.

And I irritated her. She told me I was too concerned with my health. She didn't like how I used an alcohol wipe to clean the tops of the Coke bottles I drank, how I didn't dare try the ice cream or custard because I worried about the bacteria in Nepal. Last trip I followed the health suggestions offered in my Nepal travel books and I stayed relatively healthy. I didn't want to tempt the fates this time. This trip meant too much to me. I didn't want to miss a thing if I could help it. And I don't like custard, anyway.

I think I was responding to things in Christina that I was responding to in the culture. She was a victim of that same culture. But the bottom line was, we were becoming like fingernails on a chalkboard to each other, even as we depended on each other, so far away from home.

It took Christina a long time to get ready before touring the city because she'd have to put on makeup. She complained of headaches, of being tired, of diarrhea. I told her she should lay off the custard and the laxatives. She didn't welcome my comments.

THE HIGHLIGHT OF our time in Kathmandu, for me, was returning to Boudhanath. As I circled the stupa, spinning the prayer wheels, climbing atop the different levels, offering rupees to the beggars, I was once again home.

I was still amazed that I had entered this space once, let alone twice. I felt happy. I missed Steve. Part of me could have stayed there forever.

Before I knew it, we were boarding the tiny little aircraft, gliding past and through the snowcapped Himalayas. As each peak passed, one summit higher than the next, so close you could almost touch it through the dirty airplane windows, we'd ask Pasang excitedly, "Everest?" And he'd laugh and say, "nah."

We snapped away with our cameras at mountains whose names we'll never know, until suddenly we fly next to a mountain and no spot is higher. We point, bang on our windows with such excitement that I fear they could break, shatter in this tiny little thing we are flying in, masquerading as an aircraft. "Everest?" we asked.

Pasang smiled and nodded, "Everest."

We snapped photos through the filmy windows and took out the cotton balls we had stuffed in our ears to lessen the noise of the engines.

Pasang laughed. "Save your pictures, you haven't seen anything yet!"

Miraculously, the plane came to a cough and halt on an airstrip that is the size of a long driveway, carved into the cliff of a mountain. We stepped off the plane and porters began busily taking care of duffels and gear. We met our cook, Dawa, and Tashi, Pasang's younger brother, who would be joining us on our trek.

Our group then explored Lukla, a village that welcomes trekkers and expeditions and is the gateway to Everest. It is situated at nine thousand two hundred feet, and we feel it as we wind down little alleys and up the hillside.

We watch the people of the village carrying baskets full of everything on their backs: chickens, babies, blankets, tables, bricks. Dzo (female yaks) fill the roads. They are big and hairy, reminding me of part cow, part llama. They ring while they walk along the dirt path, their bells clanging. We won't see the longer haired and woollier yaks until we reach an altitude of eleven thousand feet.

Each time our group began laughing about something, we had to stop and gasp for air. It was the altitude.

Pasang kept telling us how important it was to stay hydrated. I stopped into a small wooden room where soda was being sold. Pictures of the Dalai Lama filled the walls. I bought a Sprite and used an alcohol wipe to clean the dirt off the can. I looked to see if Christina was watching. Christina and I were keeping our distance.

The group meandered through the dusty streets looking at the offerings of Lukla. There were T-shirts with maps of Everest embroidered on the front hanging in stands along with maps of the Khumba region. Maps of Everest were printed on bandannas and caps. All of these tourist enticements were sold beside backpacks, crampons, ice axes, hiking boots, sweets, Cokes, and individual rolls of rough toilet paper.

Christina pulled me aside to tell me that she had spoken to Pasang and requested her own tent. She doesn't want to share one with me after all. Pasang had told her that was fine, he had extra tents.

I was both relieved and furious. I hadn't wanted to share a room or a tent with her either, but I hadn't known how to get out of it. I only wished she had talked with me first, so we could have approached Pasang together. It would have felt better.

"What to do?" I looked forward to my privacy.

After lunch, we began a three and a half hour trek down to eight thousand eight hundred feet to Phakding, which would help us adjust to the change in altitude. The sun was warm; the snow-capped mountains glistened against a bright blue sky.

I couldn't believe my good fortune in walking along this trail, in this country, at this moment. So when the blue sky changed to an overcast smoky gray, the top of the mountains blending into the clouded sky, I let out a sigh of gratitude to witness the changing afternoon air. I thought my photos would capture the changing mood of the weather quite well. Since it rarely rains in March, I didn't concern myself with any problems trekking in this change, only in capturing the mood.

After two hours, it began to sprinkle. Suddenly, with thunder roaring in the distant mountains, it began to pour. The rocks we stepped over were slippery; it turned a nasty, raw cold. The camera was long forgotten, and I cursed myself for packing my raincoat in my duffel rather than with me in my backpack.

We were all drenched, listening to the sound of thunder getting louder, sounding closer, as Pasang kept saying, "This is very rare."

I forgot to stay in the moment, and instead kept wiping the rain from my face and checking my watch to estimate how much longer we had until we made it to Phakding. We walked on and finally reached our camp, cold and wet. Our cook and helpers served us hot chocolate and cookies in a small teahouse filled with warmth and smoke from a fire. There was nowhere for the smoke to go, so the room was soon covered with a layer of soot. It was only 3:30 P.M., and all of us just wanted to go to bed.

After a brief nap in my tent, I felt content. I was relieved to be alone. My sleeping bag was warm, and the sun had returned. Our camp was beside a river, and I imagined this could be a spot where Siddhartha, in Hesse's novel, might have spent a night or two.

I listened to my *Everest* CD from the IMAX movie while I dozed on and off. I remember thinking that there couldn't be a more peaceful place on Earth.

After dinner we prepared for bed, standing outside of our tents, brushing our teeth with our boiled water, spitting into the dirt. Snuggled in my sleeping bag at 11:15, I feared I had to pee. I kept hoping I would fall back asleep and not have to venture out into the cold, to the "red tent" over the latrine the porters had dug that afternoon. Finally, the allure of the "red tent" won.

I took out my headlamp and in the darkness of the night found the hole, then ran back to the warmth of my sleeping bag. At 2:45 A.M. I repeated the sequence—the struggle to ignore the urge, to try to fall back asleep, but my bladder would have none of that. This time as I ventured out of my tent, I was so happy for my weak bladder.

The moon had risen, a great white ball in the blackness that bathed the snow-capped peaks in light. The mountaintops were bright white against the sky, like vanilla frosting on a chocolate cupcake. I put my hands together as if in prayer, and breathed in deeply and fully.

Then I peed contently and snuggled back into my tent.

"I can do this," I whispered to myself. "I can do all of this."

THE NEXT DAY we were up at dawn, preparing for the day's journey. Along the old, worn path, we saw people: young, old, bent, thin, spry, weak, all carrying goods and clucking chickens, shepherding dzos with ringing bells on their necks. They were all walking to Namche for the Saturday Bazaar. It is their "rush hour," like Friday traffic out of Boston to the Cape.

Our trek took us around mani stones carved with Tibetan mantras, and across high bridges suspended over the Dudh Kosi river with broken wooden planks, the sides hung with prayer flags snapping in the strong wind as a blessing for a safe passage. The first few hours were a warm-up to the rest of the day's trek. It was a long day's climb, as we trekked from eight thousand eight hundred feet to eleven thousand two hundred seventy feet over steep hills.

We had to move slowly because of the altitude, but the group was wonderful. We all kept each other laughing, which wasn't always good because we couldn't walk and laugh at the same time; the altitude was too demanding.

Christina was a strong woman. Quick legs and easy stride. She was often in the lead, but would sometimes hang back with Pasang, talking, smiling.

We had not had a view of Everest since our flight into Lukla, but on this stretch of the trek, we were promised to see Everest; it said so in the brochure.

"Is that it?" we'd ask Pasang again, like we had on the Lukla flight. "Is that Everest?"

"Nah," he'd say. "That's Khumbuyulhe. Sacred Mountain. No one is allowed to climb it because it is considered sacred. Prohibited."

A few hours later, while we had been rewarded with spectacular views, we were still waiting for Everest. Pasang pointed to a place in the distance. "It is foggy. The clouds have rolled in. That is Everest over there, but today, because of the weather, you can't see it. What to do? Tomorrow." Pasang is a wonderful, walking lesson in patience.

Some people in the group were having a hard time on the trek, and Pasang stayed back to assist them. It was strenuous, and we had been trekking for over six hours. The altitude can take a lot out of you. We had seen signs nailed onto trees warning us to "Go slow . . . altitude kills." We had no doubt.

When most of the group arrived together at Namache, we were happy and exhausted. We posed and took pictures under the welcome sign. We didn't know we were celebrating prematurely. Our camp was another 200 vertical feet up, which at that point took us another 30 minutes!

It had been sleeting a bit, especially the last half hour of the steep climb. By dinner, we had a full snowstorm. Later that night, in the dining tent, Pasang explained that a snowstorm like this, in March, was "most unusual."

I was glad it was snowing so hard. I told the group I felt like Jon Krakauer. Like I was on an expedition.

When we left the dining tent, we saw the full effect of the snowstorm: about four inches had already fallen, and snow covered everything. We had to wipe the snow from our tents. I laughed and said if this were home, my kids would be hoping for a snow day from school.

The porters had built what I thought was a rather strange looking snowman. "No," Pasang had explained. "They built you a snow stupa!"

In the morning, I awoke to icicles in my sleeping bag, frozen water in my water bottle, and nostrils stuck together.

I smiled. "I'm doing this!" I thought to myself.

AFTER BED TEA, Pasang took us on a short fifteen-minute hike to Sagarmatha National Park. In the early morning sky the sun was bright and warm, glistening over the white snow crunching underfoot and atop the snow-covered peaks. Looking out across the pass, we had a view of Ama Dablam, considered to be the most beautiful mountain in Nepal. Then, to the left, we were staring at Everest.

It was awe-inspiring. It looked like clouds were coming off the top of its peak, but it was actually wind. Pasang said the wind on the summit is over one hundred miles an hour.

I asked Pasang how it felt to stand here with us, looking at the highest point on Earth, where he had already been twice, and would be back again next month.

He looked at me, laughed and said, "It feels warmer standing here!"

We took pictures for over an hour, with each person in our group standing with Mount Everest behind them. It was magical, standing in the midst of the great Himalayas, waking up in the morning and receiving the gift of that view.

"This and Boudhanath," I thought. "I could spend forever in these two places."

Pasang told me the name of the peaks surrounding us, against the flawless blue sky: Khumbuyulhe, Taboche, Nuptse, Everest, Lhotse, Peak 39, Ama Dablam, Thomserku, Kusumkang, Konde, Pharchamo. I counted my blessings to the rhythmic flow of his naming.

I knew the first mountain he named was considered the sacred mountain, but to me, everything about this place was sacred.

ANITA, ANOTHER WOMAN on our trip, invited me to do some yoga with her in the snow. Facing the top of Mount Everest, we practiced the sun salutation. I will always remember lying in the snow in the cobra posture, head and neck raised, back arched, and ungloved hands buried in the wet, white flakes. I felt like I was offering my spirit to the gods and goddesses of the mountains.

This day was built in as our rest day, a chance to allow our bodies to acclimate to the higher altitude, the thinner air. Many of the people on our trip had developed a deep cough. Out in the Khumba region, this is common, and the name for the cough is "The Khumba Cough." No problem; if anyone needed it, I had plenty of Robitussin.

One woman on our trip developed altitude sickness and found the trek at the higher elevations too demanding. It was agreed that she would rest here in Namache for a few days while we continued our trek.

We visited the Tibetan and Nepali booths, filled with their wares. I watched yaks walking alongside villagers, their bells clanking with each step, announcing their arrival and suggestion that they receive the right of way. Sherpas, their faces browned and wrinkled, hauled sixty- to one-hundred-pound bundles on their backs. There was constant movement: the pouring of water out of buckets from a window, the washing of pots and pans in a stream with the slop of water splattering back and forth, the clucking of chickens, the cries of children.

I became used to sharing the paths with yaks, goats, water buffalo, and chickens. I enjoyed passing the monks, cloaked in their maroon and saffron robes. I often watched them making a game of kicking a Coke can left on the sandy road. I saw mothers coaxing their children to take a bath that was given in a metal bucket of water set in front of the house.

In this town, where Pasang lived, we visited his wife, Lhakpa, in her teahouse. On the dark, thin walls of her small shop were Pasang's summit pictures, and a map of the United States.

Lhakpa spoke no English, but her smile was sweet and warm, like her tea. When she was not in her teashop, she was home knitting woolen hats and socks made from sheep and yak wool.

THE SNOW HAD ALL but melted, the temperature reaching into the high sixties. There was a solar heated outdoor shower. It was heaven.

I had taken to crawling out of my tent a few times each night, of course because of "nature's call," but also because of nature's pull. The night was so still, so quiet, and so full of beauty. I'd stand outside in the freezing cold air and think about life, about Steve, Allison, and Matt, who were so far away. About how I loved this place, this wild land, the mysteries it held.

I had spent so many nights in Boston worrying about venturing out of my tent in the middle of the night, in the cold. It turned out that that was one of the best parts. Even now, at home in Boston, I sometimes fall asleep with that picture in my mind: the moonlit sky bouncing light across the mountains, electrifying the peaks where no electricity exists.

THE NEXT DAY was the day I had dreamed about: the trek from Namache to Tengboche where the peaks of Everest and Ama Dablam would be continually in view. Where we would ascend to thirteen thousand feet at Everest and I would focus on nothing but placing one foot in front of the other. Where I would listen to my *Everest* CD.

The day was sunny and warm, close to seventy degrees. I felt strong. After my shower, I was the cleanest I had been in days, or would be for the duration of the trek.

I marveled at the way I got dressed now. I would take out the "cleanest" of my dirty clothes. I brushed my teeth, spitting out toothpaste in the dirt. I put my hair in a ponytail. I had a pocket mirror somewhere in the bottom of my backpack, but I never bothered to look for it. What would be the point? Everything had a purpose: warm hiking socks, trekking pole, layered clothing, and boots. Function.

I told members of our group that today I was being anti-social. Today I was choreographing my trek with the *Everest* CD; my view would be even larger than the IMAX film had provided. They understood.

We began our trek. I pressed "play" on my CD Walkman, and my world fell into place. My dream was now my reality.

The music seemed to go beyond the call of duty, like it had consulted with the scenery. I'd hike around a sharp turn and just then, when the views became even more spectacular, the crescendo of a song would hit.

I wanted to dance, to leap across the mountain passes. I couldn't have taken that smile off of my face if I had tried.

WE QUICKLY LEARNED to move aside when the yaks needed to pass. This was the season of expeditions to Everest, and we'd already passed teams from Spain, Canada, and Germany all aiming to summit. Yaks would carry huge blue cargo boxes printed with the destination EVEREST on its side. The cargo was filled with gear that would be taken to base camp for the expedition.

Whenever a climber would ask what CD I was listening to and I told him, he would slap his forehead and say, "Why didn't I think of that!"

Many of them asked to listen for a minute. I'd give them the CD Walkman and watch them put the headphones on. They'd smile that same smile, looking out at the Himalayas. We all smiled that same smile.

FRED, THE IMPLICITLY CHOSEN leader of our group, kept talking about getting to Tengboche to hear the monks chant and to meet "The Red Carnation Lama." He was funny, big, tall, and strong, but he always insisted on being the authority, on being right. He acted like he knew almost everything, and I suspected when he didn't, he just made things up. I liked his company, but not always his manner.

Every time he talked about "The Red Carnation Lama," I thought I'd heard him wrong. "Red Carnation Lama?" What was he talking about?

For some reason, I felt unable to question him about this Lama business. Like I'm not supposed to challenge this big male, who everyone thinks knows everything. So towards the end of the trek, as we were coming closer to Tengboche, I said, "Fred, tell me the name of the Lama we are going to see." I was thinking I must have misunderstood him.

He answered, "The Red Carnation Lama."

Finally I said, "Fred, I don't think there's any Lama called the Red Carnation Lama."

Fred insisted there was, and seemed annoyed with my challenge.

"No," I said, "He's a *reincarnate* lama."

Fred looked at me doubtfully. "Pasang!" he called. "Come here."

Pasang left Christina and Anita and jogged up to Fred and me.

Fred asked, "Who is the lama at Tengboche? Isn't he called the Red Carnation Lama?"

"No, no," Pasang explained. "He is a reincarnate lama. A great lama called the Reincarnate Lama Tenzin Ngawang Janspo. But we won't see him. He is on vacation in Kathmandu. What to do?"

"All this time I thought he was called The Red Carnation Lama. I figured he wore a red carnation on his robe," Fred explained.

"You know, Fred, " I began, "You're allowed to not know everything, to even sometimes be wrong. We'll all still love you. And I'm allowed to speak up, even to a big guy like you. It took me four days to finally question you. We both have to work on this."

THAT NIGHT, in our small dining tent, we listened to the monks performing their evening chant. It was colder at this altitude, and we huddled together in the dining tent in our parkas, hats, scarves, and gloves.

Pasang was telling us Tibetan folktales, like a father gathering his children around a fire on a cold night. Then we started asking Pasang questions about his summits. Like kids, we never tired of hearing his stories. Sometimes we even asked him to repeat some of our favorite parts. "Tell us again about the time…" and he would.

That night, he talked about the 1996 disaster. He talked about Jon Krakauer and David Breashears. He talked about his good friends, Scott Fisher and Robert Hall, expedition leaders and expert climbers who died on the mountain in that terrible storm. He talked about crossing the Khumba Icefall, about setting up ropes, about the South Col and the Hillary Step. About peeing in their water bottles because it's too freezing to leave the tent at night. About having no appetite. About being so cold you think you're going to freeze to death. About how he needed the money to pay for his children's education. Then he smiled and said "good-night."

That night I meditated in my tent and then fell asleep to the handful of monks still chanting in the monastery, their voices rising across the night air, and, I imagined, landing on top of Everest.

In the morning, we joined the monks for meditating and chanting in the monastery, and then readied ourselves for our day's descent. Pasang had told us that we should all come back to Nepal next year, and he would take us to base camp. He told us we had already trekked the hardest part of the hike to base camp, we'd just need a few more days to build in time to acclimate to the higher elevations. "You've already done the steepest part. It just gets colder and higher," he explained.

"I'd come back to do that next year!" Christina said as she powdered her nose and then tossed her compact into her backpack.

The weather turned much colder, and a new snowstorm had begun. We trekked hours until we came to Khumjung and visited the monastery where the yeti skull was housed, where the climbers had received blessings in the IMAX film as Jamling Tenzing Norgay lit butter lamps.

We saw a school that Sir Edmund Hillary had built, where an empty oxygen canister retrieved from Everest hung from a pole and was used as the school bell. The children trekked two hours each day from Namche to Khumjung for school.

Back in Namche, we stopped one more time at Lhakpa's teahouse to wish her well and say our goodbyes. We took pictures, and I thought how we had spent more time with her husband in just two weeks than she had in months. Then, following a lovely Nepali custom, Lhakpa presented us with a kata, a thin, white scarf that is offered as a sign of hospitality, kindness, and respect. I watched Lhakpa as she draped the kata gently around Christina's shoulders, and then felt the softness of the material as she placed a kata around me.

Finally, after eight full days of trekking and camping, we were back in Lukla, singing Hindi folk songs the porters had taught us along the way and drinking San Miguel's. We spent the night in our tents literally a few feet from the airstrip. When a helicopter landed, it blew the red tent over our latrine right off.

The next morning we waited for the small plane to land on the tiny airstrip. The air felt so easy now, compared to the higher altitudes to which we had grown accustomed. We were able to laugh and run and drink all at the same time.

While waiting to depart from Lukla, I was standing near Anita, who was about 5 feet 2 inches tall. We were talking about the showers that were waiting for us back in our hotel rooms in Kathmandu. Christina had arranged again with Pasang that she and I have separate rooms. We were getting along okay, but neither of us wanted to spend that much time alone together. As Anita and I were talking, she put her hand on my head, patted it, and said, "My gosh! You are a little person!"

I looked her in the eyes and thought about what brought me here, about my yearnings, about the strength of my physical body that allowed my spirit to return to Nepal, about my hopes and dreams, and I said to her evenly, "Oh no, Anita. I'm not a little person at all. I'm a really big person who happens to be very short."

WE RETURNED TO Kathmandu, marveling at how we survived the take-off from Lukla, where the plane moves a mere few feet before falling off the cliff of a mountain into flight. It was like a terrifying, exhilarating ride at an amusement park (without any height requirement). After eight days of trekking in the Everest region, the fact that there were no working seat belts on the plane didn't even faze us.

Returning to the hotel, I enjoyed the best shower of my life. A few of us decided to go back to Boudhanath before dinner. Christina and I shared a cab and both of us attempted to smooth over the differences that had accumulated.

We had a good time together that afternoon. We spun the prayer wheels and I gazed in wonderment at the way the stupa looked at dusk, bathed in the soft fading light of the day, the prayer flags reaching toward the pink-orange sky.

We lit butter lamps and lingered at the stupa, not wanting to leave, not knowing when, or if, we'd ever be back. We both seemed to let go of the frustrations about each other we'd been carrying. Maybe because the hardest part of the trip was behind us we could relax a little more, tolerate our differences a bit easier.

We went to a Sherpa restaurant in the town of Thamel that night. Suddenly the whole group was starving, ordering food and beer. As is the custom in Nepal, we were seated on pillows on the floor, which many in the group found uncomfortable but I loved. Sitting crossed legged for me was easy, and I didn't have to deal with a chair where my legs dangled and grew tired not being able to reach the floor.

Christina sat across from me, and I sat on Pasang's right. The whole group was laughing, sharing our private jokes from the trek, and just letting loose.

Pasang and I started talking about Buddhism. We talked about the teachings, about his wish to be a monk in his next life. I told him I had entertained thoughts of being a Buddhist nun in my next life. We talked and we laughed.

Christina and I both got up to use the bathroom at the same time. We were happy. I told her how I thought Pasang had been such a great guide, how I was enjoying our conversation about Buddhism. She looked at me and said, "Oh God, Ellen! I can't keep it in anymore. I've been dying to tell you! Pasang and I have been sleeping together!"

"What?!" I asked.

"Yes!" she said excitedly. "Pasang has been sneaking into my tent at night! He's so sweet! He would say to me, 'Christina, just promise not to moan, yes? We can't let anyone hear us, just don't scream out!'"

I didn't know what to say. I thought of how she wanted her own tent, her own room in Kathmandu. I'm sure some of it was because of our differences; I had wanted to be alone, too. But how much of her anger at me really had to do with her desire to be free for Pasang?

"We're in love," she blurted out. "But you can't tell anyone, Ellen. Not anyone."

I thought of Pasang, of the adoration he received from our group. How we all looked up to him. He was a wonderful guide; there was no doubt. But we all projected our notions of who he was: Sherpa, climber, and spiritual embodiment of the Nepali culture we wanted to imagine. This Shangri-La that we knew didn't really exist, but yearned for all the same.

I thought about Lhakpa, alone in her little teashop at eleven thousand two hundred seventy feet. Of her hardly seeing her husband. About how she must sit and wait and hope that he doesn't die on his way to the summit of Everest. Of how Pasang has been to the States, loves Burger King, loves California, and of how Lhakpa has never left Nepal. Of how the map of the United States took up a good portion of her back wall, next to Pasang's summit pictures.

I remembered watching Lhakpa put the kata around Christina, not knowing she was placing the scarf of respect on the shoulders of a woman who was sleeping with her husband.

What I said to Christina was, "Be careful. Make sure you use a condom," and I hugged her.

I was quiet at dinner. Back at the hotel, Christina told me that Pasang was going to sneak into her room that night, so she wouldn't be joining the rest of us on the terrace. She was going to feign tiredness to the rest of the group. Then she asked me to give Pasang her key; she wasn't sure where he was just now, and she was going to go up to her room to take a shower. I knew that by asking me to do this, she was crossing some invisible line, wanting to let Pasang know that I knew about their liaison.

I walked over to Pasang when I saw him a few minutes later and did as Christina asked. Pasang froze. He looked at me before averting his eyes. He opened his mouth as if to say something, but let out a sigh instead, took the key from my hand, and walked away.

I didn't join the others on the terrace. I found Anita, and we passed the evening playing slot machines in an Indian casino. Every time we hit a jackpot, we'd get excited and frustrated. We had no idea how Indian rupees compared to Nepalese rupees, so each time we heard the clinking of coins we had no idea how much we were winning.

"Let's simplify it," I said to Anita. "We'll just play until we have no more rupees left. Then will know we're down to zero. Nothing in any country is still nothing."

I WAS QUIET the next day, and found myself pulling away from the group on this, our last day in Nepal.

Christina had told the group she wasn't going to go sightseeing with us on our free day, because she didn't feel well. I knew she was lying, as she had already told me earlier that morning that she and Pasang were planning on spending the day alone. Pasang had told the group he had some things to take care of in Kathmandu concerning his upcoming expedition.

Without Christina, our group visited Pashuputinath, Nepal's holiest Hindu temple. On the banks of the Bagmati River, considered a sacred river because it eventually flows into the holy Ganges, I watched the cremation fires burn. I watched a man sweep the ashes into the almost dried up river waiting for the monsoon season. Downstream from the main ghats—areas of stone set aside for cremation—smaller funeral pyres were burning on the sand along the river. Those were the cremations of the poorer people and people of low caste who are not allowed to be cremated within the temple complex itself. I watched as discrimination continued even into death.

That night, as we ate at a traditional Nepalese restaurant, we all signed the back of a group picture we had taken for Pasang, which he vowed he would bring with him next month to the summit of Everest. We all wrote a message to him on the back of the photo.

I wished him well on his summit bid, and then added, "Remember, it's the internal Everest that's the most challenging of all." I believed it for myself, and for Pasang as well.

THE NEXT MORNING, we prepared for our return to the States. As promised, I gave Pasang my ski jacket, Patagonia pullover, boots, and sleeping bag, because they were all the perfect size for his eleven-year-old daughter. I figured they could sit in my closet indefinitely, or be put to good use daily in Nepal.

I also wanted to focus on the positive aspects of my relationship with Pasang, and on the happy memories we had shared. We had said little to each other since the night before, when I gave Pasang Christina's hotel key.

I watched the group members say good-bye to Pasang with hugs and promises to stay in touch. Pasang looked at me and then cast his eyes downward. We hugged each other, and I thanked him for everything, and then wished him safety on his expedition.

I watched Christina and Pasang at the airport, hugging goodbye, tears running down her cheeks. I hated her and felt for her all at the same time. We hadn't said much to each other over the last twenty-four hours. I felt burdened by her secret, the way, I realized, some of my friends must have felt burdened by mine.

We found ourselves sitting next to each other on the plane. Of course, we had booked our seats together what now felt like a million years ago. I had hoped we wouldn't need to have any further contact, but now, here we were. The plane was full, nowhere to move, what to do?

I offered her a Kleenex. I said it must have been hard to say good-bye. She nodded and then said, "I feel like you're being so judgmental! It's not like you haven't done what I did."

"I know," I agreed. "I guess it's just hard to watch. To be on the other side. I didn't realize how many people could be affected, of how hurtful things can be on so many levels."

"Well, I love him. And I'm so proud of myself for doing this trip alone. I feel so independent. And I didn't really think of Jack at all!"

Before I could stop myself I blurted out, "You know, Christina, I'd imagine that fucking the Sherpa would sort of take the edge off of that affair."

She was understandably furious with me. "Hey, look!" she said angrily. "You told me you called Carl from LA before you left. You'll get back with him when you go home."

"No," I said to Christina, with a conviction that surprised me, "I won't. This trip has made me even more committed to living the life I imagined. I feel independent and strong and more devoted than ever to Steve."

"Well, maybe you and Steve have a better marriage than Paul and I do. But I deserve some happiness. I have to take my happiness where I can find it." She thought a minute and said, "You know, with Pasang, listening to his stories, it was like all the books I've been reading these past few years. All of those incredible climbers. To think that Pasang knows them, is one of them. That he's actually climbed through all those camps, through the Hillary Step, and stood on top of Everest! I love being part of that."

It hit me. Hard. Again. Like a lone light bulb hanging from a single string, lighting up a dingy interrogation room. What Joshua and Jeff and Kevin and Carl were about.

It sounded so familiar. Christina's relationship with Pasang elevated her in some way. She was tall, but she still had her own reasons why she felt unseen, why she felt she didn't "measure-up."

She responded to a culture that told her to stay thin at all costs. She popped laxatives day in and day out. She needed to take responsibility concerning her actions, just as I did for mine. But she was a victim, a casualty of the culture, too. She had tried to find fulfillment in her life through attempting to shape her body according to elusive, cultural standards. She became a wife and mother at the age of twenty-one, before she had a chance to develop her own identity.

"Christina, you don't have to have an affair with someone who climbed Mount Everest. If you want to be a part of it so much, you can climb yourself. You don't have to live vicariously, offering your body to a man living out your own dreams." I had meant those words for Christina, but I knew they were for me, too.

Christina continued to talk about Pasang, whom she loved the idea of being with, though she found the sex "wasn't really all that great." While she shared details I didn't want to know, I thought about Christina, about the chances of our meeting in this lifetime. About how I wanted this trip for so many reasons, like gaining insight and clarity in my life.

And now, through a lousy situation highlighted by Christina sleeping with the Sherpa, I got it. The lesson I needed to learn. The other position I had to assume, standing on the outside watching a woman filled with her own uncertainties and her own passions play them out through men who are living her dreams.

At first when Christina told me about her relationship with Pasang, I was upset and angry. I felt like my trip had been lessened in some way. I had spent the flight to Nepal hearing about Paul and Jack, and the way home hearing about Paul and Jack and Pasang. But it didn't lessen my trip. It *was* my trip, my life, and my lesson.

I was so blessed to have been given the opportunity to watch a drama unfold and use the plot and its ending to continue to rewrite my own.

I don't want the complications of distractions, of living any kind of secret life. I could hear, in what Christina was saying, that she had felt special and important because of her relationship with Pasang. She liked that she knew him in a different way than the rest of the group. She liked that while we all adored Pasang, he had chosen her as the favorite. How often I had felt that way, with Carl most recently.

Now, on the outside of this drama, I saw it for what it was. I saw it as Christina's willingness to act in a supporting role of someone else's film, and under someone else's direction. To settle for the silent applause from an invisible audience.

I just wanted to be under my own direction, with my own speaking part.

I LISTENED AS Christina counted off the virtues of Pasang. Then she stopped, "There is one thing I don't love about Pasang. He's too short. He's so handsome, but I wish he were taller. Most of the Nepalese men are too short."

I thought about my conversation with Anita in Lukla, about my height. I thought about Christina, who knew all about my feelings regarding stature, about being short, about the book I was writing.

She said again, "Pasang's too short, don't you think?"

And I was grateful for the wisdom not to respond.

THERE WERE TIMES, I realized then, when it made sense to speak my mind, and other times where it seemed futile and I would just learn to let go. I was glad that I spoke my mind with Anita, and glad that I let it go with Christina.

All of us, especially Christina, looked to Pasang with awe and respect as he described his ascents up to the peak of the highest point on earth. Yet she still described him as "too short."

Fred is big and tall, commanding respect; the group looked to him for leadership. He trekked his way up the mountain hoping to meet "The Red Carnation Lama."

We are all so human. Going to nine thousand feet, or thirteen thousand feet, or to the summit, it doesn't matter. We are all both dwarfed by Everest and beyond measure.

It's the character you bring to your climb—your internal and external climb. It's the care you take of your soul on the journey, and the respect you offer to the other souls along the path. I think it's learning to keep an open heart, and swimming in the joy and pain of life that allows you to keep on growing.

Chapter Eight
LIFE IS SHORT, AND SO AM I

Go confidently in the direction of your dreams!
Live the life you've imagined.
HENRY DAVID THOREAU

April 7, 2000

I AM HOME now, and not sure what to do with myself. Where to file things. Where I belong. I know I need to start writing again, but where to begin? With Everest? Christina? Pasang? Myself? So many stories and threads and layers interwoven into a cloth, creating designs and patterns I cannot always follow, yet I continue to wrap myself in.

I want to put my hiking boots back on and walk along dusty dirt paths, and climb over rocks. Instead, I walk along the sidewalk near the ocean at sea level, where the air is thick. There is a fence along its side. I close my eyes, letting my fingers brush along the cold iron, pretending I am at Boudhnath, spinning the prayer wheels.

I want to hear the familiar bell of the yaks and move out of their way as I watch the cargo strapped on their backs, the big blue barrels marked EVEREST. I want to see the porter with the long whip keeping his yaks moving on. Next come the villagers in rubber flip flops and short, torn pants, carrying heavy loads strapped across their foreheads to secure the weight on their backs. Women my size, some shorter, carrying enormous loads; men carrying tables, wood, trees, anything that needs to be moved, on their backs.

I think of Everest, the stark summit with the plume of wind rolling off the top. It is not for humans up there, yet climber after climber ventures forward.

"Because it is there," is the frequent answer to the question, "Why?"

"Because *we* are *here*," I think, instead. As if we want to announce our presence to the highest point on Earth; an affirmation that we exist, an announcement to the gods and the goddesses and to each other.

In some Buddhist shrines, there sits a large bell. Upon entering the temple, the worshippers are to chime the bell loudly. The purpose of this ritual is to announce one's presence to the gods. Is that the purpose of summiting Everest? To announce our existence? To show our human strength and spirit? To defy our humanness? To make us feel small and humble? Big and invincible? Connected? All simultaneously? I wonder.

Should I have found a trip that climbed higher? Do I need to go higher? If so, why? To prove myself? To garner respect? To see with my own eyes the Khumba Icefall? To challenge my body, mind, and soul? To distract?

I want to cry. I'm not ready to be back, and neither did I want to stay in Nepal.

Base camp. That's where I am in my heart, neither here nor there. Ready to go on to the next challenge, or ready to turn back to safety.

I wanted clarity, and through Christina and Pasang I had a glimpse. That one glimpse was what I so needed to resist my need for distraction. I knew my Achilles heel, and how it craved a stiletto.

When I felt "too short," too inadequate, I sought a place to hold my passion and power. I knew that a short high after being with Carl would be followed by a big withdrawal. It comes down to that one phone call that has the potential to send me back into a cycle I don't want to be in. Carl's phone call.

The cost is too great, the benefit too small, too elusive. When I feel the pain of it all, the pain in my heart and the pain I've caused, I feel so lonely. I dread that feeling. I think I would feel less lonely and scared alone on the South Col. I would feel the kindred spirits of others and their passions.

On the outside, with my family and friends, I pretend I am happy. That I am fine. Meanwhile, the Everest within is being bombarded with avalanches.

I fear there is nowhere to retreat. Nowhere to dodge the danger that lurks everywhere.

Fearful of being swallowed up in the mad, rolling drifts, and at the same time, wishing for the oblivion. Wanting my integrity, worrying that my hesitancy, my fear in fully realizing my own passions and dreams, will lead me back into Carl's arms.

I don't want to be torn apart again, like an earthquake that shakes the mountain, leaving my heart in rubble.

AND I THINK that was the end of it for me. The last heave, the last retching that I needed to purge from my system.

I was done vomiting.

IT TOOK ME a good month or so to phase myself back into my life at home. I felt like I had been on two very different journeys. One was Nepal, with moonlit night skies gracing the snow-covered peaks, and one that was Christina, Pasang, my ghosts, and me.

The more I thought about the trip, the more I was able to see the exquisiteness of the trip. The trip was a mirror to the most awesome scenery in the world, and, also, a mirror of the truth about myself. It was a point in my life where I learned to let go, and truly let in.

It was time for me to pour energy into my marriage. To try to earn back Steve's trust. I had been running away, scared of intimacy for so long, scared of being vulnerable to another person. Now I was ready.

I SPENT MY DAYS writing, running, and dancing. I reasoned that if I could manage to escape to Nepal alone, I could certainly arrange to spend a day in Cambridge, at a meditation center forty-five minutes from my home, even if it meant arranging for someone to pick up the kids from school sometimes.

I could structure my days so I could write, walk, and meditate. I could take the Buddhist precepts formally, acknowledging publicly that which my heart held alone since I was a young girl. I could integrate my life in a way that held both sides of me and made me whole.

I marveled at what the kids taught me, and what the kids had learned from me. How easily they spoke of both Judaism and Buddhism, of yaks and summits. How often they volunteered to their teachers, "My mom can come into our class and show you her slides of Nepal and Mount Everest."

"Follow your dreams," I would tell them. "They're your own special road map." I'd watch them jump into a freezing lake in the White Mountains of New Hampshire and think, "They're already doing it. Jumping right in, taking a juicy bite out of this ripe life."

I, of course, would refuse their requests to join them.

"Mom," they'd say. "You slept outside in four inches of snow in Nepal. This water isn't that cold. Come in!"

I'd shake my head no, and wrap them in dry towels when they came out of the water shivering, fingertips wrinkled and lips turning blue. I'd hug them close and say, "You look like you had so much fun!"

Other times I'd join them in their escapades, much to their surprise.

Allison and Matt have a favorite restaurant in Chicago called Ed Debevic's. The waiters do crazy things, the kids order chicken fingers, and they have a grand time. This spring my kids and I were there having dinner with my parents, sister, and brother-in-law, and my niece and nephews.

We had our favorite waiter, who was even crazier than the other servers. One of the things this waiter does is to bring little ice cream cones for dessert, and then shove them right into the kids' faces. Allison and Matt had heard of this, but had never witnessed this "mess." On this night, they begged the waiter "get ice cream in our face!"

One by one, the waiter shoved an ice cream cone in each kid's face, the vanilla ice cream dripping down their cheeks, chocolate sauce hovering on their chins and necks. The kids were cracking up. This was the greatest! An adult waiter smacking ice cream sundaes in their faces and the adults just calmly observing!

All of a sudden I said to the waiter, "Me too!"

The kids peered at me with gooey, messy faces, and my parents said, "What?"

My sister said, "Oh Ellen, you don't mean that."

I looked at the waiter and said, "One sundae in the face, please."

He looked around our big table of ten, shrugged his shoulders, and walked over to me, pushing the ice cream cone into my nose, my eyes and my cheeks. The kids were hysterical with laughter. My parents, sister, and brother-in-law just stared at me, and then started laughing along with the kids.

I took a napkin to wipe under my eyes and licked some of the vanilla ice cream and chocolate sauce that lay near my lips. I said to everyone, "You've just witnessed the first action of my new motto: Life is short, and so am I!"

Everyone was laughing and using napkin after napkin to clear their faces, throwing them in an ever-growing, messy pile on the table. I noticed that I had gotten some chocolate sauce on a shirt I was wearing, one of my favorites. I smiled to myself.

I didn't need to use Shout or Spray'n Wash. I didn't care if I ruined my shirt and stained it forever. It felt good to have a reminder to let loose and stay free. Life is short, and so am I.

I THINK I'VE gone through the growth spurt I needed. Maybe not the one the doctors or my parents had hoped for all those years ago, but an even better one. I grew into myself.

People still comment about my height, make jokes about me being short, and ridicule me. And sometimes it is still painful. Like last month, when I took my son and his friend to dinner at Friendly's restaurant.

There was a group of girls, probably around fifteen or sixteen years old. They were tall, thin, dressed in Abercrombie jeans riding low on their hips and tight-fitting shirts cropped at their belly buttons. When I was standing to leave, the girls pointed at me and laughed in hushed and not so hushed whispers over and over as I stood in line to pay the check.

As one girl passed me, towering over my height, she said aloud to her friends, "Did you ever notice how short some people are?" and ran back to her friends, where they all burst out laughing.

I was glad Matt and his friend were waiting outside and didn't hear this. I felt embarrassed and angry and jealous, just like I did back as a child.

But it was silly that I was relieved Matt didn't hear. I'm sure he'll have his own comments to deal with as he grows up. We all will, in one fashion or another. That's why I felt good about confronting our rabbi the other day, in front of my children.

During the children's service after Sunday school the other week, our rabbi was telling the congregation a story about the conquests of Alexander the Great, saying, "Not bad for just a short guy," motioning with his hand to indicate a person of short stature. After services I went to the rabbi's office while Steve and our kids watched and waited for me.

I asked the rabbi if I could have a word with him. Then I told him that even though I knew he made that comment as a joke, he would never stand before the congregation and talk about someone saying, "Not bad for a fat man," or "Not bad for a black woman." That he wouldn't like it if someone said, "Not bad for a Jew."

I asked him why he thought it was okay to make jokes about short people. I told him about growth hormone treatment, and the physical and emotional risk children are placed in when social prejudice is treated with medical efforts.

He agreed and apologized, and thanked me for pointing this out. He assured me, "It will not happen again."

I thanked him for his time, and Steve smiled along with the kids as I left the rabbi's office. I told the kids how important it was to speak up about things you believe in.

I wish I had spoken up to the rabbi of my childhood, who laughed at me and told me I was too short to become a rabbi, that I wouldn't be able to reach the pulpit. I was glad I had my voice now.

I HAVE TALKED with so many people about stature, about being short, about finding one's place in this world. I wanted so much to talk about the very real prejudice against short people that exists but is rendered unimportant, or turned into a joke. I watched the extremes of this prejudice being played out through growth hormone injections in the NIH experiment.

I spent ten years treating women who fought with their bodies because the culture told them their bodies were their enemies—unless their bodies were tall and thin, then they were their best friends. Friends with connections that would offer the best seats in the house. But fair weather friends, who could turn on you at any time should a pound return, a gray hair sprout, a wrinkle expose itself.

I read magazine articles that scared me because of the direction our society is heading, this constant emphasis on appearance, on the outer body rather than the inner life. I knew firsthand the cost of such an emphasis.

In an article entitled *Designer Babies,* Michael D. Lemonick writes, "Within a decade or two, it may be possible to screen kids almost before conception for an enormous range of attributes, such as how tall they're likely to be, what body type they will have, their hair and eye color . . ."[67]

Later in the article, he quotes Jeremy Rifkin, the biomedical watchdog who had tried to stop the NIH study on human growth hormone. He states, "It's the ultimate shopping experience: designing your baby." Appalled by the prospect, he continues, "In a society used to cosmetic surgery and psychopharmacology, this is not a big step."

The article then goes on to say that

> The ethical issues raised by techniques emerging from the genetics labs are likely to be even more complex. What if parents can use preimplantation genetic diagnosing to avoid having kids with attention-deficit disorder, say, or those predestined to be *short* [my italics] or dullwitted or predisposed to homosexuality? Will they feel pressure from friends and relations to do so? And will the kids who are born with these characteristics be made to feel even more like second-class citizens than they do now? Even thornier is the question of what kinds of genetic tinkering parents might be willing to elect to enhance already healthy kids.[68]

The practice of using growth hormone treatment with healthy short children clearly falls into this latter category.

And still later the article states, "There will always be people with enough money—or a high enough limit on their credit cards—to pay for what they want."

Lee Silver, a biologist at Princeton and author of the book *Remaking Eden,* states, "Medical researchers are moved by a desire to cure diseases more effectively. Reprogenetics [a term Silver coined] is going to be driven by parents or prospective parents, who want something for their children. It's the sort of demand that could explode."[69]

When I read this article, I couldn't help but think of that summer when Steve and I went to hear the Dalai Lama speak in Bloomington, Indiana. After his talk, the audience was allowed to ask questions. Someone wanted to know what he thought of the Human Genome Project, which seeks to map human genetics.

The Dalai Lama said he was skeptical that science could create a better human being. On the other hand, he said that if we can make human beings who are compassionate, who have a sense of caring for others, that is most welcome.

December 2000

I TOLD MY HUSBAND and kids last week that I was going to book myself into a small hotel in York Harbor, Maine, for four days to write. I told them that four days alone, writing, was equal to two months of writing at home, in fits of stops and starts, trying to do too many things at once.

"I want to finish writing my book. I'm going to leave next week," I informed them.

"Fine," everyone agreed, not thinking much about it one way or another. Four days? In Maine? An hour away? My kids took it in stride.

I've come to realize that my trips to Nepal made so many things relative in comparison. Nepal acted like a key that easily opened doors that once presented obstacles. That was an unexpected, and most welcome, gift.

So this past Thursday, I loaded up my Montero with backpacks full of notebooks and pens and my laptop that I didn't fully trust. Allison saw me heave my duffel into the trunk.

"You over packed, as usual," she declared.

"Comfortable clothes are more bulky," I explained. "They take up a lot of room."

Allison simply rolled her eyes.

The kids piled into the car with their backpacks filled with schoolbooks. Heavier, I would always tell them, than any pack I'd carried in Nepal. My plan was to drop them off at school and be on the road by 8:00 A.M., checked into the Stageneck Inn by 9:30, and writing by 10:00.

"Shoot for 11:00, mom. You should stop and have breakfast," Allison suggested.

Good point. I went over the plans for the next few days: how Lupe would pick them up from school, and how daddy would be with them at night and all weekend. I gave them big hugs and kisses before we left our garage, because at nine years and eleven years old, they'd die if I did that in front of their respective schools, in front of their friends.

After I'd dropped Allison off at middle school, I drove toward Matt's school.

"So you're leaving now, and you'll be back by Sunday afternoon?"

"Right," I answered Matt.

"Wow, mom. If you were going back to Nepal, that's not much longer than the flights would be!"

"Ha! You're right!"

"That's nothing, mom. Good luck finishing your book!" he said, jumping out of the car. He walked up the hill to the front of the school, turned around, and waved.

AN HOUR AND TEN MINUTES later I was driving into the parking lot of a charming hotel set upon a portion of land jutting into the ocean—the rocky ledged coast where land moves into water, connected, continuous, and the sea birds call out, announcing their flight. I thought back to the poem I wrote a few years back, "There," which I put at the beginning of Chapter Five.

I sat in the well-appointed lobby furnished in warm greens and reds. Chairs and couches with coffee tables—each supporting a festive poinsettia—filled the room. The right wall housed a huge, roaring fire that invited guests to sit, to relax. Where else was there to go?

A large Christmas tree decorated with gold and red ornaments and threads of red and gold tinsel stood welcomingly in the corner. The walls were covered with black and white photos of ocean, beach, and fishing boats. There were shelves with books about Maine, and New England, and fishing. And there were baskets of nuts on the table and a large setting of coffees, teas, apples, and cookies.

I know now, around 3:00 p.m., the hotel staff will set out cheese, offer a glass of wine. Ask me how my writing is going; is the book done? I feel held.

The length of the back wall is a window with a cushioned bench under the square-glassed panes. And here, the small grassy area outside falls off into the blueness of the ocean and across from a piece of black, rocky earth that stretches out into the water like a lover's arm thrown easily over his lover's body in sleep.

I drink my coffee and I smile.

Here

Here in the clearness!
I know it exists
Even when the fog rolls in.
I am here,
Not on an island,
But on an inland
Where earth, water, fire and sky meet.
Not only for a mere glimpse
But for eternity!
No longer hidden,
But open.
I am here!
Watch me walk into the mysteries
Watch me dance in the clearing
Watch me bathe in the tearful salt water
Watch me dry in the sand of existence!
Here, where I belong,
Where I am seen,
Where I can be.

Notes

1 Johnston, J. (1994). *Appearance Obsession: Learning To Love The Way You Look*. Florida: Health Communications, Inc. pp. 39-40.

2 Globe Staff. (2000, October 12). Campaign Journal: Stop Squirming. The Boston Globe, p. A21.

3 Deck, L.P. (1968). Buying brains by the inch. *The Journal of College and University Personnel Association*, 19, pp. 33-37.

4 Kurtz, D.L. (1969, April). Physical appearance and stature: Important variables in sales recruiting. *Personnel Journal*, pp. 981-983.

5 Keyes, Ralph. (1980). *The Height of Your Life*. Boston: Little, Brown and Company. p. 25.

6 Rauch, Jonathan. (December 23, 1995-January 5, 1996). Short guys finish last. *The Economist*. pp. 19-21.

7 Keyes, Ralph. (1980). *The Height of Your Life*. Boston: Little, Brown and Company. p. 252.

8 Todd, T. (August 1, 1983). The steroid predicament. *Sports Illustrated*. pp. 65-74.

9 Rubenstein, S., Caballero, B. (March 22-29, 2000). Is Miss America an undernourished role model? *Journal of the American Medical Association*., 283 (12): p. 1569.

10 Smolak, L., Levine, M.P., & Striegel-Moore, R. (Eds). (1996). *The developmental psychopathology of eating disorders*. New Jersey: Erlbaum Associates.

11 Reich, Robert, B. (1997). *Locked in the Cabinet*. New York: Alfred A. Knopf. p. 44.

12 Kimbrell, Andrew. (1994). *The Human Body Shop*. San Francisco: HarperSanFrancisco.

13 Bercu, Barry, B. (1996, August 21). The growing conundrum: Growth hormone treatment of the non-growth hormone deficient child. *Journal of American Medical Association* 276 (7) p. 567.

14 Hindmarsh, Peter, C. & Brook, Charles. (1996, July 6). Final height of short normal children treated with growth hormone. *The Lancet*. 348 (9019).

15   Rose, Susan, & Cutler, Gordon. Letter from Department Of Health & Human Services. *Clinical Center Study of Short Stature.* National Institutes of Health, Bethesda, Maryland.

16   Baron, Jeffrey. Letter from Department Of Health & Human Services, sent May 10, 1993. National Institutes of Health, Bethesda, Maryland.

17   Consent to Participate In A Clinical Research Study, Institute: DEB, NICD. NIH. Principal Investigator: Gordon B. Cutler, Jr., M.D. Study Title: A Randomized, Double-blind, Placebo-Controlled Clinical Trial of the Effects of Growth Hormone Therapy on the Adult Height of Non-Growth Hormone Deficient Children with Short Stature. p. 1.

18   Ibid, pp. 2-3.

19   Ibid, p. 3.

20   Minor Patient's Assent to Participate in a Clinical Research Study. Institute: NICD. Principal Investigator: Gordon B. Cutler, Jr., M.D. Study Title: A Randomized Double-Blind, Placebo-Controlled Clinical Trial of the Effects of Growth Hormone Therapy on the Adult Height of Non-Growth Hormone Deficient Children with Short Stature. p. 1.

21   Mestel, Rosie. (1994, January). It's a tall world. *Discover.* (1) p. 83.

22   Lee Hotz, Robert. (1993, June 29). Experiment to aid growth of short children resumes. *The Los Angeles Times.* p. A17.

23   Editorial. (1993, July 10). Ethics vs. genetics. *The Seattle Times.*

24   Staff reporter. (1992, June 25). NIH hormone test with children draws criticism of group. *The Wall Street Journal.*

25   Lehrman, Sally. (1992, June 28). Kids used in U.S. bid to 'cure' shortness. *San Francisco Examiner.*

26   Ibid.

27   Sandberg, David, E. (1999). Experiences of being short: Should we expect problems of psychosocial adjustment? In: Eiholzer U, Haverkamp F, Voss LD, editors. *Growth and Psyche.* Gottingen: Hogrefe and Huber Publishers, pp. 15-26.

28   Zimet, Gregory, et al. (1995, August 4). Psychological adjustment of children evaluated for short stature: a preliminary report. *Developmental and Behavioral Pediatrics.* (15) 4, pp. 264-270.

29   Voss, Linda & Mulligan, Jean. (2000, March 4). Bullying in school: Are short pupils at risk? Questionnaire study in a cohort. *British Medical Journal.* 320 (7235), pp. 612-613.

30   Cutler, Leona, et al. (1996, August 21). Short stature and growth hor-

mone therapy: A national study of physician recommendation patterns. *Journal of the American Medical Association.* (276) 7, pp. 531-537.

31   Erling, A., Widlund, I & Albertsson-Wikland, K. (1994). Prepubertal children with short stature have a different perception of their well-being and stature than their parents. *Quality of Life Research.* 3, p. 425.

32   Staff reporter. NIH hormone test with children draws criticism of group: Foundation files a complaint over use of healthy youths in experiment on growth. (1992, June 25). *The Wall Street Journal.*

33   Erling, A., Wiklund, I, & Albertsson-Wikland, K. (1994). Prepubertal children with short stature have a different perception of their well-being and stature than their parents. *Quality of Life Research.* 3, pp. 425-429.

34   Young-Hyman, Deborah, L. (1990). Psychosocial functioning and social competence in growth hormone deficient, constitutionally delayed and familial short-stature children and adolescents. In *Psychoneuronendocrinology: Brain, Behavior, and Hormonal Interactions.* (Ed) Holmes, Clarissa, S. Germany: Springer Verlag, pp. 51-52.

35   Lehrman, Sally. (1992, June 28). Kids use in U.S. bid to 'cure' shortness. *San Francisco Examiner.*

36   Samaras, Thomas, T. (1995, Jan-Feb). Short is beautiful: so why are we making kids grow tall? *The Futurist.* (29), 1. p. 30.

37   Ibid, p. 29.

38   Saltus, Richard. (1992, June 28). Tests on children raise questions about growth drug. *Boston Sunday Globe.*

39   Ibid.

40   Tauer, Carol A. (May-June, 1994). *The NIH trials of growth hormone for short Stature.* IRB: A Review of Human Subjects Research, Volume 16, Number 3, p. 2.

41   Kimbrell, Andrew. (1993). *The Human Body Shop.* San Francisco: HarperSanFrancisco. p. 155.

42   Press Release: (1992, June 22). The Foundation on Economic Trends in Conjunction with Petition to Halt National Institutes of Health Sponsored Testing of Human Growth Hormone on Children.

43   Ibid.

44   Mestel, Rosie. (1994, January). It's a tall, tall world. *Discover.* (15) 1, p. 83.

45   Taur, Carol. A. (1994, May 10). Human growth hormone: A case study in treatment priorities. Prepared for The Hastings Center Project on Priorities in the Clinical Application of Human Genome Research, p. 12.

6   Tauer, Carol., A. (1994, May-June). The NIH Trials of Growth Hormone for Short Stature. *IRB A Review of Human Subjects Research*. A Publicaion of The Hastings Center, p. 4.

47   Ibid, p. 5.

48   Ibid, p. 5.

49   Bercu, Barry, B. (1996, August 21). The growing conundrum: growth hormone treatment of the non-growth hormone deficient child. *Journal of the American Medical Association.* (276) 7, p. 567-568.

50   Letters to the Editor. (1988, May 21). Leukaemia in Patients Treated with Growth Hormone. *The Lancet.* p. 1159.

51   Rifkin, Jeremy. (1990, February 6). Petition calls on agencies to conduct long-term studies of the possible causal relationship between HGH and leukemia. Press Release, *The Foundation on Economic Trends.*

52   Rifkin, Jeremy. Press release. (1990, July 5). Genetically Engineered Human Growth Hormone Linked to Leukemia. *The Foundation on Economic Trends.*

53   Minor Patient's Assent to Participate in a Clinical Study. National Institutes of Health. A Randomized, Double-Blind, Placebo-Controlled Clinical Trial of the Effects of Growth Hormone Therapy on the Adult Height of Non-Growth-Hormone Deficient Children with Short Stature.

54   Tauer, Carol, A. (1994, May-June). The NIH trials of growth hormone for short stature. *IRB: A Review of Human Subjects Research.* (16) 3, p.6.

55   Lamb, Lynette. (1994, January-February). Do short guys finish last? *Utne Reader.* 61, p. 30.

56   Brown, David. (1992, July 6). Growth hormone for healthy teens: Treating shortness with shots. *The Washington Post.*

57   Kowalczyk, L. (2003, January 12). Thousands seek obesity surgery. *The Boston Globe,* p. A1.

58   Stein, Robert. (October 19, 2005). Stomach surgery's risks higher than were believed: Finding may affect Medicare coverage. *The Washington Post*, A14.

59   Cosmetic Surgery Quick Facts: 2003 ASAPS Statistics. {online}. (2004, February 18). The American Society for Aesthetic Plastic Surgery. Available: http://www.surgery.org/press/news-release. php?iid=326&section=news-stats. [2005, February 10}.

60   Underwood, Anne. Will he measure up? [online]. (2003, September 22). *Newsweek Health.* Available: http://msnbc.msn.com/id/3068882/. MSNBC News. (2004, November 17).

61   Bober, Joanna. (1995 September). Skin and bones: The body-shaping craze in lingerie is giving everyone a slim chance. *W Magazine*, p. 148.

62   Simmons, Ann, M. (1998 October 18). In Nigeria, girls learn that big is beautiful. *The Boston Globe*. p. A20.

63   French, Howard, W. (1997 February 26). In the land of the small it isn't easy being tall. *The New York Times*.

64   The First Noble Truth is that there is suffering. Birth, sickness, old age, and death are unavoidable. Pain, grief and despair, and not getting what one desires bring suffering. The illusion that anything is permanent brings suffering. The Second Noble Truth is that there is a cause of suffering. Craving, desire and ignorance of the way things really are cause suffering. By craving and desiring what we feel is pleasurable, we suffer. None of the pleasures, such as beauty, money, fame, sights, sounds and tastes, last. Even if these pleasures are repeated, we suffer as we try to make them last forever, or grieve when they ultimately disappear. Craving leads to an endless cycle of desires that lead to suffering. The Third Noble Truth is that there is an end to suffering. An end to suffering comes with the diminishing and extinction of craving by liberating and detaching from this thirst of desire. The Fourth Noble Truth is the path that leads to the end of suffering. This path is called the Middle Path, as true happiness can be found in avoiding the extremes and following a life of moderation. The steps to achieve this are laid out in the Eight-Fold Path, which includes: Right Understanding, Right Attitude, Right Speech, Right Action, Right Livelihood, Right Effort, Right Mindfulness, and Right Concentration.

65   Steinem, Gloria. (1993). *Revolution From Within*. Boston: Little, Brown and Company, p. 154.

66   Ibid, p. 153.

67   Lemonick, Michael, D. (1999 January 11). Designer babies. *Time,* pp. 64-44.

68   Ibid.

69   Ibid.

About the Author

photo by Stuart Garfield

ELLEN FRANKEL, LCSW has worked in the field of eating disorders since 1987 in both outpatient and residential settings. She is the co-author of *Beyond a Shadow of a Diet: The Therapist's Guide to Treating Compulsive Eating* and *The Diet Survivors Handbook: 60 Lessons in Eating, Acceptance, and Self-Care.*

In addition to writing full-time, Ellen speaks at conferences and serves as a consultant. She lives in Marblehead, Massachusetts.

Visit the *Beyond Measure* website at www.beyondmeasureamemoir.com.

About Pearlsong Press

PEARLSONG PRESS is an independent publishing company dedicated to providing books and resources that entertain while expanding perspectives on the self and the world. The company was founded by Peggy Elam, Ph.D., a psychologist and former journalist.

PEARLS ARE FORMED when a piece of sand or grit or other abrasive, annoying, or even dangerous substance enters an oyster and triggers its protective response. The substance is coated with shimmering opalescent nacre ("mother of pearl"), the coats eventually building up to produce a beautiful gem. The self-healing response of the oyster thus transforms suffering into a thing of beauty.

The pearl-creating process reflects our company's desire to move outside a pathological or "disease" based model of "mental health" and "mental illness" into a more integrative and transcendent perspective on life, health, and well-being. A move out of suffering into joy.

And that, we think, is something to sing about.

PEARLSONG PRESS endorses **Health At Every Size**, an approach to health and well-being that celebrates natural diversity in body size and encourages people to stop focusing on weight (or any external measurement) in favor of listening to and respecting natural appetites for food, drink, sleep, rest, movement, and recreation.

While not every book we publish specifically promotes Health At Every Size (by, for instance, featuring fat heroines or educating readers on size acceptance), none of our books or other resources will contradict this holistic and body-positive perspective.

WE ENCOURAGE YOU to enjoy, enlarge, enlighten and enliven yourself with other Pearlsong Press books, including:

Unconventional Means:
The Dream Down Under
by Anne Richardson Williams

Taking Up Space:
How Eating Well & Exercising Regularly Changed My Life
by Pattie Thomas, Ph.D.
with Carl Wilkerson, M.B.A.
(foreword by Paul Campos, author of
The Obesity Myth)

Romance novels and short stories featuring Big Beautiful Heroines by Pat Ballard, the Queen of Rubenesque Romances:
Abigail's Revenge, Dangerous Curves Ahead, Wanted: One Groom, Nobody's Perfect , His Brother's Child, A Worthy Heir

The Singing of Swans
a novel about the divine feminine
by Mary Saracino

FIND THESE BOOKS AND MORE at www.pearlsong.com or your favorite online or offline bookstore.
Enjoy!

Printed in the United States
55226LVS00005B/112-291

9 781597 190053